CATALINA URETA
MARIANN DÁVILA

SOMATIC HEALING IN THE AGE OF TRAUMA

The Points Holding Process™ (PHP) and 30 Self-Help
Exercises for the Nervous System and Vagus Nerve

First Edition
© SOMATIC HEALING IN THE AGE OF TRAUMA
Catalina Ureta & Mariann Dávila
Contact: www.somaticinstitute.com

Published by: First Edition IngramSpark
ISBN: 978-956-416-517-2
Editing, layout, and cover design: María Alicia Pino
Proofreading: Sasha Rondell
Cover image & inside book illustrations: Fiorella Secchi Lagos
Box images with content summaries: María Alicia Pino
Photograph of Mariann Dávila: Constanza Maldonado
Photograph of Catalina Ureta: Naomi Kaneda
Translated by: Carolina Varela Ortiz
Audio book editing: Idan Mehir
Audio book voice-over: Sophie Ilys

Disclaimer:

The authors of this book do not dispense medical advice or prescribe the use of any technique as a form of treatment for physical, emotional, or medical problems without the advice of a physician, either directly or indirectly. The intent of the authors is only to offer information of a general nature to help you in your physical, emotional and spiritual well-being. The use of any information in this book is the reader's own choice and the authors assume no responsibility.

Please note: Circled image numbers are used as markers for the audiobook only. Numbered images and cited references are available in both the print and audiobook versions.

Somatic Healing in the Age of Trauma

The Points Holding Process™ (PHP) and 30 Self-Help
Exercises for the Nervous System and Vagus Nerve

ACKNOWLEDGMENTS

I would like to express my deepest gratitude to Prem Rawat for teaching me a lifetime of wisdom, inspiration and the gift of self-knowledge. Prem Rawat is an International Ambassador of Peace, founder of the world-renowned Peace Education Program (PEP), a program that works with people in prisons, universities, schools, and community groups in many countries around the world. Prem Rawat is the author of the #1 N.Y. Times bestselling book, "Hear Yourself". I would also like to thank Marolyn Rawat for her loving care towards me and my family.

I don't have enough words to thank Mariann Dávila Coggiola, author of the book "Bitácora Chamánica". Mariann, my soul friend, has been a tireless and patient writing and teaching partner in Chile since 2006. Her ability to write and organize the concepts in trauma is what illuminates this book, without her, this book would not exist. She has a lot of experience, both as a psychotherapist and as a teacher and facilitator of The Points Holding Process™ (PHP) and as a Somatic Experiencing® practitioner. I am so grateful for the inspiration, patience and understanding.

Special thanks to Judith Johnson, teacher and workshop partner and dear friend of thirty years. Your dedication to the progress of this book has been a blessing to me and to all humanity. Your legacy in the field of Psychoneuroenergetics™ (PNE) will be a milestone for future practitioners and a benchmark for the ages.

A thousand thanks to Dr. Peter Levine, founder of Somatic Experiencing®, and author of the groundbreaking book "Waking the Tiger" and nine other important books in this field of trauma work. I had the great fortune to study the work of trauma resolution directly under his supervision. He opened many doors within me to experience and understand the mind-body connection.

Many thanks to our Chilean editor, Maria Alicia Pino, the fairy who transformed our text into a living manuscript, shaping our ideas into an essential book for people. She and her understanding of connecting writer and reader are priceless, along with her illustrations that lent a playful aspect to delivering a more specific explanation. Thanks also for her beautiful cover design work. Truly an exceptional editor, this book became a jewel with her.

Many thanks to Fiorella Secchi Lagos, our illustrator, who created almost all the diagrams in this book, a great woman who immediately managed to understand our concepts of the exercises, very professional and dear.

Thank you, as well, to Sophie Ilya (voice over) and Ian Mehir (editing) for their professional excellence on the audiobook.

Thanks to Alex Hänel Muñoz, teacher and facilitator of The Points Holding Process ™ (PHP). His dedication, wisdom and experience helped us immensely in reviewing the material throughout the process. With a lot of patience, he helped us enormously in this journey, without his guidance it would not have been possible to produce this book.

Much gratitude to Dr. David Calderón Thayer, Surgeon of the University of Chile with a vast academic trajectory and professional practice of more than 30 years. He has ventured into very diverse fields of medicine such as: exercise physiology and sports medicine, metabolic diseases, nutrition and obesity, complementary medicines such as Chinese medicine, Ayurvedic and lately neuroscience, trauma and human development. He considers himself a specialist in integrative medicine, considering the relationship between man and his environment as an object of development and quality of life. He has been a book and scientific research publications' editor since 1988 to date. David is the expert reviewer of the clinical information in our book. His help and understanding contributed significantly to the work quality, his comments completed and reinforced the understanding of more complex issues.

A sincere thank you to my life partner Bob Schwarz for his immense help with technical support, translation and content improvements. Your love and understanding of this work have been a great inspiration and blessing to me. Although it may seem informal, I can't help but tell you that I love you very much and you are the best company for me and my work.

Thanks for the help and support of my dear friends Paz Baraona, Tatiana Brooke, Carolyn Reynaud Eglash, and Monica Berg, Co-Director Kabbalah Centre, all of whom I love very much.

Extra special thanks to my daughter Sasha, who was an enormous help in translation and proof-reading, and has always supported me in this path of life. Her mother-daughter love is an inspiration in my life.

Thank you to my dear son-in-law Erik, an exceptional father to my grandchildren and an adoring person.

Special thanks to my grandson Spencer for always being so loving and understanding this work.

Special thanks to my grandson Danner for his love, affection and always good vibes.

Thanks to my father of indefinite age, Ezequiel Ureta; thanks to my brothers Exequiel, Rodrigo, Max and Luis and my dear sister Monica, who has supported me enormously throughout my life, always connecting us with our family in Chile; she is a great inspiration for me, her affection and love are in my heart.

Finally, thanks to all my clients and those who trained and certified in PHP and PNE, and have chosen to embrace the teachings for the benefit of others who seek relief from the burden of trauma in their lives. Thank you.

Ancestors and Trauma

Mariann Dávila

Over time I have understood that there are invisible threads that link our past with our present. People's life and stories, belonging to our lineage, the family we never knew; have marked our unconscious and have defined much of what happens to us today, and how we behave in response to each event.

This is the importance of our ancestral line, our old and forgotten ancestors.

In our daily life, when we are faced with adverse situations, with unthinkable problems, we do not manage (sometimes we do not even think of doing so) to relate the present traumatic events with causes that have originated in the past, decades and perhaps centuries ago.

Why do habits such as alcoholism, drug use, domestic violence, mental illness, even suicide, appear in the family and cross from generation to generation? Trauma seems to be incorporated repeatedly in family systems, in lineage: alcoholic grandfather, alcoholic children and grandchildren, but also, if we unconsciously add an alcoholic partner to our experience, this replicates the branching pattern.

What needs to heal this system? The system itself. How does one heal an ancestral system and its beliefs?

These two questions are the key that opens this research work. The need to solve a suffering that does not belong entirely to us, an inherited suffering.

When we reflect on the origin of trauma, our thoughts go back to the history of our mothers, fathers, grandparents, great-grandparents and so many others. How many painful situations, sorrow, anguish, suffering, survival difficulties, grief, struggles, must have indelibly marked them?

By doing the exercise of looking at ourselves, we can recognize their life stories imprinted in our genetic patterns. Their intense learnings are also in us, as they have been unconsciously transmitted through our DNA. This is how we generate our own stories in parallel with their stories, and at some point, we relive some ancestral pattern without realizing that we are reproducing the suffering of another. It is here when the opportunity appears to recognize in us unconscious patterns of responses, somatic traces, and memories that are activated, passing on the unsolved to the new generations.

Although we did not know these ancestors, we did inherit from them how they felt in times of war, the fear of hunger that they did not overcome. The guilt for mistakes was left behind and is passed on with the firm purpose of healing.

When I think of stress and trauma, I see the suffering of children directly affected by problems that parents could not overcome because they did not have the means or the way to do so. Children damaged by phrases from patterns that may not even belong to their own parents and resonates in them in beliefs such as "you don't love me", "I'm a problem for you", "I deserve to be abandoned or beaten" and many more. Deeply rooted childhood beliefs surface and become an internal torture, debilitating mental schemes, disorganized personality structures that, in order to solve them, the psyche itself develops behaviors and responses of compensation or denial of the acts, generating models of violence, abuse, mistreatment and self-destruction in most current systems. For some years now, parents have been aware of the need to be mentally and psychologically healthy for their children, to have a life with more regulation, more attachment and self-confidence. It is not enough to focus only on offering a good school and university education, we need to educate emotions, we need an education system that also considers the emotional dimension of each individual, their need to generate self-regulation and attachment; their need to learn, to recognize their own anxiety, to identify the relationship between psychosomatic illnesses and a dysregulated nervous system, and how all this impacts on the feeling of being unprotected, uncared for and unloved.

In recent years, we have obtained research results in neuroscience, medicine and psychiatry that show how neurophysiological trauma patterns are activated in situations of conflict, life-threatening or life-threatening situations and how these traumas, sometimes inherited and unresolved, provoke weak or erratic defense responses, harmful behaviors, violence or guilt, shame and fears, which are replicated and inherited, if not worked on to be healed.

This book shows how the overwhelming experiences of trauma can only be understood by integrating various fields of knowledge, such as neuroscience, developmental psychopathology, and interpersonal neurobiology. The clarity of vision of this work makes it very accessible to understand and adequately treat traumatic stress.

We have integrated, through our adaptive capacity, a defense system in our body that is linked to the Autonomic Nervous System and its survival responses. For example, knowing when to escape and when to attack or when to freeze, which allows us to survive dangerous events and to move forward. I think today of ancestors, of all ancestors, with the certainty that evolution challenges us all to take charge of our personal difficulties and to solve what others could not or did not know how to do.

It is of utmost importance to thank our lineage, our clan and family for their struggles to survive, for their efforts to move forward, since these efforts have provided resources for our own development, and thus keep going with this continuous evolutionary process from generation to generation.

I am grateful to be able to synthesize in this work, experiences that are rooted in my own challenges, resolve my own traumas and duels, signify failures and learn to take care of myself and believe in myself. This synthesis becomes a contribution to those who read this book.

We have all lived through trauma. We know what it has been like to experience this suffering and to make efforts to overcome it. So, I sincerely wish you all peace, that you feel life is a gift, and I thank each and every one of you, for sharing in this work.

I dedicate this work to my great-great-grandmother Magdalena, my great-grandmothers Pierina, Dolores, Grandmothers Lily Haas, Maria Manuela, and my mother Sonia.

INTRODUCTION
CATALINA URETA

In this book, we want you to learn how to work with life events that leave traumatic imprints in your body and nervous system so that you can understand how danger, stress, illness, and other past traumas affect your present physical, emotional, and mental well-being, even when experienced before birth. The goal of these chapters is for you to learn first how stress originates. Then, the various defense system responses to danger. Finally, how trauma healing is approached today through the reorganization of those same defense responses. Such reorganization can be achieved through mind-body therapies such as Somatic Experiencing® from the revered Dr. Peter Levine, and The Points Holding Process™ (PHP) which focuses on dissolving crystallized belief patterns in the body.

For over twenty-five years we have facilitated radical changes in many people's lives. They have manifested positive results after undergoing Somatic Experiencing® and PHP therapy because they have been able to understand how thoughts become imprints that calcify into limiting beliefs, crystallizing life into patterns that stifle and clog energy.

The feelings of being lost, disconnected, and without meaning in life can be mitigated through the methodologies presented in this book.

The experiences of our ancestors are also transferred to our DNA as information. Ancestral traumas, family traumas, collective pains are transferred to our cellular memory creating an energy in the body that you feel is not yours, and that gets trapped in a belief system. For example: "I am bad", "I don't deserve it", "I always do badly" and other thought mantras that accompany us all our lives.

When we are very young, we can feel what our parents are feeling, what affects them and what makes them suffer. We perceive it both energetically and sympathetically. The child incorporates this energy into their body and stores it as "calcifications." Generally, this process of accumulation takes place in the spine since it is the nerve nexus of the body. It is precisely there where we can work on dissolving those calcifications. That is the moment when deep changes and healing really takes place. Eckhart Tolle, in his book "The Power of Now," refers to this as "The Pain Body."

In the therapy of dissolving calcified belief patterns through Points Holding, some people have experienced spontaneous regression to past lives, or an exploration of their deep subconscious memories, to heal what affects them in the present. The therapist her/himself may even experience spiritual assistance through the channeling of forces that guide her/him in healing and reinforcing a radical change in the client's body. Through the pressure of the calcified points, we can access layers of memories and recognize the roots of trauma.

The therapeutic process also aims to teach the regulation of emotions. We learn to use the body as a container capable of holding and processing emotions, to know what their function are, and how to harmonize with them.

In this work we have integrated advances in neuroscience, especially in the understanding of the brain and the autonomic nervous system. Both play an important role in understanding the matrix of our thoughts. We are not raised to correlate mind, body, and emotion; however, the body is the container of all our past and present experiences.

We are continually developing and improving techniques that help people to live with meaning and purpose. We conduct international trainings with focus on The Points Holding Process™ (PHP), Somatic Release Technique™ and neuroscience courses as applied to trauma. We apply the work of nervous system regulation, the Polyvagal Theory of Dr. Stephen Porges, and Vagus Nerve healing exercises.

Our goal is to enable you to work with the body through these therapies. You will learn to recognize belief patterns and integrate them into your psychological and emotional self-awareness that may have been dissociated or repressed by involuntary defense mechanisms. You will find exercises that have been specifically selected to use daily to meet the requirements of your healing process.

Each person must focus on their own individual needs, but these self-regulation exercises will permit anyone to cultivate a sense of direction and feel grounded. You will also be able to purposely recognize your capacity to heal through the "felt sense" in the body, which supports reconnection with yourself and others. The felt sense also brings you to an integrative and loving perspective, focused on empowerment, deepening the sense of connection with oneself, and allowing us to adapt to what surrounds us. This allows us to reclaim the inner space needed to recover from the exhaustion of everyday life and accumulated stress. We often do not realize how shut down we have become until dysregulation, insomnia, and anxiety appear.

Many of us experience living in survival mode, often in hostile environments, overwhelmed by confusion and uncertainty, and saddled by the difficulties of getting ahead in life. This reactive way of brain and nervous system behavior confronts us with specific patterns that make us feel agitated, and unconsciously defensive. We can feel helpless as control slips out of our hands. Our body asks us for an internal change. It asks us to learn to self-regulate and take care of our inner ecosystem in order to create security, and to feel compassion and empathy for ourselves and those around us. It is from this space that PHP allows us to release stuck or frozen energies, to resolve unsettled situations that fill us with guilt, shame, or remorse, and to reorganize our tolerances and regain peace of mind. HEALING THE BODY IS POSSIBLE!

We intend to share practical knowledge on how to deal with life events that have left negative imprints and traumas in our human experience. Through research, there has been much knowledge gained about trauma at every stage of development from before birth through adulthood. Life is full of experiences fraught with danger, stress, symptoms, diseases, and other traumas that affect our development, physically and psychologically. From the very beginning of our lives, we have the capacity to face great challenges, to navigate complex learning processes, and to develop our unique talents. However, we are also forced to face pain, illness, loss, and accidents that challenge us to surmount the difficulties of life. We are challenged to find our inner richness, to connect with others, to create a family, to care for loved ones, to create a better world for all and for the future of humanity.

In these chapters we will find simple answers on how to recognize and manage the internal and external stress factors that accompany us day to day. We strive to rise above both conscious and unconscious emotions that upset us, mostly anger, fear, and grief. We can learn to level the high stress curves that elicit defensive responses, instigate aggression, and provoke terror in the face of a possible threat or danger.

We ask ourselves:

- How do we release limiting beliefs, family inherited patterns, and in what way can we heal our emotional wounds via the body?
- How can we proceed to ease traumatic memories, and free ourselves from a negative internal self-image based on exposure to violence, abuse, or sexual harassment? Or physical harm from an assault, robbery, or accident?

Relying on our hands-on experience with many patient sessions and PHP trainings, we have compiled exercises that have been designed to be used daily. We hope that these exercises, together with therapies mentioned, allow for the complete recovery of your personal well-being. In addition to having a daily self-care routine, we also recommend shifting away from harmful habits by examining and reconditioning your daily practices.

CHAPTER I

HEALING THE BODY IS POSSIBLE

The Body and Emotions

In each person, there is a need to work on those physical aspects that strengthen both the psychological and emotional centers. The body is the container that has the regulatory patterns and mechanisms that allow people to reconnect with their own sense of orientation, securing the changes that are needed, and freeing the breath's energy to circulate to all bodily regions.

The body sustains the mind. It stores family and ancestral memories through genetics and is designed to regulate processes so that physical systems and organs function in a healthy way. This essential balance is called, "homeostasis," an internal regulatory mechanism that we require at the physical level to provide stability in an ever-changing environment. Homeostasis is accompanied by the need to maintain a mind in balance, with thoughts that allow us to live a meaningful life.

A balanced body, mind, and emotional state is essential for spiritual well-being where peace and harmony can be present in our daily life, despite external challenges. This allows us to be more flexible and resilient when facing situations that generate fear, anger, or pain.

Recognizing one's own natural capacity to heal and connect with oneself is also a way to repair the inner apparatus that generates social engagement, establishes lasting bonds, and creates loving relationships. Sustaining positive self-esteem, living with empowerment, and a sense of connection with oneself and one's surroundings allows us to adapt and evolve as we were meant to.

In each chapter you will find life stories that have been shared by people who have overcome serious illnesses and traumas, recovered their emotional tranquility and restored their zest for life.

We hope that this compilation of our knowledge, exercises, recommendations, and testimonials all make it easier for you to TAKE YOUR DESTINY INTO YOUR OWN HANDS!

HEREDITY AND GENETICS

The gift of ancestral wisdom in our body.

We have inherited through our ancestors the ability to survive the external environment, the dangers of nature and catastrophes. This ability to adapt is essential for being able to deal with change, resolve difficulties and take actions that allow us to move forward in life.

For more than 120,000 years as Homo sapiens, we have experienced life's challenges. We have needed to provide ourselves with food and reproduce, overcome diseases, pandemics, and heal wounds. All these experiences have created evolutionary learning processes at the genetic level, which are observed through the expression of innate behaviors, that also allow us to interact and modify our environment from hunting in groups, to living in today's world of telecommuting in large cities. The nervous system and brain have developed in an increasingly specialized way, generating more efficient changes and adaptations. It conditions responses to danger unconsciously through the Sympathetic Nervous System (SNS). We call these defense-oriented responses: attack, flight or freeze. When observing danger and the possibility of facing a threat, our body activates hormones, neurotransmitters, adrenaline, epinephrine, cortisol and neuropeptides such as ACTH and TRH. At the same time, our cerebral amygdala reacts instinctively, provoking a bodily experience that leads us to face these challenges and then resolve them, freeing us from fear and stress.

This bodily and nervous system ability to discharge arousal or activation is the essential key to self-regulation. This arousal is preceded by shaking, hyperventilation, sweating, crying and other bodily responses depending on each individual. This discharge mobilizes, in the nervous system, waves of energy and a chemical response that allows us to restore the internal balance, as well as restoring the sense of vital security that we need to move through life, improve self-confidence, increase vitality and enhance the ability to actively participate in resolving the stress or event that generated the trauma. An adaptive process that leads us to a more focused and balanced sensor of well-being with our body and mind is very important.

How to understand my mind, my brain and my traumas?

If you experience a series of strange symptoms in your body that you cannot understand, it is possible that they come from some old incident that your brain remembered in an unexpected moment; maybe you do not even have memory of the event and when you perceive strange sensations in your body, you start to believe that you are crazy. You go to a psychologist, or a doctor, you try to hide this strange sensation from others and you start to get depressed; you don't eat well, you can't sleep well. You think there is no way out and that you need medication to stop this strange feeling in your body and make it go away.

You ask yourself, what's wrong, I feel tingling, trembling, energy moving under my skin. You have the tingling sensation under your skin; you just think you have to get rid of this strange sensation. The mind is altered and fear appears - fear of dying, of getting cancer or another disease. The symptom of a trauma starts some months or years after what provoked it. For example, a person who has suffered a serious car accident, his body mechanism makes him forget the incident thanks to the mechanism of dissociation or denial, which helps us to navigate in critical moments; the nervous system freezes to protect the body.

The Nervous System in the body

It is important to know that the body knows how to heal itself and that all these strange sensations are part of the nervous system recovery.

The nervous system center is between the brain and the spinal cord. The peripheral nervous system is made up of several fibers and branches that originate in the spinal cord and extend to all parts of our body.

The brain sends messages through the spinal cord to peripheral nerves in order to control muscles movements and the function of internal organs.

The basic unit, where the work of the nervous system is carried out, is called a neuron. The human brain contains more than 100 trillion neurons.[1] A neuron consists of a cell that has a nucleus, axons and dendrites.

---

[1] Extracted from the website:
https://www.nichd.nih.gov/health/topics/neuro/conditioninfo/parts

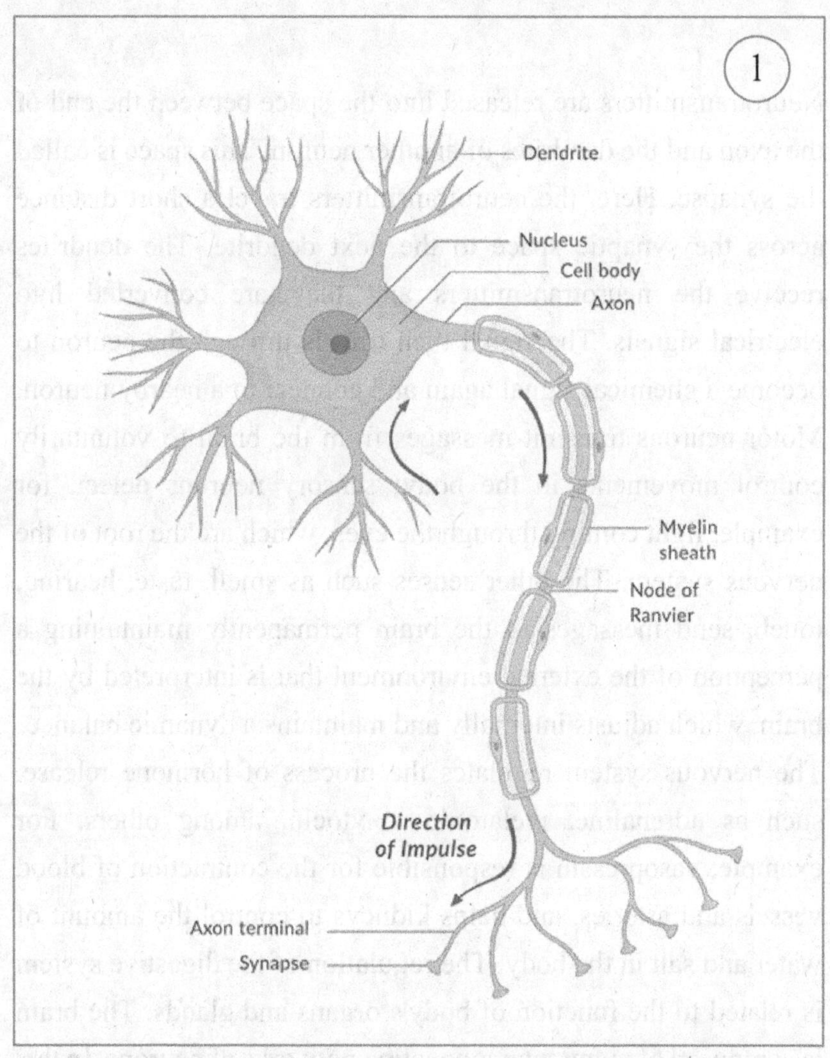

Neurons communicate with each other by axons and dendrites. When one neuron receives the message from another neuron, it emits an electrical discharge that travels through the neuron's body to the end of the axon. The electrical charge is converted into a chemical signal, and the axon releases messengers called neurotransmitters.

Neurotransmitters are released into the space between the end of the axon and the dendrites of another neuron. This space is called the synapse. Here, the neurotransmitters travel a short distance across the synaptic space to the next dendrite. The dendrites receive the neurotransmitters and they are converted into electrical signals. The signal then travels through the neuron to become a chemical signal again and connect to a nearby neuron. Motor neurons transmit messages from the brain to voluntarily control movements in the body; sensory neurons detect, for example, light coming through the eyes, which are the root of the nervous system. The other senses such as smell, taste, hearing, touch, send messages to the brain permanently maintaining a perception of the external environment that is interpreted by the brain, which adjusts internally and maintains a dynamic balance. The nervous system regulates the process of hormone release, such as adrenaline, melatonin, oxytocin, among others. For example, vasopressin is responsible for the contraction of blood vessels and arteries, and helps kidneys to control the amount of water and salt in the body. The regulation of the digestive system is related to the function of body's organs and glands. The brain is composed of many interconnecting networks of neurons. In this way the body parts can "talk" to each other and work together to send the message to the rest of the body, that is, there is a body interconnection at all levels. This interconnection of information allows one to maintain an effective and permanent communication between the different body organs and a better general functional and organic balance.

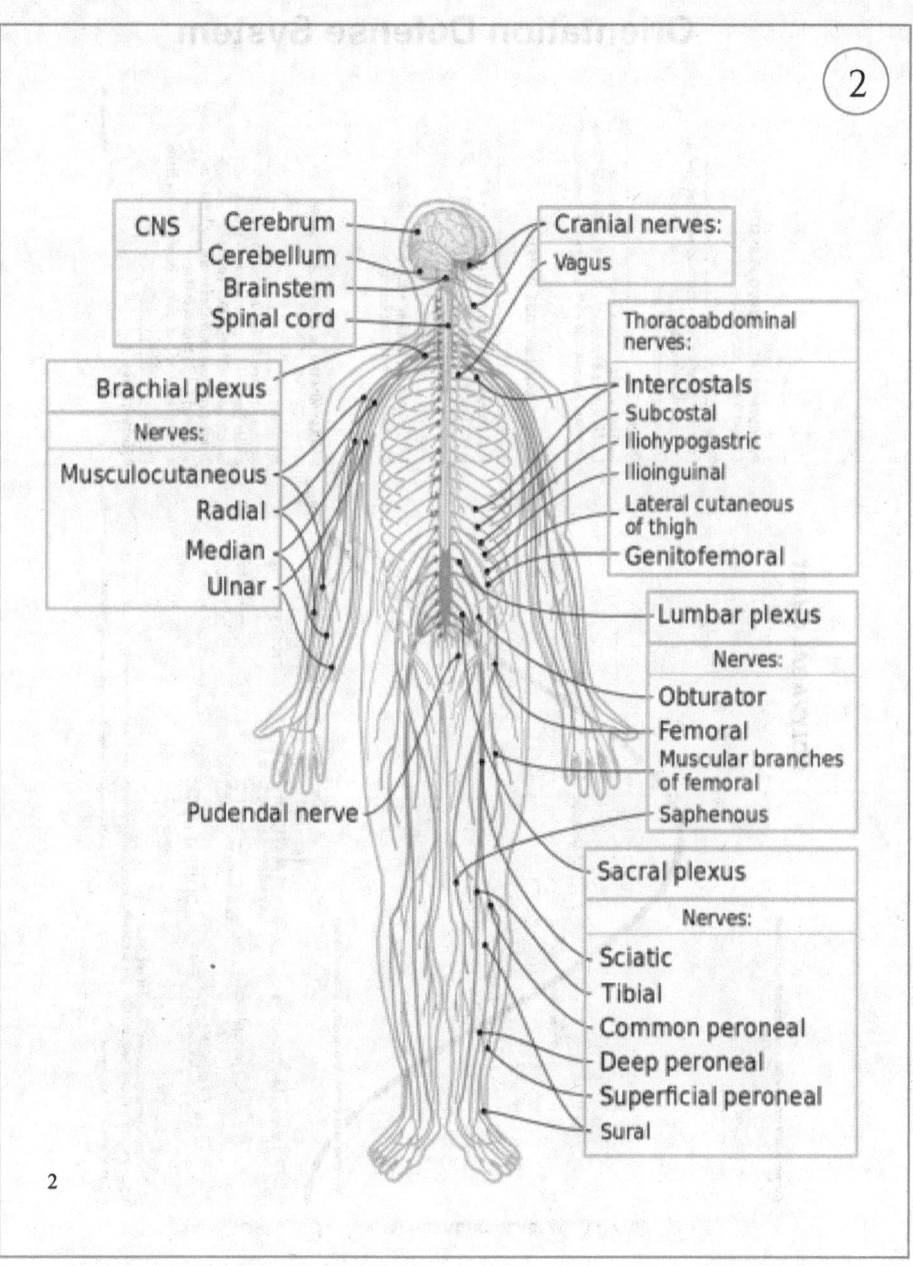

2

---

[2] Ref: Lumen: Biology for Majors II. Module 13: Overview of Body Systems.
https://courses.lumenlearning.com/wm-biology2/chapter/nervous-system/

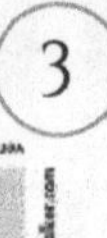

Orientation Defense System (3)

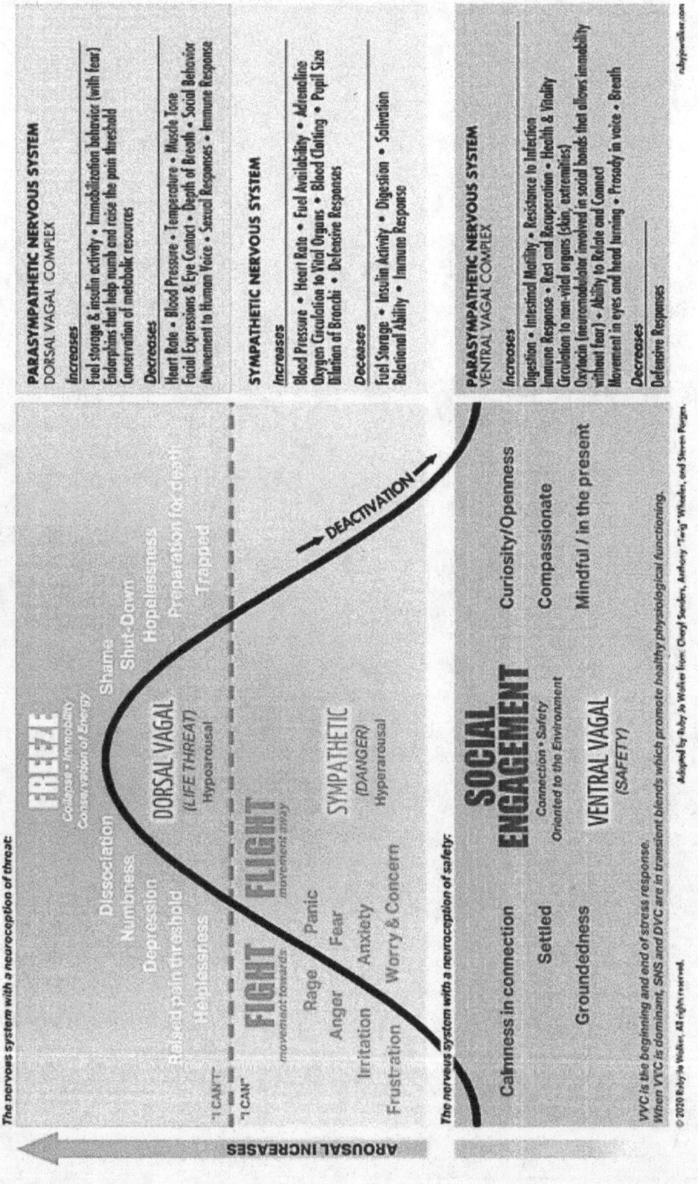

3

---

[3] Ref: https://static1.squarespace.com/static/5d9e25df25a9e9342e56e931/t/605a6b2f78c3fe3607e3ec49/1616538424232/Polyvagal+Chart.jpg

1. Social connection: Ventral vagal response, defined as a safety response and orientation towards the environment.

2. Flight or fight: Sympathetic, active response that allows the subject to make the decision to flee or fight.

3. Freeze: This is a dorsal vagal defense body collapse response and manifests as immobility.

AROUSAL OR ACTIVATION OF THE NERVOUS SYSTEM IN THE CONTEXT OF TRAUMA

Arousal is an organism's physiological state in response to internal and external stimuli. It is a response of cortical and neurochemical excitation of high energetic intensity. We can observe its effect on the autonomic nervous system: change in pupil size, tingling, changes in skin color and tremors, among others.

In PHP, the way to work with the arousal discharge, is to mobilize this energy through pressure on those points where it has stagnated and crystallized. This action allows the arousal discharge that was trapped in the body for not being able to complete the defense response, to be reorganized and above all released.

In synthesis: the objective of working with arousal, is to facilitate in people the stress discharge or trauma that was dysregulating the nervous system. As arousal is a sympathetic activation peak, PHP collaborates in lowering this curve.

Trauma is the trauma independent of its cause. In this process we need enough time to experience the sensations that accompany it, that is to say, to identify and pay attention to the sensation of the trauma (felt sense).

When hyper arousal is not discharged, it is divided into three main responses:

1. Hypervigilance and constrictions
2. Impotence and freezing
3. Dissociation.

These three responses are part of the box's third level: Freezing.

Effects of Regulation and Dysregulation of the Autonomic Nervous System

Hypervigilance and Constriction

Hypervigilance is a compulsive version of the orienting response. It is a traumatic mental state of heightened alertness, extremely sensitive to the environment, unconsciously having the need to find the source of the threat. Even if the source is found, hypervigilance will continue.

Characteristics of hypervigilance

There is a defense-oriented system that links the senses of vision, hearing, smell and the neck musculature that allows its rotation. The eyes, in a state of hypervigilance, look everywhere, looking for the origin of a possible danger. The ears do the same, searching for noises that could represent threats. The sense of smell detects and the rotation of the neck directs full attention. Hypervigilance is an exaggerated response from seeking a defensive orientation.

Exercises to work on Hypervigilance

Exercise 1: Expansion

We invite you to work with "expansion", that is, to observe your surroundings and listen attentively, to obtain more details that will prevent you from entering into the frantic response of seeking orientation. We invite you to keep your attention on an object that catches you long enough for orientation response, to reorganize, and expand the feeling of coming out of the hypervigilance state. After this, ask yourself: What do I notice in my body?

If after this exercise the hypervigilance continues, repeat it until you achieve your goal. During this exercise, micro movements may appear, these are small involuntary muscular adjustments as responses of the body to the stimulus of the exercise; they appear alone and produce in the body a sensation of natural relaxation. Their function is to regulate the defense orientation mechanism. When they appear, it is important to be aware of them and to perform them slowly and smoothly in order to integrate the experience.

Exercise 2: Pinching

Being in an active state of hypervigilance, generates a state of general muscular contraction in the body. What we recommend, is to gently pinch the contracted areas, such as the neck, head, arms, and relax. Then, check your internal state, breathe and relax.

Freezing / Impotence

Another characteristic of trauma expression is freezing and helplessness. Freezing is a survival response mediated by the Vagal-dorsal system, manifested in the autonomic nervous system. Its main characteristic is dissociation and immobility, which serve as defense mechanisms.

Impotence is the sensation of not being able to face a danger and appears after the immobility or freezing response. When this manifests itself permanently, it produces in the person a lack of empowerment behavior that becomes part of his or her identity. Instead of active participation, the behavior reflects a chronic state of helplessness and passivity.

Helplessness, which is that state of not being able to defend yourself, is going to manifest itself in the body as a frozen muscle or body part. Sometimes it will be in a muscle, sometimes in a shoulder, in the chest, the jaw and it will depend on the degree of freezing if it involves other parts of the body.

Trauma produces a blockage of nervous activity. The mind goes blank and the brain shows reduced autonomic activity accompanied by possible fluctuations in blood pressure and heart rate.

Exercises for working with Freezing

Exercise 1: Limits

First, do connection exercises, activating muscles to the limit. For example; putting your palms over someone else's and pressing them forward to connect muscles of shoulders, arms and breasts. Simultaneously, verbalize the word, "HOLD."

Exercise 2: Personal Resource Development

This has to do with the work of empowerment and development of resources that the person already possesses. For example: if you like music, or walking, in the face of dysregulation, you can sing, if you like walking, you can go for a walk around the neighborhood; it is about allowing you to access what you have as a personal tool and provide you with a self-regulatory response, which will allow you to be more resilient in the face of adversity, both neurologically and emotionally. You can make a list of activities such as walking, singing, painting, etc.

Exercise 3: Felt sensation

The goal of this exercise is to work with the development of a somatic sense of self, through the felt sensation.
Sensations are the somatic language. They come from the body and allow you to perceive how you feel inside. For example, your neck hurts when you are looking at your cell phone for a long time. That pain is a message for you to realize that it is not doing you any good and to change your position.
This exercise helps you concentrate on a pleasant sensation that captures your attention so the body will notice it. When the body detects that you are paying attention to its expression, it will then generate other sensations that will lead you to a spontaneous self-regulation. This is called Sense Sensation. The body expresses its sensory language through the brain stem.

Wave of Coherence

Dr. Peter Levine discovered the body's ability to generate coherence waves naturally in the nervous system. He made these discoveries by studying different animal behavior for several years. When he found the coherence wave, he asked himself: do we have this ability in the human body, and if so, what is the way to harness it? From this, he researched and developed Somatic Experiencing® therapy.

What we want to achieve in a traumatized person is to open healing through the body's own response by generating a wave of coherence (Coherency Wave). For example, if you observe the sea attentively, you will notice that the waves are constant and balanced. If you stay observing this movement for a period of time, it generates a relaxing effect and, therefore, gives the body a wonderful balance, peace and relaxation. There is an amplification of the wave in a natural dynamic regulating movement to all other systems, causing relief, restoration and integration of processes.

This wave of coherence manifests as an autonomic nervous system in equilibrium, being the variability of the heart rate a clinical predictor of this phenomenon, that measures the relative balance between the sympathetic and parasympathetic systems. When we breathe in, we stimulate the central nervous system, which results in an increased heart rate, exhalations increase the parasympathetic nervous system, reducing the heartbeat in normal people. Inhalations and expirations produce constant and rhythmic fluctuations of the heart rate, that means a variability of heart rate, and therefore a good parameter of human well-being.

Model of an Unhealthy Nervous System

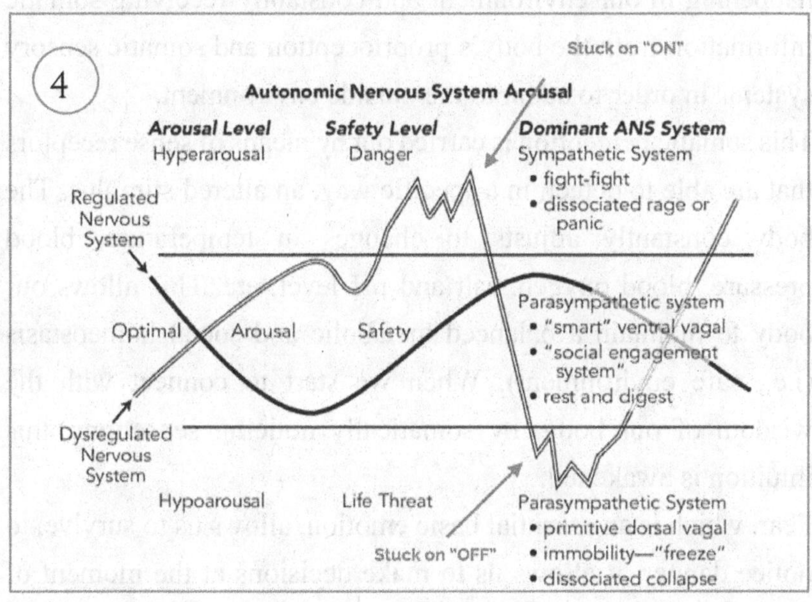

4

Neuroception

Neuroception is the body's innate ability to sense of the environment. It is important to understand that we have this subconscious ability to recognize changes in the environment, through what Stephen Porges has called, Neuroception. It is an innate capacity of the body to detect changes in our surroundings. Animals, as well as humans, operate by sensing whether the environment provides them with a sense of safety or danger. It is important to understand that we are instinctively and permanently

---

[4] Ref: Trauma Informed Yoga Alliance Teacher Online Training. Module 1: The foundations of Trauma. https://www.atiratan.com/wp-content/uploads/2020/07/TIY-Online-PDF-Manual-Compressed.pdf

alert, ready for attack or flight. We are always processing what is happening in our environment and constantly receiving somatic information from the body's proprioception and somatic sensory systems in order to adapt to the outside environment.

This somatic perception is carried out by means of sense receptors that are able to detect, in a specific way, an altered stimulus. The body constantly adjusts to changes in temperature, blood pressure, blood oxygen, salt and pH level, etc. This allows our body to maintain a balanced metabolic and social homeostasis (i.e., safe environment). When we start to connect with the wisdom of our body, by somatically noticing sensations, this intuition is awakened.

Fear, which is an essential basic emotion, allows us to survive, to notice danger; it allows us to make decisions at the moment of threat. Fear can be regulated to the extent that the risk is not so high and there is the possibility of renegotiating the defense response to the threat, being able to gradually and consciously calm down and get out of the situation. However, above a higher level of danger, (arousal[5]) involuntary unconscious responses inevitably appear. Fear activates the defenses in an intense way, releasing hormones and neurotransmitters that will impact the brain, activating the cerebral circuits and the attack, flight or freeze reactions, and selecting the most appropriate one for that moment. For example, animals in the jungle intuitively perceive when there is danger and prepare for attack or flight.

---

[5] Arousal: Excitement

The Body Posses Instinctive Intelligence

We naturally have the ability in our body to maintain the balance of multiple functions that allow us to live: the ability to maintain a flow in breathing, sensitivity to external temperature change, heart rate, blood flow in the body and other unconscious and involuntary mechanisms.

Through attention to bodily or somatic signals: heat, cold, tingling, itching, weight, pain and more, we can consciously track or perceive consciously changing sensations; by noticing these changes and sustaining them, emerge somatic reorganization responses that generate internal changes. These allow us to achieve the proper balance of fluids, oxygen in the blood, respiratory rate and in the whole process of homeostasis, experiencing the proper regulation of all body systems, which act in a synchronized way for an optimal integrated body functioning, mind and emotions.

Through the complex mechanism called "perception", sensory stimuli allow us to make contact with the body, learn to recognize the warning signals – pain; and recognize where the tension or symptom is. This is called the "voice of the body" and represents an unresolved, crystallized or calcified emotion often manifesting as pain in the muscles, jaw, neck or back. These are the emotions, memories, thoughts and beliefs that become encapsulated in the body and weaken our physical and mental health.

Since our gestation, we are constantly learning, incorporating information through different means, and simultaneously perceiving signals of threat or safety from the environment. From that early moment on, we seek to resonate, tune in and connect with others; to feel that we belong to the social group or herd, integrating ourselves into socially safe spaces.

MEMORIES FROM THE PAST DWELLING IN THE PRESENT

Trauma, family and transgenerational memory

Our ancestral life history, along with the psychic memories of our parents, grandparents, and great-grandparents, accompany us permanently through genes we inherit. Unconsciously we share ancestral patterns and traumas, which mark and reinforce specific behaviors for survival. In today's world, these can become maladaptation patterns that significantly alter our experience.

For example, surely on some occasion, as a result of feeling out of place or hurt, we have shouted at someone in a moment of confusion. Then appears, from within, the uncontrollable rage, where even oneself is frightened and wonders, how is it that I have no control over myself?

This is the neocortex, or cerebral cortex, which is connected to thoughts and inhibited defense. It is also connected to the program we learn from childhood, from how my father treated my mother, or my grandmother treated her son. This can have consequences for many generations to come, transmitting and sustaining the trauma from generation to generation and thus causing suffering that often does not seem to belong to us.

Socially, aggression, as a defense, is frowned upon, often inhibited, which prevents us from expressing rage and activating physical defenses: scratching, biting, hitting and attacking. We remain inside obfuscated, contained, with holding any defensive action, which has repercussions on our physical and mental health. In behaviors of aggression, we can observe how the brain stem connects with unconscious mechanisms that inhibit emotional control (prefrontal cortex) in extreme moments, generating uncontrolled impulses to act in self-defense. At other times, the impact of the threat may be such, that we cannot contain the defense and we react instinctively. This happens inevitably on some occasions. Dysregulation, trauma and violence can be generated from toxic and destructive emotions from childhood, both in the family and social environment. This damage, inevitably, has caused a negative impact on the victims and in many occasions these behaviors give rise to extreme situations of social impact, people who have lost the ability to measure the consequences of their actions and represent a danger at the social level. Individuals who attack schools, gunmen in supermarkets. The extreme case of violence is represented by the psychopath, who feels no remorse and rather enjoys harming others.

The TTG are those traumatic experiences of our ancestors that we are unaware of, that affect us, and that often repeat themselves in us, without knowing where they come from, because they are the product of repetitions of unconscious family patterns. They can express themselves in difficulties, from small addiction problems to sexual violence, suicides or traumas. Through the recognition of these patterns, thoughts, feelings, and limiting beliefs we can reorganize the life experiences that have provoked crises, psychosomatic illnesses, emotional blocks, distorted thoughts, irrational fears, guilt, failures in relationships, and insecurities. We can understand that traumatic events may have been generated before birth, from the family context. Our progenitors are loaded with experiences that implant a representation or image of what it means to be a son or daughter, for example, and how siblings are incorporated into the family unit. Underage mothers, unplanned or unwanted children, fathers who do not participate in family support create chaos. Conflicts or intra family violence and economic difficulties generate high levels of stress, depressive moods, anxiety, threat and insecurity that affect the mother directly and this is incorporated into the body and is transferred to the fetus in high levels of cortisol, the stress hormone. The prevailing environment of care, including nutritional and social support during gestation, affects not only the physical health of the pregnant mother, but also the way she internalizes emotional support and protection. A toxic environment, lack of tranquility, loneliness or fear are elements that will provoke, in some cases, negative effects on the pregnant mother and the fetus. These toxic environmental, emotional and relational conditions of insecurity could provoke an ideal context for early trauma in the newborn.

From gestation onwards, deep unconscious sensory and motor imprints are generated in the fetus, precursors of unconscious patterns that will generate restlessness, hyperactivity, sleep dysregulation, food allergies, and other neurodevelopmental alterations. Reactions and fears are traces intimately linked to the psyche that will mark the baby's future.

At birth, we receive our first impressions of the external world. We come from a warm, fluid, liquid space and quickly change to an air space, with environmental variations in temperature that impact the newborn. Like a vinyl record, from the center to the periphery, we record memories, memories in the neural circuits that are our own early neurobiological, preverbal, sensorimotor and unconscious base, which will give rhythm to the song of our life.

As the nervous system develops in the baby, an increase of genetically established neural networks is generated to activate a basic system of survival and adaptation.

The baby's capacity for survival responses, is organized on the basis of stimulation, that is, the child receives stimuli that make it activate these natural defenses; for example: it cries when it is hungry, then receives food and calms down; it cries when it has a belly pain and mom gives it something, and it calms down. This action that the baby and the mother perform intuitively is transformed into a dynamic that reinforces the infant's security through the mother's response, which calms and regulates him from that moment onwards. This is how the attachment bond is built.

The capacity of imitation or vicarious learning (learning that takes place through the observation of the other) allows learning to take place. Mirror neurons generate the phenomenon of empathy (putting oneself in another's place) and mentalization (reading another's behavior, or what is going on in another's mind and in our own mind). At the same time, neural networks and circuits of responses to the perception of danger and safety develop. In this early stage of infancy, we are totally dependent, we have the intrinsic need to be cared for, in order to achieve a healthy body, an organized mind and a stable psyche, which allows structuring the Self. With an integrated Self, we will gradually be able to structure a healthy personality, which will allow us to develop psychological and emotional aspects, the current diagnostic systems emphasize behavioral management without recognition of interpersonal trauma.

The continued application of multiple different comorbid diagnoses to traumatized children, has important consequences in relegating a small part of the child's psychopathologies, rather than promoting a comprehensive treatment approach.

Attachment repair can be a therapeutic process to reinforce and repair the individual's self-confidence and ability to build healthy relationships. Secure attachments allow for trust in the other, to have stable emotions and harmonious affections.

In an ambivalent attachment, the capacity to establish relationships will be hindered by anxiety, dependence, and stress, with attacks of fear, jealousy and insecurity, characterized by intense emotions, affections, easy breakups, and difficulty to accept and understand the other as an independent person. These types of relationships could be intermittent and unstable, and difficult to navigate in face of stress, feelings of restlessness and insecurity.

In avoidant attachment, we suffer from excessive, obsessive self-control. We wish to have control over our circumstances so as not to require the presence of the other, that means to avoid it. We need to be in charge of everything, to make demands on ourselves; we distance from others because we distrust them. At the moment of relating to others we distrust them and we are distant and defensive, unable to create bonds and establish stable relationships of mutual cooperation. It is possible to have important difficulties in being in a relationship.

The greatest attachment disorganization is observed in children with a high degree of trauma. They present a disorganized attachment to close bonds, they are rather solitary and reserved, with little physical contact, restlessness, anxiety and internal chaos, emotional instability and inability to integrate bonds or have relationships, they may even present aggressive behaviors. For example; in the world in general and especially in the United States, many young people between seventeen and twenty-one years old have already bought or used a gun involved in a mass shooting in a school, theater, temple, market, or mall, resulting in the death of many innocent people. These children have never had a familial attachment to a father or mother and view society with anguish, resentment, and jealousy to others, who have had or who have social ties and better opportunities. This is social trauma, just like terrorism.

It is important to know that the development of secure attachments in a child is vital, because if it is not established at an early age, it can have many consequences in the future, such as delinquency, aggression, and violence.

The quality of future relationships will be a product of this stage of the infant's psychic life. The style of attachment will be maintained until adulthood as it has already been organized. In the case of being ambivalent, anxious, avoidant or disorganized, it will be possible to work therapeutically on reworking the attachment style to bring it towards a healthy attachment.

After the construction of the attachment, at around four years of age, the development of the primary Self begins. The psychic recognition of the "I," the not "I" (the recognition of the others), informs the child's capacity to make contact with others and with reality. The child's incipient character traits appear: shy, introverted, sociable, confident, insecure, restless, quiet, playful, and explorative.

Starting from ages six to seven years old, autonomy begins to develop and reaches maturity around twelve years of age, the beginning of adolescence, along with great physical and emotional changes. Adolescence is a difficult stage, tinged with insecurity, a search for identity, and the need to relate to other peers and build self-esteem. This is a period of great sensitivity and vulnerability, especially due to the awakening of sexuality, as well as the need to feel capable of achieving social status with their peers and in their studies.

At the age of eighteen to twenty, we are expected to be able to develop a defined sexual identity within an organized personality; a personality, that is to say, that has an internal structure with its own characteristics. It is the beginning of young adult life, where decisions will be made based on the needs and preferences of how one build's their own life. The relevance of accompanying reflection is essential at this stage in order to develop reflective thinking and self-observation, which will help define their life alternatives.

At this stage, we seek to be recognized, integrated, and to belong with self-confidence. When we feel in good spirits, with clear thoughts and are achieving our goals, we feel positive and open. Early childhood abandonment, parents with major illnesses, bullying from teachers, peers or groups, abuse, violence due to social or sexual discrimination and trauma, make life become hell itself, which goes along with us throughout life. When we feel disconnected, afraid, insecure, tight, physically and emotionally sore, we feel we have no energy, everything taxes us, we are working with negative unconscious beliefs and patterns, which stops us and fills us with stress and frustration; we do not value or take care of ourselves and, sometimes, this exposes us to negative habits, to groups with risky behaviors, to drug use, looking to find a place to belong, in any way possible.

This is why it is very helpful to understand how to activate the body's healing processes from a somatic, psychological and energetic point of view.

The traces of experiences that overtake us are memories that become unconscious. However, we can recognize some traces of these, through observation and attention to the body, somatic sensations, emotions, behaviors, meaning and image. The SIBAM model of Somatic Experience®, Dr. Peter Levine, is a model to detect the way in which trauma hides, dissociated or not integrated by our mind; it hides in unpleasant sensations, isolated symptoms that emerge for no apparent reason, non-specific pain, tachycardia, panic attacks, anguish, phobia or anxiety. Through these symptoms we can find the trauma's tip of the iceberg, and begin to recover the energy to live.

The "descent into hell" is the journey into the parts of ourselves that are separated, disowned, unknown, unwanted, outlawed and exiled in different underworlds of consciousness. The goal of this journey is to reunite with ourselves. This homecoming can be surprising and painful. To realize it, we must first accept it and not exclude anything.

THE BODY THROUGH THE POINTS HOLDING PROCESS (PHP)

An experience of Therapeutic Session

When you attend a PHP session, there is a reason, a very deep motive that leads you to this healing experience.

PHP consists of a construction of stages, a "container" of emotions, that is, a body container. You can, in the first stage, relearn to sustain the processes of discharge in the nervous system; that occur in parallel with the processes of psychological integration of the experiences, that have caused you dissociation. With this we recover our center, balance and security, we integrate the experience and signify the patterns of negative beliefs, causing changes in the schemes of destructive thoughts and thus stop feeling dejected or without energy.

In the PHP therapeutic process, we give support to the nervous system by recommending to the client a natural mineral supplement in order to prepare the body for the session. The objective of activating the nervous system response to the stimulus; we seek to create a space of containment and calm that allows the body to begin to travel the path, to resolve what is stuck. The blockages will be discovered to the extent that the client feels her/his body.

The connection with the therapist in a safe space, together with education about the work to be done, is essential. Questions and answers based on an understanding of the trauma and how to resolve it, are part of the treatment; this is called psychoeducation.

The client is given an understanding of how negative psychological, mental and emotional belief patterns affect his or her life.

During sessions we hear stories of much suffering: tiredness, loss of meaning in life, how the loss of a friend or the death of a loved one weighs heavily, severe sleeping difficulties or disconnection with life and/or sexual pleasure. Car accidents, cosmetic or emergency surgeries, falls, assaults, sexual or work harassment, fears and phobias, mental exhaustion, fears that isolate us, doubts, depressive emotions, anger or memories generate hopelessness and motivate us to seek ways to free ourselves from them.

In the Process Holding Points™, the work is focused on what is hidden in our mind: Our debilitating thoughts, the beliefs learned in our family, inherited or learned from our parents, and the patterns that alter the regulation of our life, moods and emotions.

With PHP we know that working with trauma must be specialized; it requires an understanding of the categories of trauma and how to work with each one of them. This is why we have created a specific chapter dedicated to understanding these categories and how we can address them.

We will describe cases and show exercises that will help you on a daily basis to become safe or secure in your body again. In The Point Holding Process™, the work is focused on what is hidden in our mind: our debilitating thoughts, the beliefs learned in our family, inherited or learned from our parents, and the patterns that alter the regulation of our mood and emotions. Guilt, shame, mistrust, and isolation are accompanied by the disorganization of the self-regulating mechanism of the autonomic nervous system. Carrying the past is not good for our life, especially when we do not feel worthy of success. We feel as if stuck in a vacuum with a feeling of deep pain accompanied by shame and guilt. These beliefs make us feel helpless and insignificant and provoke self-destructive, punishing behaviors.

With PHP, we work on developing a loving view of our processes, giving us a healing and aligning context. We enhance the reflexive capacity for learning and integration as we learn to contain the somatic processes, while changing the beliefs that lead us to renegotiate the traumatic energy.

When we make contact through the points, the trapped (crystallized) energy and accompanying dissociation that results from the traumatic shock at the moment of impact, discharges from the nervous system.

Phrases such as "you are a fool, I can't do anything right, everyone rejects me, I can't be happy, or every day my life is worse", have affected the functioning of our neurons, creating altered neurotransmitter networks, neurohormonal disorders, fatigue, mood decompensation and loss of confidence, self-esteem and the ability to adapt. In some people, weight-gain or anorexia occurs when, in a childhood stage, their parent has disqualified them by saying that their body is not beautiful or that they look bad in certain clothes. This creates a belief system in which the child feels that he/she is not accepted by others and, for example, "stores anger" inside his/her stomach, which disconnects from the esophagus and does not feel that he/she is satisfied when he/she eats. A disconnection then occurs between physical body part, resulting, for example, in this case, in being overweight. With Somatic Experiencing® and points, we help you reconnect the organs that have become disconnected.

When we begin to open the body to the therapy, it reacts by supporting the process, releasing tensions and reshaping thoughts and behavioral patterns. Emotional pain, unloaded anger, fear and rigidity as a defense gradually disappear. This is reflected in changes of behavior and perception that liberate us from having to remain restricted, hurt, and without the possibility of self-expression. To retake one's own life, to expand the creative; peace and joy make up the closure of the trauma, because it is not cured definitively; there is no turning back.

Trauma and Dissociation

Experiences that push our boundaries

For a long time, the study of human behavior has been based on comparative analysis with animal behavior. We seek to understand differences and similarities. Some social and nurturing responses and behaviors in animals, for example, show similarities with the humans' relationship, in part because we share in the fact that we are mammals. This is manifested in the concept of healthy attachment.

Mammalian characteristics have to do with caring for, nursing, protecting and nurturing the newborn. This characteristic of caring is related to the limbic system, with genetically programmed behaviors. We have memories that allow us to interpret the needs our offspring and their requirements via non-verbal expression, in order to provide care and feeding when needed. The offspring naturally seeks to be nursed, to receive warmth and to connect through gazing. We have an innate instinct to protect and regulate.

Through the stimulation of sensations, sounds and through mother's caresses, the sensory stimulation necessary for the baby's development is generated. Sounds and glances are exchanged, and the baby emits signals of hunger, cold or pain, which are interpreted by parents.

From the moment the baby connects with its mother, the baby's chances of survival increase. Through the neurophysiological process of neurobiological construction, attachment and secure bonding with a close other unfold. As mentioned above, this attachment mechanism forms the basis of the ability to relate to others and allows for the development of the capacity to socialize and create pair and family relationships. This has also been observed in other primate species such as chimpanzees or orangutans.

Another important similarity, in addition to healthy attachment, is the ability of the mother and/or caregiver to calm the baby, to provide support when the baby is feeling insecure, restless or upset. The mother needs to be able to interpret these behaviors and self-regulate, to keep her anxiety and tension at a positive level, which allows her to seek support to calm the baby. This self-regulation capacity of the mother and/or caregiver, activates the neurophysiological basis of the child and sustains it through adulthood, especially the ability to regulate anxiety, fear, anguish, other emotions and behaviors that make up the unique and unrepeatable personality, especially in times of high stress, where we need to be flexible, and adapt quickly.

To develop a healthy and stable sense of self, a healthy self-esteem, a sense of security, autonomy, the context of the home is important, the relationships of the couple, family and siblings. The transmission of values, the ability to share and communicate within the family, expressing oneself in an appropriate way, with positive emotions and adapted behaviors, will promote self-care, and will result in a regulated and more resilient nervous system, with greater potential for defense against the threat or danger of death.

Animals and humans connect with fear and threat in a similar way. However, instinct is not suppressed by the animal which in the face of danger reacts instinctively, activating its defense mechanisms, the primary memories or patterns of attack, flight or freeze (depending on the degree of threat) using all its physical and sensory resources to attack in defense of itself, its offspring or herd.

In the human's case, the development of the cerebral cortex, reasoning and interpretation of threats can, in some cases, "inhibit" the response to it. Social norms, thinking, learned conditioning, can affect the defense mechanism and generate a greater exposure to danger. For example: when we watch a TV program showing a predatory animal attacking its prey, you usually close your eyes and feel your muscles prepare for the action and tense up. Unconsciously we connect with a sense of danger. When the person did not know or could not face the danger, one's nervous system becomes dysregulated. Trauma and restrictive beliefs appear.

Dissociation is the essence of trauma. The overwhelming experience is divided, fragmented so that the evocations, sounds, images, thoughts, physical sensations related to the trauma take on a life of their own.

THE WORK OF PHP FOR RECONNECTION / REGULATION OF THE NERVOUS SYSTEM

For the Reconnection / Regulation of the nervous system the PHP work is applied, based on the Polyvagal Theory and the two branches of the Vagus nerve system: Dorsal Vagus and Ventral Vagus.

Cranial Nerves

There are twelve pairs of cranial nerves, and they have motor and/or sensory functions.

Some of the components of the face and throat motor function, are under voluntary control and others are not, so that a smile may be only partially simulated.

We automatically seek to express safety and emit these signals to others, as well as detect safety signals in others. We detect signals in the upper part of the face (acoustic, vocal and visual); we receive acoustic signals from the properties of vocalization; we pick up signals from head gestures and even from hand gestures. Gestures on our face also connect us with others as does body language. We can recognize whether the other is trustworthy or generates distrust in us through the way he/she looks at us and talks to us.

It is the cranial nerves that innervate the face, larynx, vocal cords, and especially the tenth cranial nerve, which is the base of the vagus nerve.

Our ability to interpret the basic emotions, happiness, anger, fear, sadness, disgust, are universal, which leads us to recognize, through mirror neurons, the mental state and emotional attunement of the other.

The cranial nerves regulate many critical aspects of human physiology, such as:

- Heart rate, blood pressure
- Sweating
- Digestion, stimulating peristalsis of gastrointestinal tract
- Speech
- Vascular tone
- Respiratory tract, lungs, esophagus
- Reflex (cough reflex when the ear canal is stimulated)
- 80% of the fibers are afferent, i.e. they carry information from the body to the brain
- 20% of fibers are efferent - commands from brain to body.

The five cranial nerves of the social engagement system:

- Trigeminal nerve (V. Cranial nerve)
- Facial nerve (VII. Cranial nerve)
- Glossopharyngeal nerve (IX. Cranial nerve)
- Vagus nerve (X. Cranial nerve)
- Accessory nerve (XI. Cranial nerve)

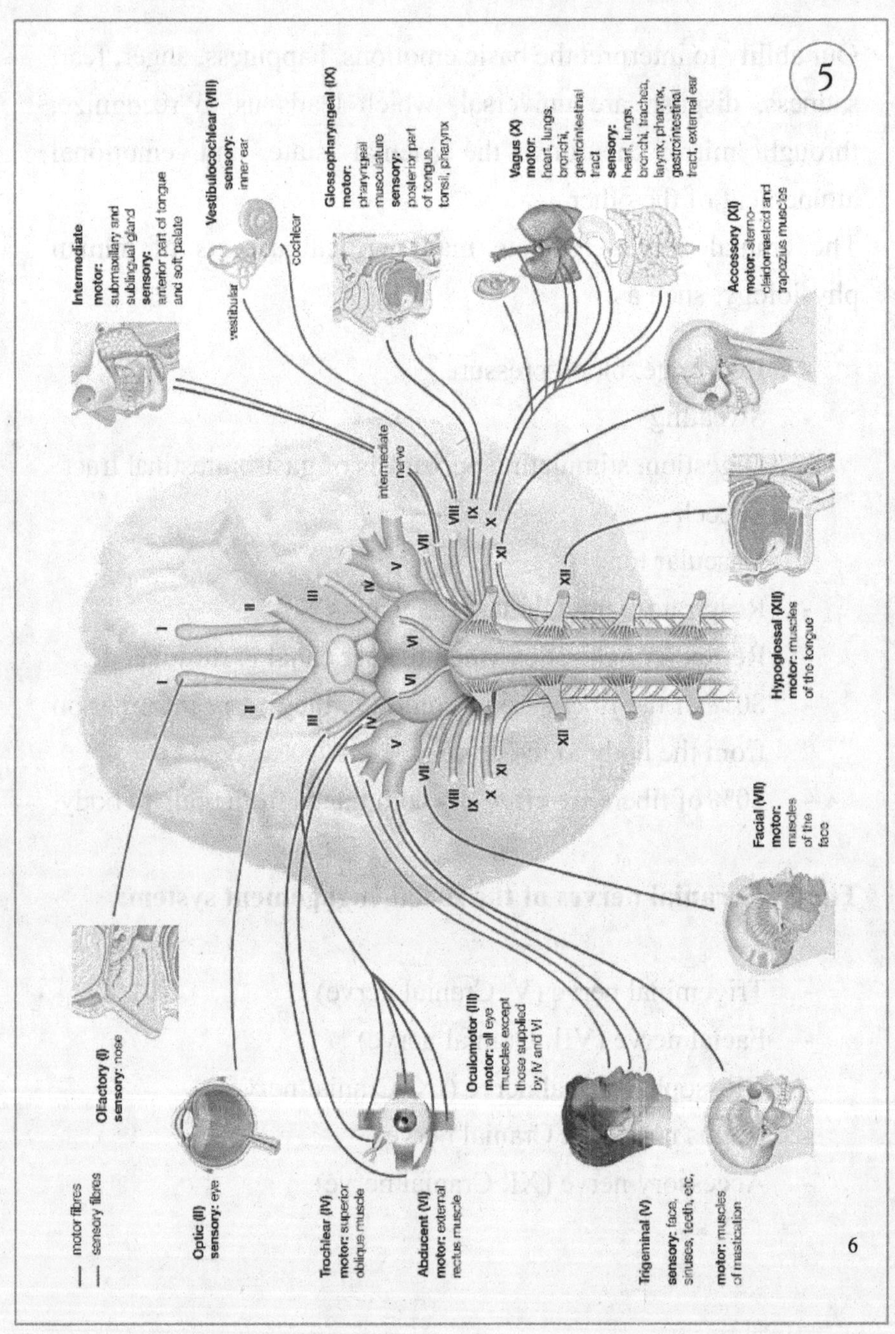

[6] Ref: Heidi Moawad, MD, Neurologist. The Anatomy of the Cranial Nerves, 2023. https://www.verywellhealth.com/cranial-nerves-anatomy-4780532

The social engagement system is related to the ventral vagus nerve. The latter is located in the viscera and is related to the function of our diaphragm and breathing. When there is a response of the sympathetic nervous system, product of the perception of a danger, the social engagement system or ventral vagus is disconnected, for example: After a road accident the individual is shocked and will not be able to accept an invitation to socialize, he will not feel socially connected, he will require time to reactivate his ventral vagus system.

In order to be connected with the social system we need to feel secure in the space we inhabit and also secure in our physical state. We are social beings, we have the need to look each other in the eyes, to contact each other, to listen to others, to share by eating, talking, singing, kissing, laughing, and sometimes feeling the heart with another individual. That is our nature. Human beings need others to survive, but they also need a deeper bond with that other, which is socialization. This phenomenon is not only psychological but also neurobiological.

Jerome Kagan, distinguished professor at Harvard University, pointed out that for every act of cruelty in this world there are hundreds of acts of kindness and connection. Being benevolent rather than malevolent is probably an authentic characteristic of our species.

Feeling safe with other people is probably the most important aspect of mental health.

When mammals feel safe, not in danger, they come out of their immobility, they don't have to change anything, they rest, recover and repair and/or prepare their resources to be ready to face a new challenge. They enter a state of fearless stasis.

When the social engagement system is active (ventral vagus active), mammalian groups cooperate and build trust. They help others in their interactions with each other. They naturally enjoy activities with the group, they trust, they bond with each other, and the significant pattern of reproduction occurs.

When mammals feel danger and their existence threatened, they need to mobilize to change the external situation and also their internal environment. They fight, overcome and/or neutralize the danger, or, ultimately, flee far enough away where the risk does not exist. This mobilization creates many defensive resources for safety.

When the mammal is overwhelmed and in a life-threatening situation, it feels annihilation and the Dorsal Vagus Nerve response is activated, causing a frozen state, in which the social engagement system shuts down, and tonic stasis appears.

On a daily basis, we are exposed to situations that mobilize us to a state of constant unconscious alertness. If there are no stimuli that represent a high risk, no response actions appear. Through the Parasympathetic pathway (Vagus Nerve), we return to a regulated Vagal Ventral tone and feel socially open, as described in the Polyvagal Theory, by Stephen Porges. A state of calmness, and security is produced, and everything returns to normal. As there is a greater degree of danger, the defenses of the autonomic nervous system are activated via a sympathetic pathway.

This alarm system and its physiological responses, commonly referred to as "arousal", are triggered and mobilize defense reactions, which are involuntary at higher degrees of threat, so that, the human being will not be able to inhibit them.

These defensive responses are socially seen as inappropriate, disruptive and many of these reactions are accompanied by motor hyperactivity, a feeling of tension, contraction of intestines, hypervigilance, sweating, impulses to hit, bite or scratch, which is seen as something natural in animals and as a lack of impulse control in humans.

Three parts of the brain

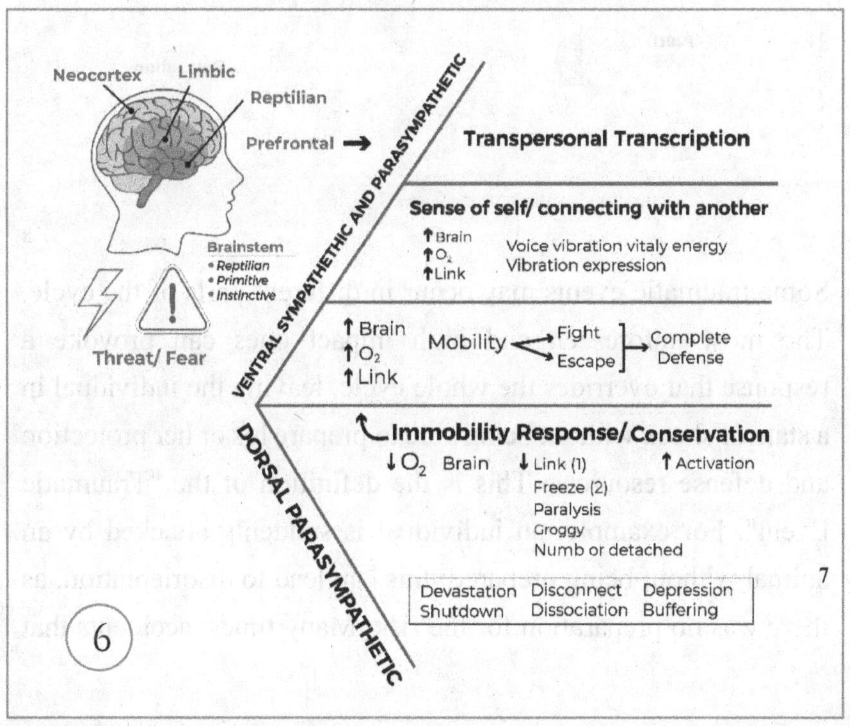

7 Image: Catalina Ureta Parot

The Defense Orientation Cycle

The orientation defense cycle is a circuit possessed by mammals that allows them to be alert to face risks.

It is constituted by four stages: the alert stage, preparation for defense, active discharge-response for defense, and relaxation.

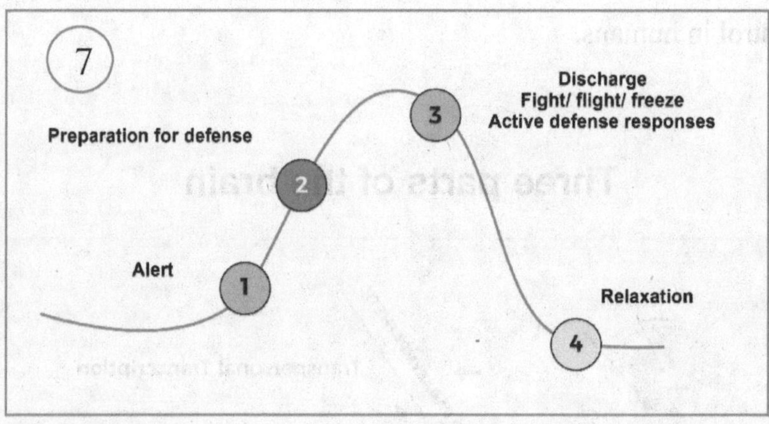

[8]

Some traumatic events may occur in different parts of the cycle. The most unforeseen and high impact ones can provoke a response that overrides the whole cycle, leaving the individual in a state of shock without being able to prepare his or her protection and defense resources. This is the definition of the "Traumatic Event". For example: an individual is suddenly attacked by an animal without being prepared; this can lead to disorientation, as there was no preparation for the risk. Many times, accidents that

---

[8] Image: Mariann Dávila

are not foreseen happen and cause shock, leaving us totally defenseless and vulnerable.

Each person has his or her own speed of response and can react differently at each stage of the cycle.

PENDULATION

In PHP's work with trauma, we seek to recognize the client personal resources that have allowed him/her to successfully cope with stressful or risky situations. These resources are identified so that they can be used at the moment of dealing with a traumatic experience in a session. These can be a memory, image, song, word, sensation, among others. These resources are an important part to develop in order to co-regulate the nervous system and learn to mobilize the overload of the system. After recognizing which are the resources to be used, we can then approach the Pendulation process, which is nothing more than paying attention to a pleasant sensation and comparing it with the unpleasant one we are dealing with.

One of the objectives of somatic work is to reestablish the balance of homeostasis. During the traumatic event, the person remains stuck in part of the cycle; the incomplete response is frozen in the body. Therefore, reestablishment will be achieved through a process of both recognition of the trauma event and Pendulation.

It is relevant to understand how our system is deregulated in trauma and how we lose internal stability. Trauma disorganizes the rhythm of the organs and impacts the autonomic nervous system, which translates into symptoms, diseases and syndromes that when treated only at the pharmacological level, attenuates and dissociates the symptoms, but does not resolve the underlying trauma. We need to integrate psychopharmacology support, complementary to corporal therapeutic processes that allows the progressive integration of the person's processes. But we also need to generate gradual changes through practices, exercises, complementary therapies, sleep habits, nutrition, and physical activity, in order to strengthen the body. That is, we need to build a new level of support, restructuring the functional processes, so that body, mind, emotions and spirituality are connected in a single holistic unit.

Self-regulation v/s Self-control

It can be easy to confuse self-regulation with self-control. The two are related, but they are not the same.

Self-control is primarily a social-cognitive skill and is learned through social norms. Children use it to keep their behavior, emotions and impulses under control.

Self-regulation is a type of neurobiological skill. It is built on a secure attachment between the infant and a mother who is able to soothe the infant. It allows children to manage their emotions, behavior and body movement when faced with a difficult situation; self-regulation allows them to stay focused and attentive. In this way they are able to be flexible and can resist giving in to outbursts of frustration. This ability develops over time. That is why it is quite common to see a four-year-old having a tantrum, but not a twelve-year-old. If a twelve-year-old has tantrums on a regular basis, it is likely that he or she has a self-regulation problem.

The master key is "Feeling Sense". As we have already discussed in this chapter, this is the sensation that you are able to pay attention to and sustain. This allows us to connect with the somatic language: with what is loose, tense, empty, burning or cold; it is the language of the brainstem, the gateway to the association networks in the brain and the pathway to the memories of the Hippocampus. The images of the Amygdala, which like a permanent witness from birth, records and classifies the experiences of our life in an unconscious way.

Alert and Relaxation Circuit

PHP's work consists of uniting the body and the word as a bridge of action that allows us to become aware, to express, to share situations that many times we have never talked about, which requires trust, respect and deep listening on the part of the therapist. We release secret experiences and memories that marked us, that we need to unveil and release, both in the mind and body. Thoughts are a subjective interpretation of experiences. Situations are experienced as two poles: negative or positive; good experiences arc linked to pleasure, and bad experiences, to discomfort and physical and/or emotional pain.

Traumatic experiences are those that are perceived and interpreted as having a high impact and that penetrate our consciousness provoking a defense response through arousal, a chemical response that involves the endocrine glands, such as the adrenal glands, which in turn release cortisol (stress hormone). This neurochemical cascade is called "sympathetic activation", composed of hormones, neurotransmitters and nerve networks that modify the balance of the sympathetic system.

What is Cortisol?

In a study at the University of Harbor, it was discovered that when there is danger, a loud sound or a dark street where a shadow appears, the brain through the hypothalamus initiates a cascade of events that prepares the body for action; the hypothalamus responds to the danger signal and creates a substance called CRH

(Adrenocorticotropic) that stimulates the pineal gland. In turn, the pituitary gland creates a molecule called ACTH (Adrenocorticotropic), which travels to the adrenal glands.

The Stress Response System

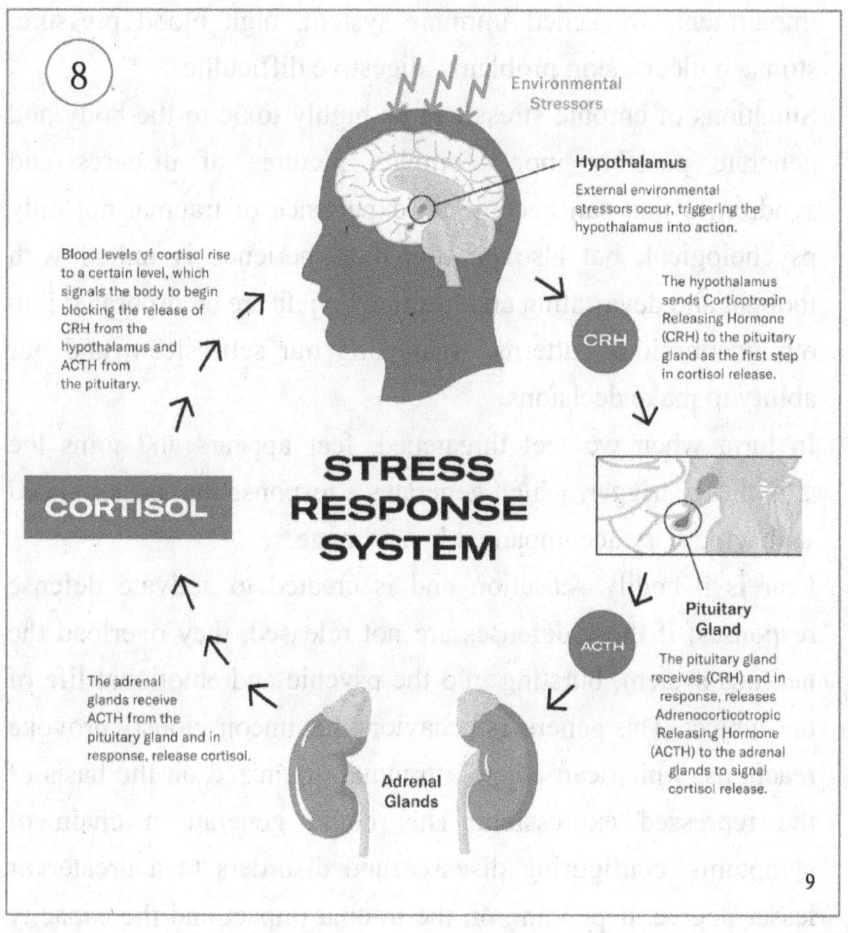

[9] Ref: https://rebalancehealth.com/pages/about-cortisol

Epinephrine, cortisol and growth hormone are other hormones that help maintain blood sugar levels. They, along with glucagon (see above) are called "stress" or "glucose counter-regulatory" hormones, meaning that they cause blood sugar to rise. If there are many years of this activation, the stress response can wear down the body. Some of the common symptoms are: memory impairment, weakened immune system, high blood pressure, stomach ulcers, skin problems, digestive difficulties.

Situations of chronic stress can be highly toxic to the body and generate possibly more complex pictures of diseases and syndromes that can become an experience of trauma, not only psychological, but also emotional. Experience is united with thought and devastating and limiting beliefs are incorporated into our unconscious patterns, weakening our self-esteem and our ability to make decisions.

In turn, when we feel threatened, fear appears and joins the stimulus or trigger, which generates a response that is associated with a memory accompanied by an image.

Fear is a bodily sensation and is created to activate defense responses; if these defenses are not released, they overload the nervous system, bursting into the psychic and emotional life of the subject. This generates behaviors that unconsciously provoke reactions, which can create a trauma, organized on the basis of the repressed expression. This could generate a chain of symptoms, configuring diseases and disorders to a greater or lesser degree, depending on the trauma impact and the capacity of each person to sustain the traumatic experience. At a younger age, there are fewer possibilities of defense, especially when the person exhibits some other health or psychological difficulty, such as endocrinological, thyroid, adrenal glands (Addinson's disease with hypocortisolism), cardiac arrhythmia syndrome, hypotension, dysautonomia, can generate a fear syndrome, product of an organic-metabolic problem.

Impact of Trauma

A human being can have early traumas, in gestation and at birth, as well as developmental traumas which affect not only the physical but also the psychological aspects. They can cause altered behaviors, activate addictions, develop mental disorders, post-traumatic stress disorder, high level of freezing and dissociation.

We can see the impact of trauma on the ability to relate to others: feeling lonely, isolation or social phobia, difficulty in maintaining healthy relationships and in creating stable bonds, maintaining a partner with a sense of mutual support, having an active sex life, maintaining a job and a positive sense of life. It is also possible to experience crises that manifest themselves in anxiety, fear, anguish and stress, causing psychosomatic illnesses such as irritable bowel syndrome, migraines, sleep disorders or allergies. Fear, as a permanent emotion, freezes us, bogs us down, with the purpose of keeping us alive; however, the level of disorganized responses and altered behaviors can lead to panic attacks, vertigo, fibromyalgia, multiple sclerosis, lupus and a myriad of diseases. These symptoms are the common thread of schemas and thought patterns that are associated with emotional blocks, often unconscious, and ideas of self that cause low self-esteem. Internal affirmations inherited from upbringing, such as: I am not capable, I am not wanted, I am useless, I cannot, are accompanied by feelings of abandonment, frustration, shame and self-rejection, which in some cases cause overweight, low defenses in the immune system and complex pictures of diseases, alterations in the lymphatic system, loss of sense of life, insecurity and distrust in relating to others.

We are like a wall, where each brick forms a wall that separates us from life, with a sense of isolation and insecurity.

The impact of trauma on a person who is already experiencing a severe depressive or anxiety disorder, or who has an obsessive-compulsive disorder, can possibly provoke major negative effects and a generation of crises, less coping capacity, destabilization and risk of self-harm or suicidal behavior.

Essential Factors to deal with Trauma

Resilience, empathy, the ability to recover, together with the ability to release the energetic and emotional blockages that affect and are specific to each person, are the essential factors that accompany a process of somatic work.

We need the desire and willingness of the person to open up to the processes of working with the body, to prioritize mental health, to feel part of life and to believe that it is possible to find new ways of thinking and to recover meaning, to assimilate difficulties and to renew the inner connection.

How Can We Recognize Trauma

Trauma has been defined by different currents, at different times and in different ways. In its beginnings it was related to traumatic psychological life events, such as the birth process, wars, catastrophes and natural disasters, when a human being lives a state of inescapable threat and is overcome by the experience, which impacts him/her for life.

These definitions of trauma have evolved until today. Nowadays, a traumatic experience is considered unique and personal, subjective and integrating different patterns that make up the experience.

Defense mechanisms, such as dissociation, disorganize the functioning of the internal structure of the person, causing problems in the ability to mentalize, difficulties to regulate aggression or fear which, without treatment can trigger psychological disorders and destructive behaviors such as the consumption of addictive medicines or drugs.

Today, trauma is also linked to the body and expresses itself together with metabolic and homeostasis functions, as the basis of psychic and emotional processes. All orchestrated in a melody, which has a tempo and a vital rhythm. It is important to mention that trauma affects the whole organism. The body continues to defend itself from an arousal that belongs to the past. Overcoming trauma means being able to put an end to this continuous mobilization of stress and to restore the whole organism to safety. We speak of trauma when the person experiences the situation of danger as a rupture of limits, without being able to defend oneself, or not to be harmed psychologically, physically or emotionally. It is to feel overwhelmed, to live the shock of the impact, to lose sometimes the conscience, the sense of reality, to receive wounds, blows, accidents or losses that make you feel "fixed" in a mourning, with the heart without affection, frozen, dissociated and without sense of life. To live from trauma is to stay in a dark place, where there is no energy. There is fear, burden, pain and struggle in feeling trapped in the past. Fragments of memories are often left deep in the unconscious, causing dissociation and simply not being able to understand what is happening to you, why situations affect you so deeply. Dissociation seeks to protect us from difficult times; however, it also disconnects us from the flow of life, energy and the body. Frozen, depressed or in a state of living death, we fail to change, despite all kinds of treatment, some of which can become invasive or risky, such as electroshock therapy.

Each person experiences trauma through different symptoms: physical weakness, chronic fatigue, headaches, dizziness, irrational fears, tension and chronic pain, bruxism, digestive, hormonal, cardiac problems, allergies, gastritis, irritable bowel syndrome, insomnia. All these symptoms are associated with psychosomatic diseases and are part of the symptomatology of chronic stress. Trauma and stress are reflected in high levels of various hormones already mentioned, especially cortisol, which acts via bloodstream and reaches deep into the brain. A persistent level of cortisol can be toxic and destroy neurons, damage tissues, cause dysregulation of internal organ systems, alter the circadian cycle and reduce working memory capacity, concentration and attention. Anxiety, insecurity, fear of the future, instability and uncertainty trigger excessive consumption of food, pain medication or body inflammation; cause social problems, phobias, domestic violence, broken relationships, loss of stability at work and financial problems, low control of aggression, sexual impotence problems, irritability, guilt, low self-esteem and social isolation. All this, as a whole, can also lead to drug dependence. Today in our society there is an exaggeration in drug consumption, that is to say a polypharmacy especially in mental and psychic aspects of the person. Thus, antidepressants, anxiolytics, antipsychotics, relaxants, sedatives, hypnotics, are part of the "arsenal" used many times to treat trauma, but most of the time they only build a mitigation and symptomatizing of a more complex problem that requires the management of resources of both the therapist and the client to overcome this situation.

Panic attacks, chronic traumatic stress of being a survivor of an accident or a natural disaster, feeling in permanent danger, as in the case of wars, can lead the person to a deep demotivation, lack of sense and total disconnection; these conditions can become indicators of severe trauma. Trauma disconnects, makes us lose the sense of time, leads us to be workaholics, have obsessive thoughts, permanent rumination, not being able to recover from an assault or an accident, incapacitates us to stop carrying out habitual activities. Extreme self-criticism also appears, we do not allow ourselves to fail, we have a deep fear to commit ourselves, to experience emotions that expose deeper feelings. All these may be signs of a more complex picture of trauma, which requires attention. Symptoms may appear six months after the event, and may even take much longer to manifest, even years.

Another relevant symptom is the abuse of alcohol and drugs, which leads the person to a state of "emotional anesthesia", trying to disconnect from the pain or grief. It is important when we reach this point or have the will to heal ourselves, to be aware of how the body feels, if it hurts and what that pain is like. It is significant to check the level of fatigue in order to detect what is happening. We can also observe trauma in children, which manifests itself through crying, not being able to calm down, having attachment problems, food allergies or lack of impulse control. All of these, are signs of difficulty with dysregulation of the baby and is not feeling contained, safe or cared for.

Surviving or Healing

What is the solution for the problem? Do we just want to survive or are we willing to work on our healing processes?

Currently the trauma's symptoms are addressed with drug therapy and, in specific cases and depending on the diagnosis, the patient is advised to compliment treatment with psychotherapy. In some cases, psychotherapy can provide support that modulates the symptoms and, at the same time, allows the person to elaborate on the trauma, simplifying the process and understanding the effect of the traumatic experience in his/her life. This can strengthen his/her self-esteem and facilitate the integration of these processes. However, the body cannot be separated from the mind.

The body is the container of emotions, the nervous system allows us to move and move forward in life, and memories connect us with previous experiences, genetically inherited behaviors in order to sustain the life's species.

Therapy based on listening and talking has been used since 1900, and as neuroscience has validated the connection of body, mind and emotion as an integrated process, we have been able to move forward in giving greater depth to therapeutic processes.

Since 1950 it was thought that drugs could cure, however, they often serve only a supportive and stabilizing function, rather than a cure. Over decades we have integrated other more ancient medicines, some dating back to 5,000 years ago, which incorporate, for example, changes in nutrition, such as Chinese Medicine or Ayurvedic Medicine. Through the incorporation of this new ancestral knowledge, we have been able to understand how breathing, its rhythm and control, allows us to be more present, as is the case of Mindfulness.

Medicine is moving towards an integrative process that conceives the human being in all its dimensions and for each of them there is a healing response.

It is not only about survival; it is possible to heal.

The Body as a Biological Basis of the Therapeutic Process

The research and development of technologies: magnetic resonance imaging, tomography, X-rays, high resolution microscopes, have allowed us to enter into the complex brain processes, which have been studied in a broader way. The aim is to improve treatments and diagnose more accurately. However, the neurochemical mechanisms approach of the autonomic nervous system, the work of Bessel Van der Kolk on stress and trauma memories, Peter Levine with Somatic Experiencing®, the contributions of Polyvagal Theory of Stephen Porges, and many other ancient and contemporary authors such as Sigmund Freud himself have all contributed. The Swiss psychiatrist and psychologist Carl G. Jung, leading physiologists such as Cannon, Seyle, and distinguished neuroscientists, have allowed us to know the complex mechanisms behind trauma, and the path of genetic adaptation has allowed an orientation towards the body which develops more attunement and resonance with the client.

That is how we have reached an important moment in the history of health: the development of Neurosciences applied to trauma.

The Autonomic Nervous System (ANS) and Self-Regulation

The Autonomic Nervous System is part of the central nervous system that is responsible for regulating involuntary bodily functions, such as heartbeat, blood flow, breathing and digestion. It regulates different bodily processes that take place without conscious effort. It is divided into the Sympathetic and Parasympathetic Branch and also into the Enteric Nervous System.

- The Sympathetic Branch regulates flight or fight responses. It also performs tasks such as relaxing the bladder, accelerating the heart rate and dilating the pupils of the eyes.
- The Parasympathetic Branch helps maintain normal bodily functions such as bladder control, slowing the heart rate and constricting the pupils and allows us to relax.
- The autonomic nervous system is also composed of a third component known as the enteric nervous system, which is located in the gastrointestinal tract.

The Autonomic Nervous System

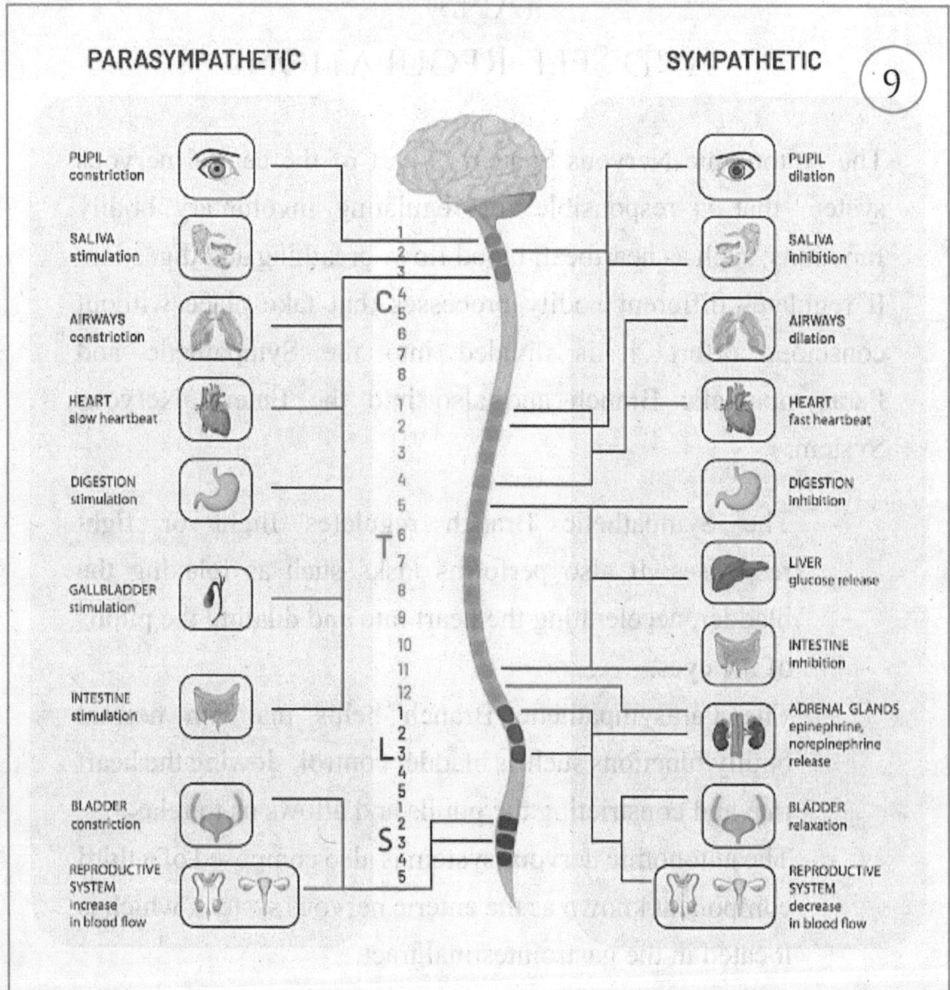

10

---

[10] Ref: Saul Mcleod, PhD. BSc (Hons) Psychology, MRes, PhD, University of Manchester. Autonomic Nervous System (ANS) Division And Functions. 2023. https://www.simplypsychology.org/autonomic-nervous-system.html

Through the Autonomic Nervous System, the body has the ability to reorganize inhibited defense responses, unload the nervous system, recover the coherence of the autonomic system and, above all, resolve the various disturbances.

Indeed, through this new knowledge of the functioning of the central nervous system (CNS), peripheral and autonomic, we can conclude today that it is a very complex system of activation, whether of need or attention or stress, related to trauma and its treatment. It is neither easy nor quick, and it is rather through safe and competent action of the therapist, that brings this delicate task to a successful conclusion. It requires a deep learning of the neurophysiological mechanisms of responses to unconscious memories on the part of the therapist, in addition to the containment and development of resources of the self and the client.

Neuroscience has allowed us to deepen the knowledge and research on the importance of the ANS in the therapeutic process of trauma. Undoubtedly, neuroscience will impact the field of cognitive and behavioral therapies, and it will also open new frontiers in the field of Neuro- Psychoanalysis. This advancement will allow us to better attend to individuals based on different clinical proposals and, as a result, make significant progress in the path of trauma healing.

Chronic and Traumatic Stress

We have recognized stress as the disease of modernity. Accelerated, with no time to rest, no time to repair ourselves, we live in a hectic way, without realizing that this overload consumes our vitality and causes us to lose the ability to feel in good spirits. Sometimes it is easy to recognize the symptoms of stress and sometimes not. The body has involuntary mechanisms that combat stress. However, when it is sustained over time and becomes chronic, stress not only affects the nervous system, but also weakens the endocrine and immune systems.

Stress curves above normal will generate physical exhaustion, inability of a tonic regulation of the muscles, alterations at the neurohormonal level. High stress curves are the neurophysiological substrate that leads to chronic fatigue, discouragement and the unconscious feeling that we are unmotivated, with poor sleep, or sometimes restless and irritable. Trauma and chronic stress can not only appear in difficult situations of the organic system, but often from a high overload of work activities. Even exaggerated sports activities, in which people are subjected to important and competitive sports competitions that ultimately take their toll on the musculoskeletal, circulatory, endocrine systems, causing wear and tear and non-recoverability of these damages.

When stress becomes chronic, the wear and tear can be observed in ailments and diseases that affect especially the musculoskeletal system jaw tension called bruxism, tensional headaches, ulcers and gastritis, insomnia, pain in the lumbar spine and neck. Many times, the reflex of extreme concern for survival, economic resources, or the ability to comply with home and work routines affects individuals in such a way that they may experience hair loss, reflux, psoriasis, or hypertension. In general, there are symptoms of physical pain, inflammation of tissues that affect organs and joints; constipation appears, problems of blood circulation of extremities. All this symptomatology and the impossibility of finding solutions generates demotivation, apathy and rigidity in the human being.

At a high level of traumatic stress, the body has already lost the ability to return to a normal level, and as stress energy accumulates, physical and mental health will be severely affected. There is an alteration effect of sleep cycles, body posture is modified, diseases that generate disability appear, such as Fibromyalgia, Lupus and ALS (Amyotrophic Lateral Sclerosis) and other diseases that require greater care; important changes in habits lead us to long periods of treatment, to therapeutic processes aimed at strengthening health through different types of support.

Today, we can say that stress is inevitably present in our activities. However, we can prevent these adverse effects through self-care, connecting with ourselves, with the body language of sensations; these are the signals emitted by the body so that we take into consideration how to take care of our sleep, regulate our working hours, perform meditation activities, exercises and, above all, listen to the voice of the body: pain, tiredness, tension and discomfort, which are the alerts emitted by our body due to attrition.

THE SOMATIC WORK

Catalina Ureta, Peter Levine and Judith Johnson (1994)

I remember Dr. Levine asked me a question in 1995, when I was learning his Somatic Experiencing® work. He asked me: Do you have any trauma? I answered: no, I don't have any trauma... He was surprised and asked me again: how many operations have you had? have you been hospitalized? I told him: I had an operation on my tonsils at the age of five and another operation for appendicitis at the age of seven and a serious car accident, in which my father was driving, at the age of eighteen; I went through the windshield onto the ground and broke the wrist of my right arm, I was taken to the hospital for surgery, which was done intuitively by the doctor; he did it by putting the bones in their normal position and also put eight stitches in my head. I had never thought of this as trauma. I thought and believed that my

86

parents' divorce at age fourteen was my trauma and the source of my love problems in relationships. Then, when I studied and understood the concept of trauma, I was able to understand that I was very wrong. I was shocked and it was at that moment that I awakened to the understanding and began to really study trauma.

Catalina Ureta

In somatic work, stress symptoms are not seen as pathology but as normal responses to an overwhelming life event. Traumas are facts of life, and most of us have been exposed to them. However, they should not be a death sentence. As human beings we are biologically designed to respond to threats and to recover from them.

We approach or engage with the living body through contact with primal sensations that support the core of self-regulation. Energy waves work at this level allowing the body and mind to speak.

In the therapeutic process we focus on mind and body awareness. When there is stress there is a kind of immobilization, paralysis; and if the excitement stays in the body, it will create symptoms and syndromes: feeling ashamed, fear, pain and discomfort. Our body is disrupted and that energy that is trapped, with a disruptive effect; we feel blocked and helpless. Without realizing it, within our body an activation of the nervous system is provoked.

At the moment we work with sensations, we reset the nervous system and it responds by balancing itself in a natural and organic way. As positive effects of "feeling our body", we will be able to sleep better and feel with more courage and strength. Our cardiovascular system will reach normality, the immune system will be balanced, and the endocrine system will complete its cycle.

The somatic work is focused on being able to pendulum in the body the daily experiences of fear and helplessness (negative pole) and readjust the nervous system (positive pole), expanding the capacity to contain and sustain these emotional variations and create an organism capable of containing and sustaining emotional processes (continent or bowl).

To be able to recover the inner life, to improve the balance of the body and to feel the inner silence, allows us to recover vitality, equanimity, and capacity to participate actively in the life of the family. Many people will regain inner peace and will manage not to freeze in a stressful situation.

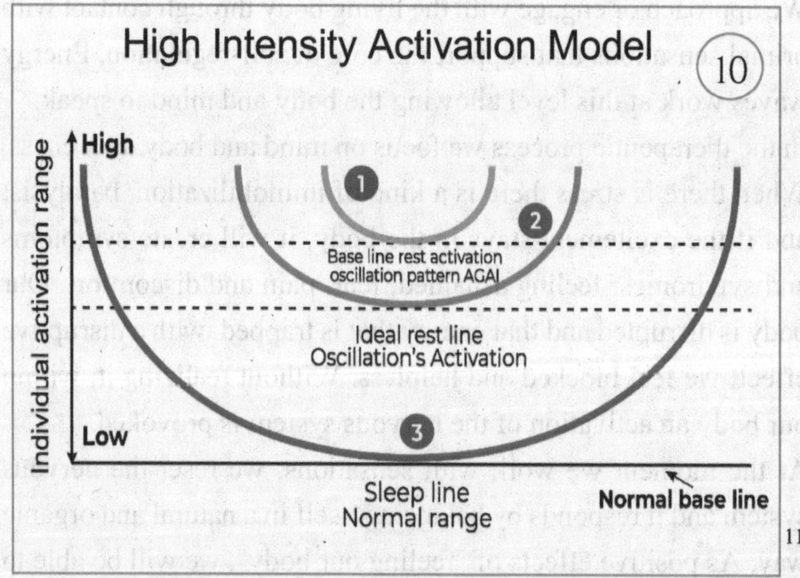

---

[11] Ref: Somátic Experiencing®, training, Module 1, Intermediary.
www.traumahealing.com

MOBILIZING TRAPPED ENERGY

In this book we will teach you how to recognize the trauma vortex and the healing vortex, allowing in a gradual or titled[12] way, to mobilize the trauma vortex and to bring from one to the other the stagnant energy. This allows one to open to the healing memory to discover these healing aspects at the cellular level in our body, in the DNA, and moving through the nervous system.

Letting the frozen energy be release in the Vortex Model

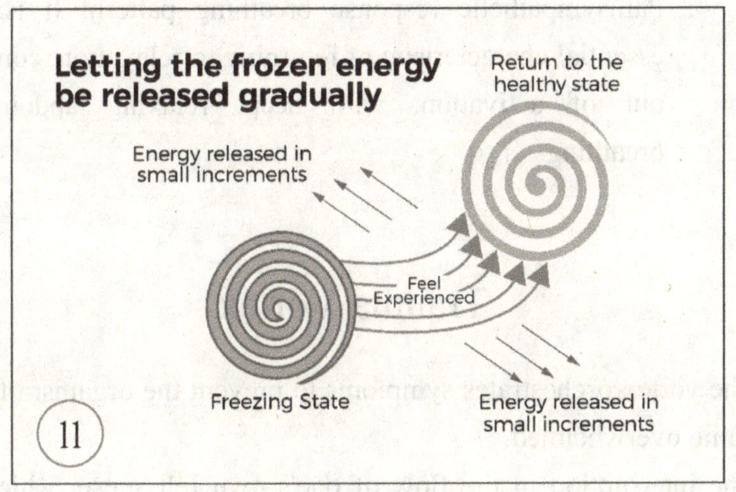

---

[12] In chemistry, it is called "titled" to that process in which the minimum is exposed. Amount of compound to create a suitable reaction possible to sustain. One Droplet of X is enough to generate the process.

[13] Ref: Text extracted from: New Insights into Trauma Therapy an introduction to the work of Peter Levine, Ph.D. John Chitty, BCST, RPP ∞ Colorado School of Energy Studies. https://www.energyschool.com/articles-and-handouts

In somatic work we need to become aware of the body's responses:

1. Constriction: Characterized by general tension, parasympathetic-dorsal vagus freezing.
2. Dissociation: The main characteristic of this process is to feel outside the body, not connected to it. What is expected at this stage is to reconnect, to feel warmth, sensation, and trembling.
3. Sympathetic response breathing pattern: The body breathes reactively through the upper chest with shallow breathing, hyperventilating.
4. Parasympathetic response breathing pattern: It is the essential characteristic of returning to relaxation, coming out of activation, with deep, relaxing abdominal breathing.

Trauma Vortex

The vortex orchestrates symptoms to prevent the organism from being overwhelmed.

The interruption in the flow of one's own felt sense, which is caused by trauma, becomes something like a vortex, out of the main flow of the stream of consciousness.

This vortex of energy is maintained by the traumatic symptoms.

Signs or symptoms of the traumatic vortex:

- Fear, compression, constriction.
- Lifting of the diaphragm and viscera.
- Feelings of being overwhelmed, as if out of control.
- Feeling of disconnection from the body
- Time is speeding up
- Lack of or low energy.
- Freezing, immobility
- Stiffness
- Dilated pupils
- Coldness in the periphery
- Restricted perception: tunnel vision.

The more you move between the trauma vortex and the healing vortex, the more turbulence you will experience: Feelings of being shaken, disturbed.

This experience is like:

- Sweating
- Change on the color of skin
- Change in body temperature
- Unfocused blinking of the pupils
- Tremors and shaking
- Skin almost vibrating
- Mental turmoil
- Goose bumps
- Breathing rapid and higher in the chest

91

- Change in pupil size
- Breathing stops
- Cold extremities
- Increased heart rate (observed in the carotid pulse)
- Vibrations in small muscles
- Exophthalmic eye movement (bulging eyes)
- Bowel movement.

The Parasympathetic system, which informs us of the felt sense, and allows when we are not in vital danger, states of relaxation and digestion, of rest and repair. It is the healing energy used by animals to shake or shake muscles that have been traumatized.

We, humans, are also designed to reorient ourselves and reorganize high-intensity survival states. We have the neocortical capacity to learn from experiences and to seek solutions to natural regulatory problems. For example, when we reconnect the three parts of the brain: brainstem, limbic system and neocortex, the shame we harbor is healed and the fear leaves our body. Through the language of sensation, we are able to utilize the innate ability to self-regulate, eliminating the incapacity of powerlessness.

If the nervous system does not self-regulate after an overwhelming experience, your body stops sleeping peacefully, the cardiovascular system becomes dysregulated, you simply develop a malfunction of the immune system, high amounts of distress appear. Also, on a psychological level these dysregulations can generate decompensation that can lead to a variety of cognitive, emotional, and behavioral traumas.

We call our inner movement our Energetic Sense or Tone. It is a regular ripple that goes through the Nervous System, and it can feel like someone hooks you up to an extra battery and suddenly you feel like you have extra energy, your breathing is more open and easier, and your muscles feel strong; you feel really alive, emotionally and mentally. Energy moves at the cellular level you feel connected to everything and everyone; there is an openness to social engagement and positive interaction with others (ventral vagal response).

The energy system that is in the spinal cord, is like a musical instrument that always plays a concert on the energetic scale, we never stay in a negative place constantly, unless we are experiencing a pathological disorder, a catatonic state that is resistant to a point where the energy of our body stagnates, right? It is important to know how love carries energy upward and anything less than love carries energy downward.

Catalina's Case: A life-changing decision

A few years ago, I attended a young man in his thirties, who for more than eight years had had many digestive problems and, despite being treated with medication, diet and specific nutrition, he felt worse every day. When he arrived at the session, he told me that he had parasites and vomiting problems every time he ate and he constantly had pains all over his body.

Emotionally he felt very angry since his mother had surgery to increase her breasts. Seeing the scars on her breasts was a profound impact on him. He felt anger towards his mother when he saw the wound. This rejection led him to be unable to have a relationship, he felt disconnected, in a catatonic state.

At the time of starting the work I asked him: How many sports have you played since you were a child? He looked at me with surprise and told me that he had played eleven types of sports.

I also asked him: How many falls or fractures have you had in your body? He answered that he had fractured the clavicle of his shoulder. At that moment I understood that we had to start by healing that trauma.

Today this young man has healed, recovered his life and after living this experience he became a teacher and therapist of PHP.

CHAPTER II
WORKING WITH TRAUMA AND MEMORY THROUGH SOMATIC AND POINTS

LAW OF HEALING

The only true healing in the physical body takes place when a change of consciousness occurs

For a shift in consciousness to occur, it is necessary to visualize thoughts (sensory experience), feelings (emotions) and word pattern (verbal and internal), on a mental level, so that they can be re-experienced and expressed as an energy pattern, thus freeing oneself from continuation of repressed thoughts, feelings and words, so that the external manifestation of the disease can be resolved, perfect DNA pattern can then manifest, and the understanding of the law must be understood and applied, so that you can come out of the bondage of your own creation.

All body balancing techniques that do not incorporate the above information, are at best temporary in their effects and do not bring about true healing. To move beyond mere balance and toward real regeneration, we must affect a shift in consciousness. The source of all disease (which, after all, is our own inner creative essence of thought, feeling and speech) must be re-experienced on mental level, so that physical enslavement through our self-imposed reactive mechanism can disappear, such is the path to ascension.

John Whitman Ray

EMERGING BELIEF PATTERNS FOR HEALING

As we saw in the previous chapter, and as a summary for the reader, The Point Holding Process (PHP) is a therapy whose objective is to achieve changes in belief system through working with the body's instinctive healing mechanisms.

In PHP we recognize the body as an organized system, an innate carrier of electrical charges (biochemical processes) that affect the human being when there are internal blockages. The electrical charge is conducted through the nerve pathways, these are neuro-electrical pathways that carry information from the external environment into the body, in response to external stimuli; the body processes the information and regulates adaptive responses in conjunction with the brain, from the inside out.

PHP prepares us to hold a point in a specific area of the body (press the point), provoking a somatic and energetic response at the nervous level. This stimulation activates innate self-regulating mechanisms. Through the electrical current of the body, the stimulus and the point that is held (pressed) are connected, which allows to generate pulsations of the latter and the discharge of the pattern connected to the point. Each point affects a specific area of the body that is related to the emotional field, the patterns of memories and unconscious beliefs that may be activated by traumatic life situations that have not been resolved, for having been frozen, or split in mind.

We focus on resolving the effect of traumatic memories, encoded in thought patterns, and negative unconscious beliefs; phrases and words inherited or acquired at the psychic, cellular and energetic level that live in calcifications that occur in our body.

"BODY ELECTRONICS" THE ORIGIN OF THE POINTS[14]

John Whitman Ray words

"Body electronics can initially be best explained by a physical demonstration in the physics laboratory. When a crystal is compressed, it emits energy and/or electric current, which can be measured with sensitive instruments. This energy or electric current is known as the piezoelectric effect. In the human body there are crystal formations at various acupressure or reflex points along the spine and other parts of the physical body. These crystals or nervous system calcifications are found within joints or in lesions throughout the body and at cranial sutures. As each crystal is compressed using acupressure on a specific point, the crystal slowly dissolves and releases energy that can be experienced by both, the facilitator and the client.

---

[14] Ref: Hearth Illia. The body Electronics Experience, John Whitman Ray. Free e-book. Canadá

In a session, the point facilitator may have one or more facilitators accompanying in holding the necessary points. The facilitator will inquire as to what is going on with the client (what is being accessed as somatic information), encourage the client (with intuition) to re-experience on the mental-present level, all memories that emerge, memories of trauma, as if they were occurring in the ever-present now.

One and a half to two hours is the average time for a session that includes the consultation and specific exercises, but there are exceptions. If there is adequate activation of the points, stress or anxiety is relieved. The time it takes to work on holding points will depend on the time limits of each practitioner's body, and this is variable from person to person. The facilitation of the points creates a healing crisis to which each practitioner must pay attention and relax as it evolves.

It is desirable to maintain an atmosphere of joy and enthusiasm when holding the points, but not to the level of distracting the client from paying attention to his or her process. We must remember that in therapy traumas and resistances are opened, which appear in the consciousness and in the dissolution of the crystal, so the client must be attentive and connected.

It is possible that during the session, the facilitator may go through a "reflex" healing crisis, (mirror neurons and transference). This is a skill we can develop when reading the physical expressions of the client while "holding" points. This should be handled in the same way until the point holding is completed and the healing crisis is over."

How to compare the reason for consultation with what the body says

In common form the conscious mind can fabricate a multitude of reasons or justifications why it performed a given behavior, or experienced a situation. However, from PHP's point of view, every issue is a reaction that comes from an unconscious suppressed programming, which may even be a genetic inheritance. By asking the client what is happening now, what brings him/her to the session, we are only situating ourselves. It is important to work in a framework of reality and certainty with this body and not to focus on speculation or fantasy about it. It must be remembered that the avoidance of reality is disguised in various ways.

The facilitator should always encourage the client to allow her/himself to hold words, feelings, images, to experience stressful experiences or traumas, in the ever-present now, as all memories are experiences that were once experienced in the ever-present now and resisted in the ever-present now.

The facilitator encourages the client to be discrete and to experience all things on the mental level while accompanying the physical body and supporting its emotions. The facilitator should encourage/remind him/her to connect with his/her/his body, to breathe deeply and regularly.

One must be patient, kind and gentle about these matters, as it will take some time to learn to master these discharges. For the PHP specialist, catharsis is not the way to resolve trauma. We must remember that little is gained by venting one's emotion and reactively flopping around like a fish out of water; we are far from it. One learns from experience, emotions and memories experienced on a mental and bodily level, but within a nervous system framework of self-regulation. If the person is taking medication, keep the indications of his/her pharmacological treatment given by the treating physician, and under no circumstances eliminate that medication.

THE PROCESS OF HOLDING POINTS

The felt sensation: the body knows what the mind has dissociated

In each PHP session we work on stress and trauma through responses to the stimulus and bodily processes, bringing the person's attention to the felt sensation. This possibility of observing how the body opens the information of its memories, allows repressed emotions to appear, deep unconsciously ingrained beliefs emerge that cause different psychological blockages, symptoms and diseases. In PHP these patterns are recognized as information crystals, scattered in the nervous tissues, which can be detected by palpation in the body.

The connection of the nervous system is a network of responses (afferent and efferent) that allow us to adapt to the internal and external environment. The effect of these interferences through crystal's, alter homeostasis, cells and psycho-emotional state. Time stops internally and the devastating effects of pain, inflammation, disease, mood disorders, fatigue and tiredness appear. People do not relate that their nervous system is altered, that their body fails to decompose toxins and crystals, which affects the ability to regenerate at the cellular level. The experiences of daily life add up to an overload on the nervous system. Understanding the importance of connecting with our body and what it wants to communicate to us is essential.

Everything starts with a discomfort, then a symptom appears, without us understanding that, behind these body signals, there are behaviors that affect our internal balance and patterns of unconscious destructive behaviors appear that lead us to repeat problems and get sick. Feelings and emotions appear that make us feel blocked, with low spirits, insomnia, anxiety and anguish at a psychological and physical level.

Emotions, the Internal Engine

We are born with an innate repertoire of emotions that define us as human beings, regardless of age, race or culture. These emotions represent our affective states and allow us to recognize ourselves and connect with others. They allow us to question ourselves when we feel sad or angry, to sense fear and detect danger, to recognize gestures that show whether we are safe or on alert.

Since childhood we learn to react to life experiences, we learn to get frustrated, to reflect, to realize our mistakes and to know if we act wrong, from the feeling of emotions. As the rudder of our state of mind, they mobilize, empower and motivate us to move forward, just as we get depressed, feel lonely and suffer from emotional pain. These emotions have been classified into primary and secondary emotions.

Primary emotions:

They are fairly simple to understand; they are your reactions to external events. Some triggering event may cause you to experience emotion. Example: You may feel sad because someone hurt you, or anxious about having to perform the next test or task.

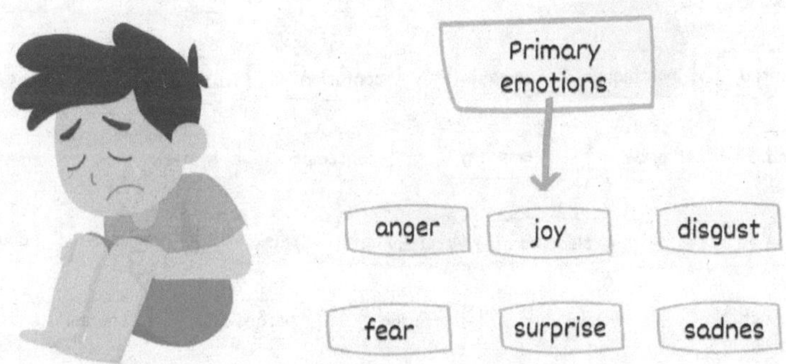

Secondary emotions:

This is when you feel something about the feeling itself. Secondary emotions turn emotions into complex reactions that increase the intensity of your reactions. By differentiating between primary and secondary we gain powerful abilities to distinguish between them. Example: you may feel anger for being hurt, but also shame for your anxiety.

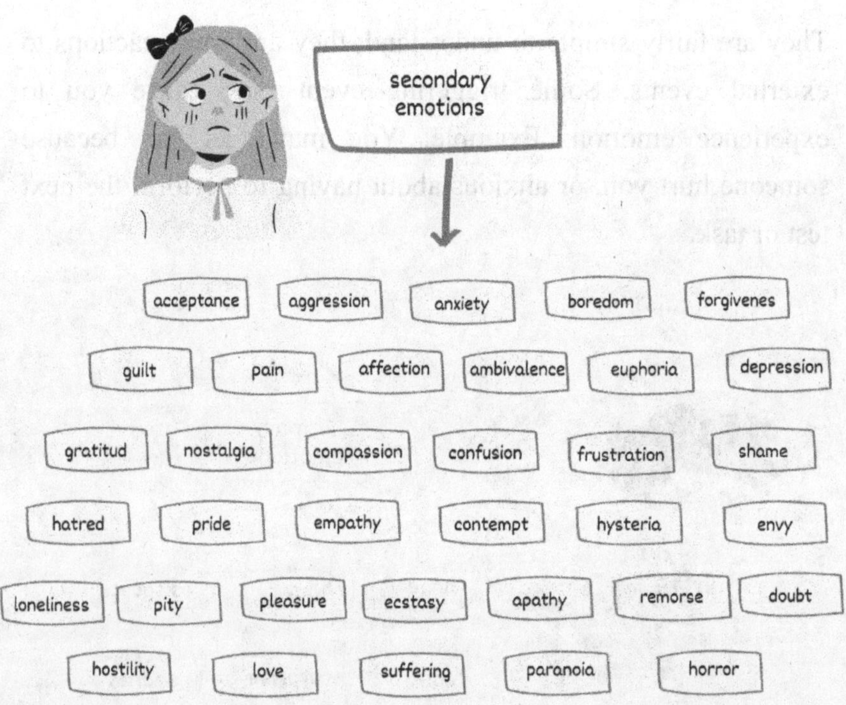

In order to differentiate between primary and secondary emotions, we can reflect on these questions:

1. Is this emotion a direct reaction to an external event? Primary
2. Does the emotion become more intense over time? Secondary

3. Do you experience the emotion more frequently than the events that provoked the emotion? Secondary

4. When the initiating event receded, did the emotions recede? Primary.

5. Does the emotion continue long after the event, interfere with your abilities in the present, and affect new and different experiences? Secondary

6. Is the emotion complex, ambiguous and difficult to understand?

Secondary in a PHP session there are sensations, emotions, and memories that are triggered by sustained acupressure (holding points). These stimuli are deeply linked to the limbic system, cerebral amygdala and hippocampus, to the nervous system. Each process in the brain responds to specific neural networks and association areas in different parts of the brain, cortical and subcortical. The brain functions in an interconnected way, with specific neurotransmitter circuits that go in different areas, connecting and activating biochemical and electrical neurophysiological processes, which we will later call "emotions".

CHANNELS OF TRAUMATIC EXPERIENCE INTEGRATION

PHP allows us to integrate fragmented memories of traumatic memories. These are moments of internal reorganization, of making contact with deep unconscious layers at the cellular and energetic level, modulating an intense release of discharge, in conjunction with the autonomic nervous system, which allows the client to open up to disconnected or dissociated emotions. When a person is in a state of dissociation, he/she feels, for example, floating, as in a cloud, or out of body flying in space.

The repressed emotions are transformed into discharges, which we observe in involuntary movements, changes in skin color, tears, heat, pressure and eye movement; as well as images, sounds, smells or words may appear as an expression of memory. The connection with the psychological is the bottom-up integration of the brain stem (sensations) and the limbic system (emotions); after this re-processing, the insight, or understanding, is integrated into the cerebral cortex (thought): sensation-emotion-thought.

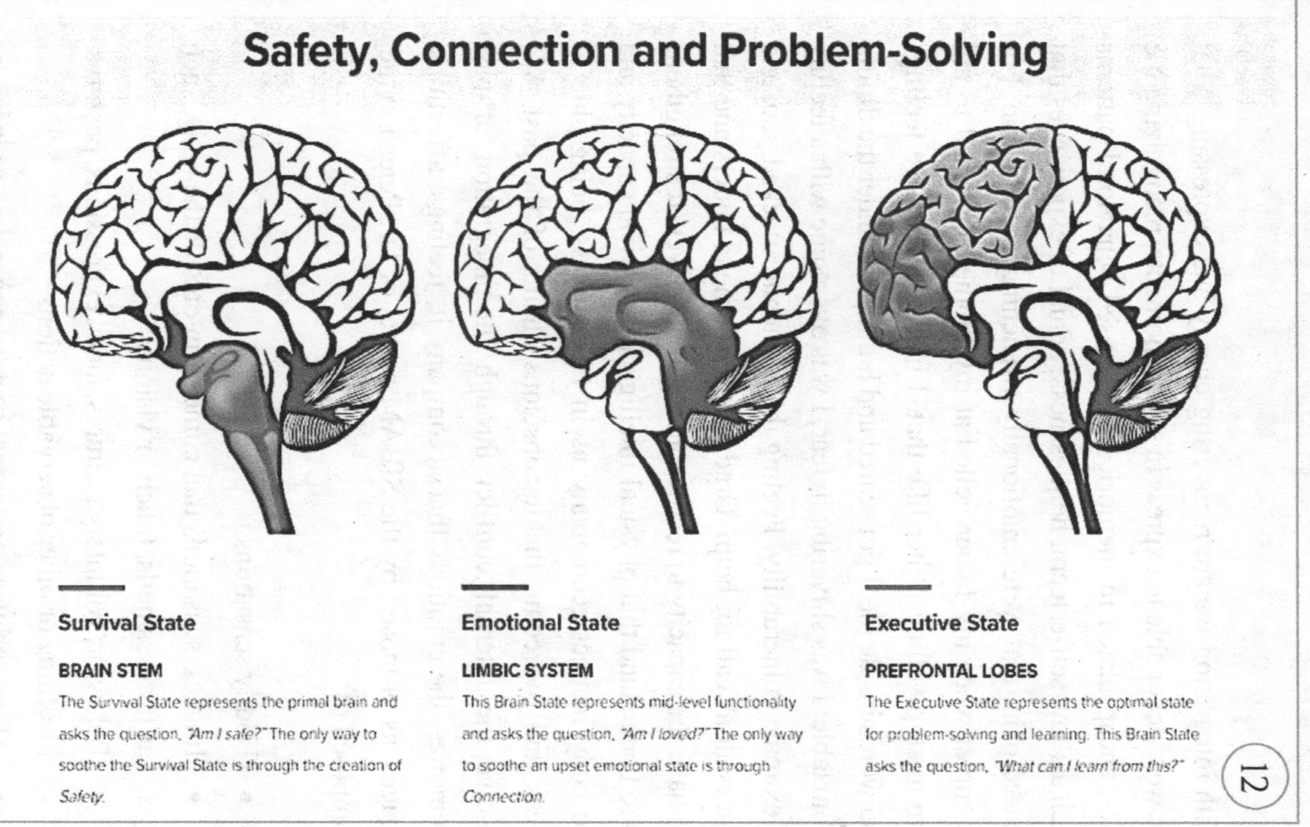

[15] Ref: The Conscious Discipline Brain State Model.
https://consciousdiscipline.com/methodology/brain-state-model/

With integration we are recovering energy and expressing what we were never able to express in shock moments, recognizing the pain, encapsulated in memories that caused behavioral patterns such as: low self-esteem, helplessness; denial of experiences that caused pain, that were emotionally wrenching or traumatic. For example: when my father yelled at my mother, I wanted to tell him to stop yelling at her like that. I had to keep these feelings and words inside me. I got scared and hid myself under the dining room table; I was shivering in fear; I was overcome with a feeling of extreme vulnerability. Feeling that someone attacked you, and you couldn't call for help. Gradually we come to understand that we have the capacity to recover and heal ourselves. It strengthens us to understand that physical intelligence, survival capacity and the body instinct accompany us in this process, being able to break and overcome the unconscious chains of the past. We resolve the internal conflict through the integration of past memories, the emotions that accompany it, feelings, affections, images, as proposed by the SIBAM model of Dr. Peter Levine, composed of:

- Bodily sensations.
- Images: sensations that come from outside the body, such as tastes, smells, touch or visions.
- Behavior: voluntary gestures, facial expressions, postures, breathing or other observable actions.
- Affect: primary emotions, such as anger, joy, sadness, or more nuanced feelings, which guide us.
- Meaning-making: cognitive thoughts and beliefs.

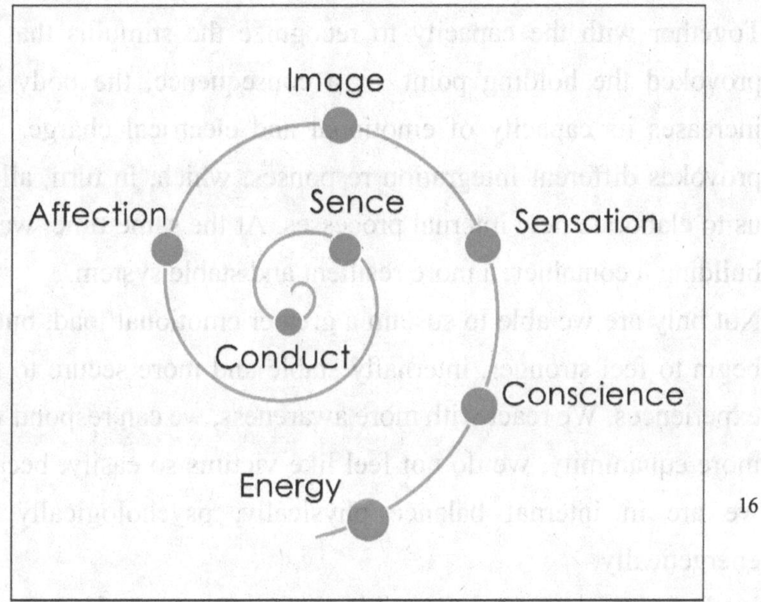

Process of Energy integration and Consciousness[16]

Based on the previous model, Mariann Dávila has incorporated the energy element (electrical response of the nervous system), as a triggering factor of the insight processes, which develops the consciousness factor, the state that allows us to access the perception of reality and then, in a different way for each person, the rest of the interaction of SIBAM factors. All these factors interact at the unconscious level and many times they are expressed as unconscious signals that reveal unresolved traumatic processes, which can be detected precisely because they are expressed, for example: headache, anxious behavior, intrusive images, together with smells or sounds; they show us parts of the unveiled history of trauma.

---

[16] Ref: Image Mariann Dávila

Together with the capacity to recognize the stimulus that has provoked the holding point, as a consequence, the body also increases its capacity of emotional and electrical charge. This provokes different integration responses, which, in turn, allows us to elaborate new internal processes. At the same time, we are building a container, a more resilient and stable system.

Not only are we able to sustain a greater emotional load, but we begin to feel stronger, internally stable and more secure to face experiences. We react with more awareness, we can respond with more equanimity, we do not feel like victims so easily, because we are in internal balance physically, psychologically and energetically.

In deeper traumas it is possible that there are early traumatic memories (gestation and first years of life), which are found in the implicit memory (sensory-motor memory). As the difficult experiences of life accumulate, they crystallize in the body without us realizing it.

The points open these time capsules, reorganize the defense responses, redirect the system energy flow, and channel the emotions, eliminating traces of complex births, birth asphyxia due to the umbilical cord on the neck, fetal distress, premature birth, among others.

The PHP session is a journey of discovery for the client with the therapist, which allows him/her to consciously mobilize his/her emotional burdens, frustrations and fears. The presence of the therapist facilitates the emergence, with awareness, of emotional burdens, the change of thoughts, leading to decisions that have often been postponed because of lack of energy and inner strength. When you go from the unconscious to the conscious, the action of new patterns of healthy beliefs is produced, which directly benefits the client with better physical and mental health.

In this book you will learn which acupressure points are used to track sensations and self-regulate emotions. This can be

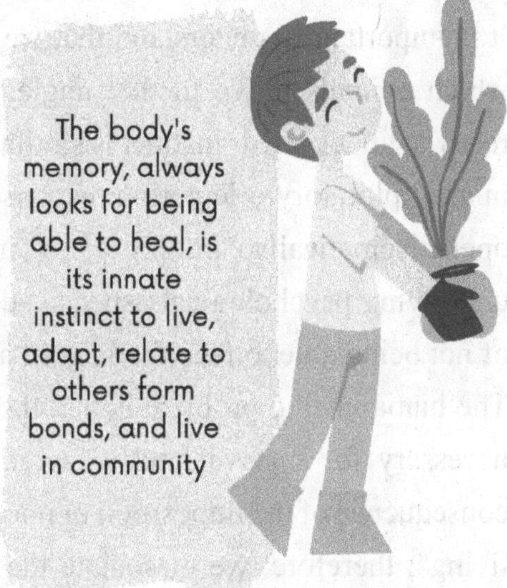

an effective therapeutic tool in moments of impact, emergency or as first aid that you can use on your own. However, regular PHP work requires the mandatory accompaniment of a certified therapist, and does not replace medical treatment.

In chapter four, you will find different self-application exercises that will help you in times of emergency.

SURVIVAL INSTINCT

It is important to understand that we share survival instinct with which animals move in the jungle; they sense danger and are ready to attack. Our instinct is similar, somatically we are always in an exploratory orientation response, on alert. When the body opens somatically, intuition[17] is unlocked along with some underlying psychological aspects, such as insecurity, the feeling of not being able to face fears, guilt and frustrations.

The human being problem is that these intuitive mechanisms, so necessary for survival and to avoid traumas, are blocked as a consequence of the imposition of norms and social rules for "good living"; therefore, we dissociate the impulse of survival, losing the capacity to establish limits, to put order in the bonds and/or to react effectively before danger.... In short, we are more vulnerable to trauma.

Vortices, Conscious and Unconscious Beliefs and Traumas

Traumas are facts of life, and most of us have been exposed to them. However, they should not be a death sentence. As human beings, we are biologically designed, as are animals, to respond to and recover from threats.

---

[17] Neuroscience recognizes the concept of Intuition as the brain's ability to predict events.

Trauma is conceived as a phenomenon of repeating a pattern or a state of immobility or freezing, "becoming fixed." Sometimes they are inherited or transgenerational traumas (transmitted at the genetic level) which often causes people to act without understanding the reason for their reactions, since at that moment the acquired traumatic memory is operating unconsciously. This is reflected in destructive behaviors, with oneself and with others, in acts of aggressiveness, impulsivity or uncontrolled anxiety.

In the PHP session, we sense the somatic-body experience which will free us from the fear and helplessness that has collapsed in our body. We aim to restore the natural balance of the nervous system, to restore the internal equilibrium by improving the resilience in it, increasing our vitality, equanimity and capacity to participate together actively in the resolution of trauma itself.

Current medicine still separates body, mind and emotion, and, in general, ignores the value of somatic therapy which links body, mind, emotion and their connection to trauma.

We approach and engage with our body through contact with sensations, which allows us to activate the vortex of self-regulation. The energy waves work at this level, vortex of self-regulation, allowing the body and mind to connect in a way that we can remember what produces dissociation, for example: a restrictive mental pattern that does not allow us to act or move but from the effort and self-sacrifice. There are also unconscious mechanisms such as denial and projective identification, where everything that happens is due to the "fault" of others, or because I see in others what I cannot tolerate seeing in my own behavior.

If we focus on mind and body awareness, stress reduction begins to come.

By working with sensations, the pendulum swings from a trauma's vortex and dissociation to a positive healing vortex will gradually create a container, a releasing energetic flow, which will modulate the nervous system, balancing it. As a result of the trauma mobilization, the shock discharge in the nervous system, and the dissolution of the patterns and crystals associated with the traumatic memory, we will sleep better, we will feel stronger, our cardiovascular system will come back to normal, the immune system will be healthy and the endocrine system will maintain its functions.

Through the somatic liberation technique, the patterns are reorganized, the experiences associated with fear and impotence are corrected in the body, the nervous system is readjusted, restoring the inner life and integrating the balance in the body; this way we are able to recover vitality, the ability to actively participate in family life, to regain inner peace, to have the ability to regulate ourselves instead of freezing or dissociating in a stressful situation.

The trauma vortex is one of the concepts that will be taught in this book, and its importance lies in that, it allows us to open to the healing memory and expand it to discover levels of vital energy at the cellular level, which are in our body, in the DNA and that move through the nervous system and its connections, opening the ability to mobilize, understand and reorganize dysfunctional behaviors, patterns of collapse, internal noise and feeling of emptiness or disconnection.

Emotional Brain

In the organization of regulatory processes, the system that allows us to relax, rest and repair is the Parasympathetic system. The brainstem or reptilian brain connects us to physical sensations. The Limbic System and the cerebral Amygdala modulate emotions such as fear, or innate and instinctive aggressiveness. The system of perception through the senses leads us to interception[18] and exteroception[19]. The concept of perception, which groups both, informs us of the sensations felt inside the body: to feel if there is something tight in the hip or in the left shoulder; it is to discover the sensations inside us (felt sense), which is what is considered in PHP as the healing energy that animals use, for example, by trembling or twitching muscles that have stored trauma.

We humans are also designed to sustain high-intensity survival states; we have the neocortical capacity for regulation through top-down cognitive processes (cortex, limbic system, brainstem), so we naturally, especially when we are not in danger, think and then act, driven by reason. In moments of emotion, such as anger, we can sometimes manage to inhibit defense responses. However, depending on the degree of danger, the brainstem is activated by the Limbic-Amygdala circuit, switching to the bottom-up circuit,

---

[18] Interception is a sense that helps us understand and perceive what happens to us, inside our body; For example: feeling hungry, thirsty, hot or cold.

[19] Exteroception, are several senses that allow us to perceive the external. Herself classified into tactile sensation, visual and auditory receptors and chemoreception (smell and taste). They are considered exteroceptive because they confer sensations that they arise outside the body.

where the brainstem and instinctive responses react modulated by the Amygdala. This activates the Hypothalamus-Pituitary-Adrenal axis, responding to the stress triggering stimulus and releasing the stress hormone cortisol.

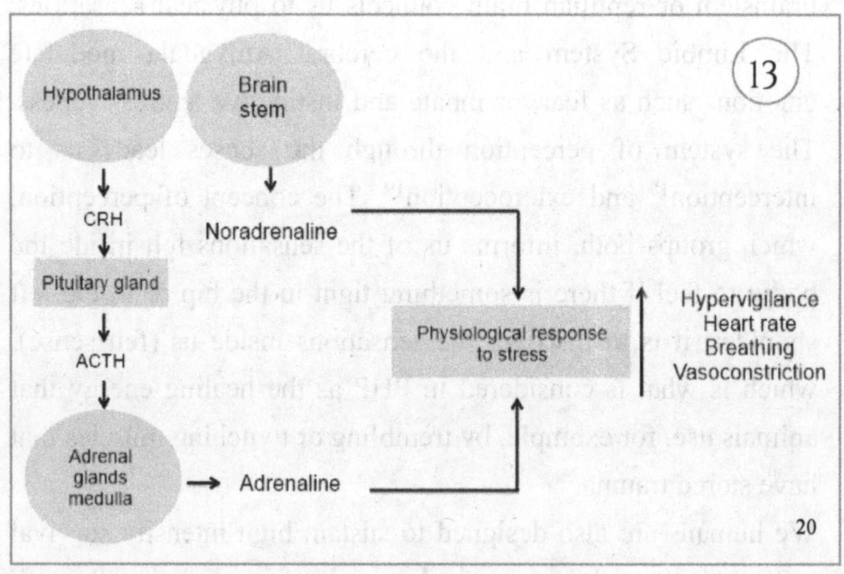

Neuroendocrine response to acute stress

If the nervous system does not reorganize after an overwhelming experience, the body loses the ability to rest, to achieve restorative sleep, the cardiovascular system is disturbed, there is poor immune system function, high amounts of psychological distress; it can also lead to a variety of cognitive, emotional and behavioral traumas.

---

[20] Extracted image from website:
https://www.uv.mx/eneurobiology/vols/2017/17/Herrera/HTML.html#bibliograpy

Traumatic Stress in Our Life

Traumatic stress is an accumulation of fatigue due to lack of real rest; the body is unable to manage this over demand of demands and, because it is a chronic and cumulative process, it is installed as depletion of the immune system, muscle exhaustion due to tension, lack of relaxation. This leads to a deterioration in the quality of sleep, discouragement, dullness, lack of motivation, becoming a vicious circle that generates a traumatic state when not being able to break this dynamic, going from fatigue to anguish, to emotional overflow, resulting in depression, panic attacks, anxiety disorder and hyper reactivity.

At the time of trauma, the energy system is like a vortex spiraling in the body, contracting intensely and generating overload. This causes energetic body exhaustion and constrictive thoughts appear. This whole process leads us to feel exhausted, internally drained, chronic fatigue, fibromyalgia and metabolic disorders appear.

Stream of Life Model with Pendulation Added

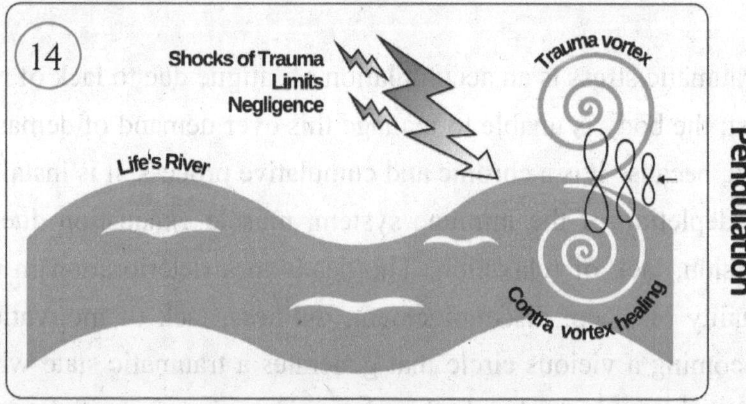

Vortex of trauma and healing - Image Dr. Peter Levine[21]

Signs of being in a Healing vortex are as follows:

- Expansion / distension
- Warmth
- Relaxation, calmness
- Settling in, sense of body's connection
- Sense of present time continuity
- Relaxation of viscera, stable center of gravity
- Tingling, moving downwards and outwards
- Fluidity
- Energy waves
- Feeling of lightness, brightness
- Awareness of the negative pole
- Abdominal breathing

---

[21] Extracted from widesite: https://lelaccarney.com/wp-content/uploads/2013/01/SE-Maps-for-recovery.pdf

Our inner movement, we call it Energetic Sense or Tone. Through the Nervous System it feels like someone is connecting you to a battery and suddenly you feel like you have extra energy; your breathing is more open and easier and your muscles feel strongly; you feel really alive emotionally and mentally and the energy moves at a cellular level. You feel connected to everything, and the Social Engagement System is activated.

It is important to remember that by loving and wanting to work our processes, we regain our love for ourselves, our self-esteem and our personal power. We become free of all bondage, especially the belief system.

Catalina: "I remember in 1995 I was in Boulder Colorado doing my workshop with Dr. Peter Levine. When I was at his house, he invited me to the back of his garden which ends in a channel where the water flows through the rocks, and he told me: *'Look at the water, as it flows and circulates through the rocks; if you look carefully, you realize that the water swirls in circles like a whirlpool. It starts to create a small circle in the water on another rock. This is the healing process beginning through a nervous system. Trauma can be healed'*.

This was very helpful in my learning, how trauma heals, and being able to use this vortex concept with every client I have worked with for so many years."

The belief system is what governs our life, it comes from way back, from our ancestors and runs from one generation to the next.

When we decide to be free and heal our body, we go into a healing crisis, and this is where we have to look within ourselves. What part within my body needs to be healed; for example, we already know if in the family there is a grandfather or great-great-grandfather with heart problems and your doctor asks you: do you have someone in the family with heart problems? You may have that problem in your body through your genetic connections with the DNA. As we work with our heart and healing, we can also connect it to the emotion or event that has created this accumulated residue and the energetic system of the belief: "I am not worthy! I do not deserve to be healthy."

The energetic points help to transmute these beliefs and heal them, when one transmutes the pain locked in the emotional and physical field, the mind is released.

DISSOCIATION

Dissociation allows us to endure a pain, provoking a forgetfulness from the conscious state. It is sometimes temporary, by means of an unconscious mechanism of protection by which an individual can be physically present, but psychologically split or separated from memories, images, feelings and recollections, disconnecting through amnesia, blocking the pain or fear of the whole traumatic experience or also retaining some memories in a diffused and partial way.

The ability to make contact with our body allows us to access our inner state, emotions that we find difficult to face because they are intense or devastating. When we have falls or accidents, we are not prepared, they are unforeseen, and the body is not able to receive or absorb the impact or prepare for the escape. We enter a space of disorientation, shock and sometimes fear, freezing, dissociation or unconsciousness. We are also affected psychologically, feeling internally disorganized, we lose, at times, contact with reality, or, if we have wounds, the pain shocks us. Anxiety states and panic attacks can appear for many years and can occur without being, apparently, related to the past trauma.

Being in a state of survival is more common than we think. Every morning we feel that life is a struggle; the dense traffic, arriving on time is an odyssey, feeling at risk of losing our job constantly, all of this brings us down emotionally, and consumes our spirits. Stress affects us, intoxicating us irremediably in a chronic way. Stress and insomnia, are signs that reinforce the feeling of being in an unstable and insecure environment. Noise, pollution, news of assaults, wars and killings, violence in all its expressions at family or social level, make our nervous system feel unstable, disorganized and activated. Cortisol, the stress hormone, affects our mental and physical health. We do not rest enough, we do not move enough; the lack of healthy routines and organic foods are still not accessible, urban commuting does not leave us time to have activities other than work. Feeling depressed has to do with the activations of the nervous system. Not being able to stop, or being in an over-demanding social system, causes isolation and depression. Added to this are the activities at home, taking care of children or the elderly, differences with a partner, unexpected expenses due to illnesses, school routines, unavoidable social commitments, and, in short, an endless number of situations that make us feel trapped, unable to find silence in our minds. The spiral of modernity of internet, messages and emails, social networks, become a way of evasion, which leads us to feel more anxious about the future and create addictive dependence, affecting relationships with children, partners, family and social activities with others.

The Pandemic left us with a strong sense of instability, as well as relationship problems within our homes. Confinement generated high stress dynamics for more than two years, with intense moments of loneliness. Families experienced crises, domestic violence, increased divorce, less work and fewer resources. It was a period that, to this day, continues to generate breakups, depression, and sequelae of Covid 19 a long covid symptoms. In addition to all this impact on mental and emotional health, there is also damage at the organic level, such as pulmonary, cardiac and lowering of the immune system's defenses. Many people who have a chronic illness or symptoms are generally more vulnerable and at greater risk of contracting COVID.

The Two Options for Help
Sympathy and Empathy

In PHP there is the concept of sympathy, which is defined as the attitude of wanting to help another to feel better. There is also the concept of empathy, which is understood as "the ability to put oneself in the other person's place". In PHP it refers to having faith that a person can heal himself or herself.

We are always in sympathy with others, we always want to help someone, even if it means sacrificing ourselves. We neglect ourselves to go to the aid of others. We need to understand that we first need to be well ourselves to help others, we cannot abandon ourselves to be concerned about others, friends, family, and animals.

Sympathy, in the context of PHP speaks of a debilitating look at the capabilities of the other.

In empathy, on the contrary, the person possesses the capacity to be well within themselves first. In this attitude we trust that the other is capable. That we are in a position to be able to help others, trusting the other, we support without being carried away. It is to have the conviction that the other can succeed.

Catalina Case:

In the year 2022, a thirty-two-year-old man came to see me because he could not connect emotionally with women. He would have sex and then disconnect from them. He couldn't have a steady relationship with anyone. In the session, he remembered that at the age of four, he hid under the dinner table while his alcoholic father very angrily tried to hang his maternal grandmother with a telephone cord while the mother watched. The police arrived and took him away, and his parents separated after that.

From that moment on, his mother never stopped checking on him every minute. Today at the age of thirty-two, he moved to California to escape his mother's control. Even so, nowadays she asks him to call her every day, and she visits him all the time. During her visits, she goes through his closet and his car. She is obsessive and possessive of him.

While having a Points Holding Session, he was recalling this situation. His body was very tense, as well as his feet and legs from the knees down. His pelvis was also very tight. He could not relate this tension to the traumatic childhood experience, and the internal effect it had, both for him and his mother. This is what is called "Fragmentation" (being broken into separate parts).

I asked him to perceive his legs, how tight they were, while signaling to him that everything would be okay and bringing him into the present moment. I sought to expand the movement of the legs. He began to shake and I said, "You have to tell your mom right now, mentally and calmly: "I am fine, mom". In that very instant, as he connected with the three parts of his brain, he began to feel warmth and tingling all over his body.

In this visualization, he realized that his mother, as a result of the trauma that they had both experienced, had been in a state of sympathy all her life, always looking out for him to be well and safe.

With this exercise, he repairs the situation internally and manages to understand why his mother acted like that. When we have witnessed something difficult in the family, we stay in sympathy mode for a long time. Very soon afterwards, he reached out to his mom and brought her to have a session with me.

BLOCKED ENERGY PATTERNS

Energy can be blocked as a reaction to any type of extreme stress or danger, whether emotional, physical, spiritual, or impacting the realm of thoughts and beliefs.

The facilitation of holding the points allows us to access blocked energetic patterns on all these levels: physical, emotional, mental and energetic-spiritual, in an integral and holistic manner. It does this through the neurological mechanisms of the endocrine and autonomic nervous system, which function and direct, in an integrated way, multiple processes of the brain and body.

Dr. Peter Levine, founder and pioneer of the Somatic Experiencing®, has shown that traumatic symptoms are not caused by the events themselves, but by the lack of release, or discharge, of energy, and/or arousal processing, which is the intense energy that is mobilized to cope with extreme life-threatening events.

In animal studies, survival behaviors are observed. One of them is when the pursued animal makes the attacker believe that it has died, in order to eliminate in the hunter, the stimulus to attack. It deceives the hunter and with this strategy it manages to survive. This is called Thanatosis.

The opossum or weasel, as well as a deer, faces danger by freezing. When the danger has passed, the animal's body trembles, discharging by shaking itself until it manages to regulate its nervous system. It will run away without any residual traumatic stress. This trembling is the liberation of the excess of immobilized energy. This is how wild animals mitigate post-traumatic stress. To achieve a traumatic discharge, they rely on their natural mechanisms. Trauma is the energy trapped in the nervous system.

Human beings have inherited the instinctive capacity and the same survival mechanisms at the level of the brainstem and limbic system. The cerebral Amygdala picks up and coordinates defense responses if necessary. If we sense danger, we respond through the sensations of fear. In the body, the heart rate and respiration accelerate, the pupils dilate in search of the danger signal, our ears and sense of smell also respond to the threat. The body first freezes, and, after the threat has passed, we tremble to release the mobilized energy. But if that energy is not released, or is encapsulated in the form of unresolved emotions, or negative or destructive beliefs, it could develop, over time, into symptoms and diseases in our mind and body.

THE IMPACT OF TRAUMA ON EMOTIONS

Guilt and shame

Guilt is related to sympathy, it´s not a normal emotion, and can be paralyzing. A person may feel guilty for something he did, for something he failed to do, or for something he thought he did. When a person causes harm to another, guilt is a natural emotional response and can mobilize you in the form of an apology, correcting the mistake and not repeating it in the future. When you have guilt, that energy is stored in the body, it becomes a calcification, a crystallization; that calcification generates bodily suffering.

Some people suffer from excessive guilt. A person who feels bad, for example, of having ill thoughts towards someone else, could feel their guilt to the extreme. They may also suffer from excessive ruminative or depressive thoughts.

Guilt and shame are two closely related emotions. While guilt usually stems from having caused some real or perceived harm, shame can be thought of as involving negative feelings about who you are. A person can also feel guilty about a specific harmful act without necessarily experiencing a strong feeling of shame.

Guilt and shame also create body calcifications; they are trapping emotions, and we recreate them over and over again, to the point where we are unaware of them and become unconscious of their presence.

If we fail to decalcify the crystals, we feel worthless, we cannot be rich because "we have to be poor"; we feel guilty for being rich. Belief systems appear that enclose us within walls, limiting us in order to have what we want: money, fame, success. We have to break these beliefs, otherwise we will always feel small, weak and limited.

Certain people are especially prone to feelings of guilt, as well as feelings of shame, and both can be expressed excessively. The tendency to feel shame has been associated with depression, anxiety and other forms of mental illness.

- Shame can easily develop in childhood, when the adult does not look at reality from a child's perspective.
- It appears when there are messages of not being good enough.
- It is related to childhood abuse trauma.

Projecting Blame onto Others

Those who feel guilty may be angry or sad, or a combination of both emotions, and can express it in the following ways:

- There are guilty parties who need others to be found guilty. To place the blame on others.
- They never take sides, they avoid.
- They judge themselves and others from pity and victimization.
- They live in a state of permanent comparison.
- They give rewards and hand out punishments.
- The idea is to make the other feel guilty and at the same time manipulate to victimize themselves, affirming phrases such as "You did it to me".

There are several types of guilt:

1. Healthy guilt, when realizing the mistake and mobilizing to repair the damage.
2. Pathological guilt, based on victimization and evading responsibility.
3. Manipulative guilt, making the other feel guilty.

We can trace guilt in our body by connecting with a specific part where the sensation associated with the memory of a past experience is located, which leads us to feel this way.

- Where do I feel guilty in my body?
- What makes me connect this emotion with the felt sense of guilt?

What would our lives be like if we were free of resistance?

Our resistances are based upon judgments, which involve identifying with one side of a duality to the exclusion of the other. Judgment and resistance involve being locked into a particular state of identity while ignoring other possible states of identity in which we have become fixated or stuck.
The goal is change of consciousness through release of resistance. Let´s suppose we have to work through a particular resistance which has governed our behavior in a given area of life up to now. We begin to experience what appears to be freedom in this area because resistance is gone, and our behavior is no longer governed by it. We may certainly call this a change of consciousness.
Resistance cannot be resolved without love or enthusiasm.

The Requirement of Health and Healing

Our body, in order to be healthy, must have an alkaline pH (8.5). The pH is a measure of acidity or alkalinity of an aqueous solution. All living beings depend on an adequate pH to be able to live, because the acid-alkaline balance is one of the basic mechanisms to be healthy.

Western medicine has long ignored the critical importance of maintaining an alkaline pH to maintain our health. It has also ignored how modern germs are highly resistant to the strongest antibiotics, leading to rare pandemics. One of the keys to preventing disease is not to avoid ingesting aggressive medicines, but to achieve the natural healthy balance our bodies need.

Through PHP's work you will learn which foods help correct pH in the short term and which foods and supplements provide specific relief for such common ailments as asthma, indigestion, hypertension, joint pain and many more.

Toni Toney is an American nutritionist who has excelled in her work called Ecotarian diet, helping thousands of people. She calls her work "Internal Acid Theory", in which she states that the secret is to sustain an alkaline environment in our body. In her book "ECOTARIAN DIET" Get clean go green (2010)". She states, "Eating too much meat increases the chance of dying prematurely. If you eat too much meat in your diet it is dangerous for your health, you are going to have heart disease, cancer, colon or rectal cancer."

She also indicates that cow's milk is dangerous for health, because it has many hormones. That some fish, such as king mackerel, swordfish, golden croaker and tuna, are contaminated with mercury and antibiotics.

Excess sugar also produces more microbes, increases candidiasis and creates metabolic syndromes such as insulin resistance, which can trigger type II diabetes.

The importance of Minerals for the Process of Holding Points

The purpose of using a mineral supplement during PHP sessions, is to introduce sufficient mineral electrolytes to saturate the body and, in particular, the cerebrospinal fluid. This provides the physical energy for a profound transformation to occur. With mineral saturation, there are enough electrolytes in the cerebrospinal fluid to create changes at all levels. To increase the electrical potential, or life force, within each cell of the body, each person must possess highly available and highly charged forms of minerals and trace elements. A wide range of minerals is required before the body can transmute them and utilize them properly for healing. Once blockages in the electrical structure of the body are resolved in one session, healing can proceed deep into the physical body.

If sufficient and readily available minerals are not present it slows down the process of removing blockages from the electrical body and can even trigger the withdrawal of minerals from deep tissues and organs. This mineral deficiency delays healing in the physical structure and causes the individual's recovery time and session work to be prolonged.

To get into balance and alkalinize your body, we recommend consuming supplements containing minerals.

Another objective of maintaining the stable health of the physical body through alkalinity is to prepare it for its interconnection with the other dimensions of being. Through the physical body we access the emotional body, and when we transmute the pain in the emotional field, we then access the mental body, which allows us to embrace the dualities of life and transmute all the resistances caused by judgment, criticism and condemnation.

It must be recognized that tissue regeneration and emotional transmutation require a commitment to build within the body as large a reservoir of essential precursors as possible.

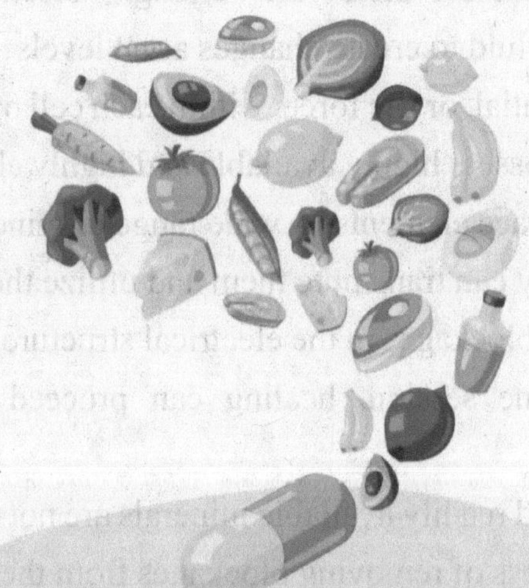

Supporting a High Nervous System Operation

The work with the points and somatic work is aimed at strengthening and reorganizing the nervous system so that it functions well. Without an optimally functioning nervous system, the deep energy reserves of the organs are in danger of being drained due to the energy needed for transformational processes. The health and vitality of the nervous system is supported by the basic lifestyle choices of:

1. Water and nutrition
2. Movement and relaxation.

The first level consists of alkalizing the body through pure, micro-filtered, alkalized water, ionized water, and a diet of fresh, raw, electrolyte-rich, phytonutrient-rich foods.

Recommendations:

- Eat 90% alkaline foods.
- Exclude sugar, salt, white flour, hot and cold drinks, and carbonated beverages.
- Eat vegetables and fruits separately at least 1/2 hour apart.
- Soak seeds and nuts for 12 hours before eating.
- Drink fresh, raw juices (one-quarter to one-half liter daily).
- Drink large amounts of plain water or water with a little lemon to make it more alkaline daily.

BODY'S RESILIENCE

To help a person to re-establish healthy energy flows that have been blocked, by a stressful or traumatic life experience, whether recent or years ago, we begin by making contact with the body. The body has the awareness to "recognize" the path of blocked energy. We just have to know how to listen to its messages. It is the direct entrance to the truth of the heart, it contains the essence of the Self, it is the source of our deepest personal truth.

Often the mind and emotions are not aligned with this deeper knowledge of Self. Thoughts and feelings are part of the psychological defense mechanism that maintains the energy blockage caused by a traumatic event. It is necessary to elaborate a trauma resolution process by channeling the energetic blockage from a trauma vortex to a healing vortex in a very gradual way. This psychological defense mechanism walls off the traumatic experience. The main objective of the defense mechanism is to protect the psychic balance, repressing or dissociating the experience, depending on the degree of traumatic shock, and thus protecting the individual from an overreaction at the moment of the traumatic event.

Therefore, taking minerals facilitates:

1. Re-establishing the connection with the body's natural healing power.
2. Regulation of the nervous system.
3. Discharging the defense responses that were incomplete and block the flow of energy.

Being connected to the body brings us directly to the heart's truth, to a space of calm and re-signification of feelings, affects and memories that, when released, allow us to align emotions and ultimately change thought patterns and limiting beliefs.

When we experience pain, insecurity, anxiety, distress and emptiness, we know that something is out of alignment. These experiences may be connected to the family's past, come from a genetic pattern, come from a mistaken belief stemming from a traumatic incident, or originate from cultural programming. The body will lead us to the mental program that created the pain.

In a PHP session, we re-experience the original source of that pattern, we do it in a safe way, accessing higher cognitive processes (limbic system, cortex and prefrontal cortex), instead of the primitive fight or flight mechanisms (brainstem) that were activated at the original moment of the trauma.

In a PHP session, we are able to access the limbic system circuitry and the self-regulation of the neuroendocrine and energetic system, through sustained pressure on the suboccipital points (STO), which are located on both sides of the spinal column, at the base of the skull.

With the stabilization obtained by holding the points:

1. We guide the process through the sensation felt.
2. We trace the signals of the trauma through the nervous system.
3. We allow the nervous system to guide and mobilize the charges, discharge the inhibited responses, integrate and reorganize the internal synchrony of the organs and systems.

In this process, tonic immobility and re-traumatization are significant elements that need to be precisely managed in conjunction with the body's wisdom.

LIMBIC SYSTEM

The limbic system is composed of a multitude of interconnected brain structures. This makes it complex to determine precisely which structures form it and the specific work of each one of them: The Cerebral Amygdala, the Hippocampus, The Hypothalamus, The Fornix and the Limbic Cortex.

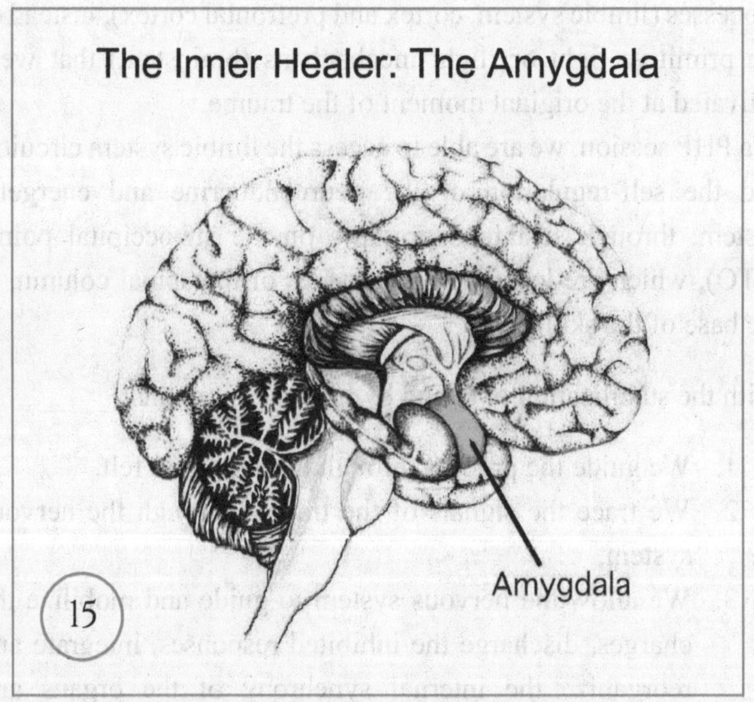

---

22 Ref: New pathways in brain's amygdala discovered. UT San Antonio, 2019.
https://neurosciencenews.com/amygdala-pathway-15199/

It is one of the almond-shaped nuclei of nerve cells, located in the posterior temporal area of the brain. It has connections with the great majority of the encephalon, being a nucleus of special relevance that can affect the whole nervous system and the functionality of the organism. It is a key element for survival, since its main function is to integrate emotions with their corresponding response patterns, provoking a physiological response or the preparation of a behavioral response.

Structure: The amygdala is made up of different structures and has the following subdivisions:

1. **The Central Nucleus:** emits messages in the form of electrical impulses to the nervous system so that we respond appropriately after processing emotions. It also regulates the function of the endocrine system. It determines according to the circumstances which hormones have to be produced. When the senses are heightened, it sends an order to synthesize adrenaline, serotonin, dopamine and cortisol, among others.

2. **Medial Nucleus:** in charge of receiving information from the sense of smell and processing it. It determines how specific smells can awaken memories, activate sexual appetite, and even make us run away from something.

3. **Lateral nucleus:** This is the main area where everything that comes from sight, taste, hearing and smell is processed. It interprets what we feel and elaborates the response signals that we are going to give to these stimuli,

and then carries this information to the rest of the nervous system.

4. **Basal nucleus:** controls our actions, not based on what our senses pick up, but on our memories.

Functions:

1. **Emotion regulation:** The amygdala is the control center of our emotions. It is the one that dictates that, in certain situations, we feel joy and happiness or fear and sadness. It is one of the protagonists in everything related to the experience of both positive and negative emotions.

2. **Responses to fear:** The amygdala processes the emotions of fear and, therefore, triggers all survival mechanisms. It directs flight responses when we feel fear, either when our senses perceive danger or when we remember something from the past.

3. **Association of memories with emotions:** The amygdala links stored memories with the emotions we feel about that event. The amygdala is responsible for remembering good moments of our life with joy, bad moments with pain. It is closely linked to emotional traumas.

4. **Regulation of sexual behavior: It** is the task of the amygdala to link different stimuli with sexual pleasure. It regulates sexual behavior. This brain structure is responsible for triggering, when we perceive specific stimuli, the reactions that lead to sexual arousal (or inhibition).

5. **Control of aggression:** It is also the control center of aggression. People with a hyper-stimulated amygdala have a greater predisposition to react aggressively and violently to specific stimuli, while people with lesions in the amygdala are more likely to have weak self-defense reactions.

6. **Appetite regulation:** The amygdala also influences the sensation of hunger. Depending on whether we need to eat or not, it regulates satiety levels.

7. **Emotional learning:** The amygdala is our storehouse of emotions. The more it develops and the more lived experiences we have, the more it learns. This is how emotional intelligence develops throughout life.

8. **Pleasure responses**: The amygdala generates all physical well-being reactions to positive emotions. This is a survival mechanism, since it is the body's way of ensuring that we spend more time away from danger.

9. **Recognizing emotions in other people:** It is responsible for the development of empathy. It is the region of the brain that allows us to interpret the emotions of others based on what they tell us, their facial expressions, their behavior. It allows us to put ourselves in the other person's shoes.

In PHP, the memory capacity of the amygdala in the brain is used to evoke the client's traumatic events in session, through the images and emotions that emerge from these memories, and to connect them to the "felt sensation". Thus, when reliving the shock, the nervous system recognizes it and performs the corresponding discharge and integrates the experience.

The Hippocampus

It is a structure of the prosencephalon. It is in the temporal lobe and has the shape of a "seahorse". It is one of the most ancestral regions of the human encephalon and is therefore the main structure linked to the hypothalamus in the regulation of the basic processes of our survival. Moreover, the hippocampus is so important that without it we would not have an identity since it is an essential area for the proper functioning of our memory, in particular the remote memory, which is what provides us with the memory of everything that has happened in the past, and therefore partly shapes our personality molded on the basis of experiences. In addition, the hippocampus is also a very important structure in learning processes. As for the limbic system, the hippocampus is primarily responsible for emotional memory. This means that every event we have lived, felt, and experienced is filtered by the hippocampus, which, together with the hypothalamus, makes it possible for us to remember not only the experiences, but also what we feel associated with them.

The Hypothalamus

The hypothalamus is essential for life as it is responsible for coordinating vital functions, by controlling the endocrine and autonomic nervous systems.

It has a very small size, and the diversity of neurons it contains is not found in any other organ. Located directly above the brainstem, together they control the body's energy levels, coordinate the functioning of the heart and lungs, the endocrine system and the immune system.

It is responsible for maintaining a constant body temperature by controlling the respiratory rate and sweating. It regulates appetite and thirst, as well as sleep and circadian rhythms. It participates in parasympathetic functions related to feeding, locomotion and mating. It regulates blood pressure and homeostatic balance. It is involved in aggressive and defensive behaviors.

The Fornix

The fornix or trigone is a C-shaped bundle of nerves in the brain that carries signals from the hippocampus to the hypothalamus, as well as from one hemisphere to the other. The fornix is essential for normal cognitive functioning, especially known for its importance in memory formation as part of the Papez circuitry. However, its main functions seem to relate to the consolidation and retrieval of memories.

Limbic Cortex

It is mainly concerned with behavior, emotions, and motivation. The limbic cortex is part of a much larger whole, the limbic system, which encompasses a complex series of neural structures in the midbrain and basal regions of the brain.

Limbic System and Prefrontal Cortex

The limbic system is integrated with the prefrontal cortex and higher functions, including executive functions, that generate actions in response to emotions. The prefrontal cortex allows us to use language, plan, reflect, imagine, play, and create future scenarios. It is the seat of empathy - the ability to feel in another person - and mirror neurons, which allow us to be in sync with another person. The prefrontal cortex acts as a watchtower, offering a view of the scene from up high, helping you realize you may be responding to a false alarm and enabling you to suspend the stress response, restoring equilibrium.

The medial prefrontal cortex is just below the forehead; one of the most dramatically changing regions of the brain during adolescence. It is the basis for the executive or higher functions of the brain. It is responsible for organizing, prioritizing and curbing impulses, crucial in decision making, concentration, attention span, and personality.

The first segment of the brain that begins to give out when we sleep little is the prefrontal cortex, where decisions are made and problems are solved. It is one of the areas of the brain most vulnerable to stress, even early childhood stress, and is crucial for homeostasis or metabolic stability, survival and adaptation.

Functions of the prefrontal cortex:
The prefrontal cortex is the seat of both decision-making processes and ethics. The main functions of the prefrontal cortex are the following:

- **Emotion regulation:** the prefrontal cortex constantly articulates our thoughts, feelings and actions through sophisticated attentional and decision-making processes. It is permanently finding more information that allows us to make difficult decisions in life.

- **It plans and organizes future actions considering the consequences:** This brain area, is activated in tasks that involve a delay between stimulus and behavioral response or that depend on recent experience to complete them.

- **Working memory:** One of its key functions is working or short-term memory. It manages the temporary memory that stores information for a short period of time. It acts in complex processes such as language or reasoning and discovers how to optimize short-term memory. Pain awareness is another function of the prefrontal cortex.

The Thalamus

The thalamus is part of the structure known as the diencephalon. Stimuli reach the thalamus and are transported to the primary motor cortex, which is responsible for producing rapid movement in the face of these noxious stimuli.

It has functions such as:

- Control of more vegetative functions, i.e., controlling automatic functions such as blood pressure or body temperature.

- Transmits pain and temperature.

- It is essential for survival, as it allows us to move away from painful stimuli quickly.
- Maintenance of postural control.
- Plays an important role in generating routines and learning them until they are transferred to the cortex and become 'habitual.'"

Reptilian Brain

It is located is in the brainstem, just above where our spinal cord enters the skull and is already activated before birth. It is the nerve center that has nerve cell nuclei responsible for the basic functions: breathing, hunger, temperature, sleep, wakefulness, pain, moisture, crying, getting rid of toxins by urinating and defecating. This is also the exit of the twelve cranial nerves. Their task is to keep us alive, with vital signs.

The subcortical structures are worked in a PHP session through the points located on the feet, which will be described in the next chapter.

Participating in a PHP Session

During the PHP session the client will lie comfortably on a massage table. The facilitator will hold one or more points on the body continuously for a period that can be from one hour to one hour and a half. If the client intends to address a particular issue, you begin by tracking a sensation in the body related to what you are bringing in to work on. By tracing the sensations that appear in the body, we connect with the nervous system and the memory emerges. There are times when the reason for consultation does not coincide with what the wisdom of the body points out about the place where we should go, revealing forgotten experiences repressed by our mind.

By holding the points, the body usually relaxes deeply and leaves the stress behind. Then sensations appear that will give rise to the emotion or memory of past events. Once the experience of a triggered event is recognized, the possibility of a resolution arises. The client, within the framework of a session, can discover and resolve one or more cycles of processes that are appearing and that involve several issues.

The points of the body, by their very nature, pulsate and give signals as to the start and end timing of the session.

The facilitator will know the moment when this homeostasis occurs. The exact nature and outcome of each session is not predictable. Each session is different.

Some people have gained insights into events of their ancestor´s lives and resolved generational patterns; they have recalled what appear to be past life events, or resolved collective consciousness issues, eliminated entities, and received profound messages and transcendent understandings. These interpretations will depend on the beliefs of each person. In the PHP session, negative energy charges are eliminated.

Many of the destructive or risky behaviors are related to transgenerational antecedents: abandonment, parental neglect; these can be precursors to acts of violence and crime, as in the following case.

In November 2022, a Florida teenager was sentenced for the 2018 Parkland school shooting. He went to the school with an automatic weapon and killed seventeen people, injuring many others, including students and teachers. After the shooting, he left the school and went to a Walmart to buy something to drink and then sat with one of the victims' brothers at a nearby McDonald's. At that moment, when the police arrived and caught him, he was calm. A few years later, the boy was given a life sentence. When in court, he was asked, 'Why did you do it?' He, being the son of an alcoholic woman who never gave him love or attention (to the surprise of all the people, parents of these dead children), he said, "I don't know, I had no control of my actions, I don't remember anything." To everyone's surprise, he was not given a death sentence, only life imprisonment.

INTRODUCTION TO THE PROCESS OF HOLDING POINTS

When the therapy is done with a single facilitator, it is very likely to begin the first session by reinforcing the body's ability to reconnect to itself, holding points in different parts of the body: for example, the abdomen, through which stress, heart and trauma are worked. It is also possible to work neck points, what we call the STO points, located in the occipital triangle, between the sternocleidomastoid and trapezius muscles, at the base of the occiput. These points have very powerful access to the nervous system and the mind-body matrix. For very specific issues or physical ailments, other points can be used as needed.

Your facilitator will ask to fill out a form. He or she will incorporate any relevant information on surgeries, accidents, past and present health problems, whatever needs to be considered to assess the client's conditions.

There are certain contraindications for holding points in general, or for working with specific points. If holding points is contraindicated in your case, your practitioner may suggest working with Somatic Release Technique™ (SRT), which involves similar facilitation to PHP, but without holding points.

How to maintain pressure on the points:

Pressure should be persistent and strong enough, but tolerable. Avoid using so much pressure that it is painful and distracting to the client.

The points are held with the intention, especially at the beginning, of provoking continuous stimulation that allows activating the process of accessing repressed sensations, emotions, and memories. The client monitors the pressure, providing feedback to the facilitator. As everyone's nervous system and sensitivity is different, it is necessary to know the appropriate level of pressure. With full presence and intention, the facilitator maintains his or her attention in service to the session and the needs of the client. The fundamental purpose is to support with love and awareness the nature of each moment that emerges, without personal judgments.

The facilitator will consider the following indicators:

- The time when the cerebrospinal fluid is released and circulating smoothly.
- The points have cooled, and small pulsations are present.
- The points settle into a light heart pulsing of 72 beats per minute, indicating that the nervous system has returned to equilibrium.
- At this point there will also be a felt sensation that the energetic charge in the system has dissipated.
- The practitioner has returned to ordinary consciousness.
- The energies of the client and the facilitator have completely separated.

What the points tell you:

The facilitator experiences deep resonance with the client at the time of the session, and, also by holding the points, experiences sensations such as numbness of fingers and dry mouth. At that moment the client is releasing thoughts and emotions, which activates the limbic system and the base of the brain. We accompany and support the space of security, giving confidence with phrases of support such as: "I am with you", "Everything will be fine" and we ask them to share with us what sensations emerge or what is happening in the body.

The nervous system of the client will perceive if the space is safe, and if the facilitator is present in the therapy, because the body is able to detect if the context is safe and the facilitator is trustworthy. Only then will such a powerful bond be generated that will allow these processes to emerge to be healed.

When the points heat up:

The heat is energy trapped in the nervous system, which begins to move; circulation is being restored to various parts of the body, the nervous system is activated.

When the points become very hot:

The biological transmutation of the elements produces heat in the fingertips as the querent dissolves thought patterns and emotional blockages out of the body.

The client begins their process and whatever is stuck in their mind or emotion comes up. The process is supervised with questions that give information to the facilitator and generate confidence and security in the client. Sensations appear, such as:

- Goose bumps / chills.
- Deep fears and feelings of threat.
- Deep throbbing in the fingers, which represents that the nervous system is integrating and restoring energy.
- Body shivering/feeling cold, both in the client and the facilitator, and represents release of traumatic energy.
- Reaching an equalized pulsation (72 beats/min) shows completion of the work with the points.

Responsibility in the healing process on the part of the client:

The person is responsible for maintaining a loving and voluntary attitude of recognition and openness to the experience, opening to share previously repressed emotions and memories that may emerge involuntarily. It requires being present and informing the facilitator of his or her sensations, feelings, thoughts and visions, and remaining in the process until his or her body has reached the time it needs to close the session.

Contraindications to point holding

These contraindications are relevant, and specific to the client's conditions, which can be physical, emotional, mental and energetic.

A PHP therapeutic process does not replace medical treatments, but rather, in general, positively enhances them. Rather, it reinforces the body's ability to recover.

If you have any doubts, it is important to consult your treating physician.

Carotid Artery:
Consult if you have presented obstructions.
It is not recommended for people with carotid artery problems, as it can affect blood flow to the brain, especially in the manipulation of the vagus nerve or STO points. At this slight point of the carotid triangle, the common carotid artery is covered only by skin and superficial cervical fascia, therefore, any manipulation can be delicate and affect the person.

Xiphoid cartilage:
If you compress the xiphoid cartilage, it could lacerate the liver. It is a contraindication.
When we hold sternal points, it is recommended to keep your hands "high" on the chest so as not to make contact with this body cartilage. It should not be manipulated.

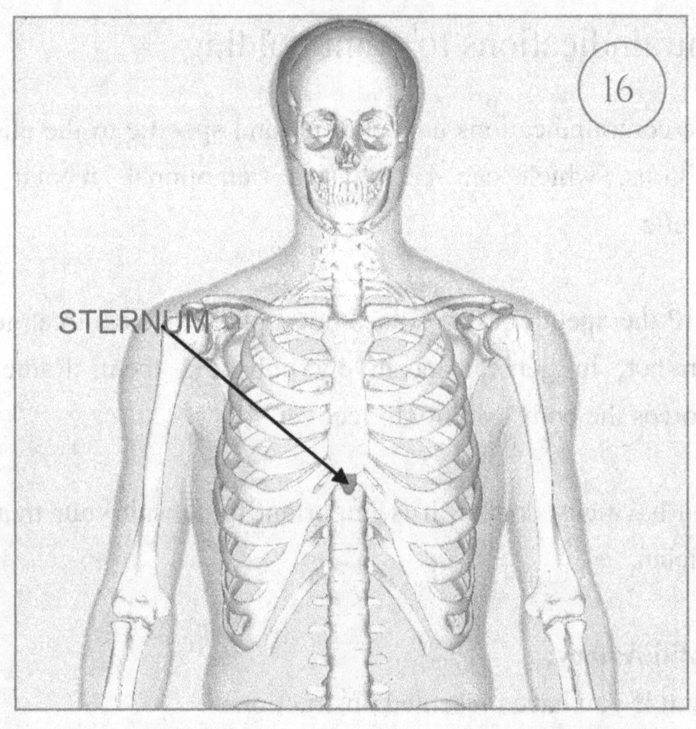

[23]

Acute injury and receiving help:

Performing a PHP session right after a person has injured a muscle may be counterproductive and inappropriate.

An acutely injured person should wait to receive a session. Otherwise, it will interfere with the normal healing process.

Severe injury is another contraindication that must be taken into account.

[23] Ref: Image extracted from: Anatomography (setting page of this image), CC BY-SA 2.1 jp: https://commons.wikimedia.org/w/index.php?curid=22529292

Intervening when a person has just undergone major surgery is counterproductive. The surgical procedure often penetrates or exposes the body wound. He or she may have undergone extensive tissue dissection or a related orthopedic process. The major surgical procedure is potentially dangerous because it can cause permanent physiological or anatomic impairment.

A PHP session inmediately after major surgery is an absolute contraindication

High fever:

When the client has a significant temperature of around 38°C or 100.4°F, it is best to wait until the fever is down and has fully recovered to perform a session. Fever is a clear indication that a person's body is fighting a bacterial or viral infection, and in both cases the conditions can be contagious. The risk of contracting illnesses is high for the facilitator, and there is the possibility of spreading it to other clients, co-workers and family members.

Hemophilia:

Hemophilia is a genetic bleeding disorder where the person experiences uncontrolled bleeding. The degree of bleeding varies from case to case. A person may have mild symptoms or be declared a moderate or severe hemophiliac Even the slightest trauma to the joints and muscles can cause internal bleeding in people with moderate and severe hemophilia.

People with severe hemophilia usually show no signs of the condition. This makes a condition of hemophilia a total contraindication for a session.

Addictions:

A PHP session should be postponed if the client presents under the influence of alcohol, drugs or specific medications. This should be reported, if applicable. Giving a session to a client intoxicated by alcohol or drugs can be risky, since the effect of that state is to be without an active consciousness, to be numb or desensitized. Their sensations may be unreliable at this time. Honest feedback from the client is needed to provide a session in optimal conditions.

Shock, heart attack or stroke:

A client who is in shock should not receive a session. Shock is a potentially life-threatening condition when the body's blood flow drops suddenly, restricting the level of nutrients and oxygen delivered to the body's vital organs.

If you have just had or are having a stroke or acute myocardial infarction, under no circumstances conduct a session; it is recommended to seek emergency medical help.

Conditions such as these, emphasize the importance of knowing the medical history or condition of the client or physician's approval before conducting a session.

Brain Injury:

Occurs as a result of a traumatic brain injury, resulting from a blow, impact or head jolt; this is called a closed head injury. Brain damage can also occur when an object penetrates the skull, and this is known as a penetrating injury. Brain damage may be accompanied by the following symptoms:

- Dizziness, vertigo
- Headache
- Fainting
- Memory problems
- Nausea

Mental contraindications:

- Schizophrenia, psychotic outbreaks
- Loss of consciousness
- Apathy, state of disinterest and lack of motivation, indifference to any external stimulus.

Work with sensations and breathing, to make sure they are in control of their emotions before going to the work point.

Make sure the client is in control of emotional reactions before working with the points, that they can titrate (go from one vortex to another), step by step, resolving and modulating emotions.

Emotional and physical contraindication:

- Traumatic anger
- Severe anxiety or anguish
- Fear, terror

Other contraindications:

- Diarrhea
- Kidney disease
- Severe pain
- Acute conditions requiring medical attention.

Before and after a session:

We recommend an alkaline diet rich in enzymes and electrolytes for best results. Your facilitator will offer you a dose of liquid trace minerals to increase electrolyte levels in your body immediately prior to the session. A healthy diet and mineral electrolyte intakes during the day, leading up to your session, will increase your body's reserves and facilitate nervous system processes.

Give yourself time to rest, relax and continue the integration process after the session. Drink plenty of water, alkaline filtered water or water with lemon is the best, as your body can continue to eliminate toxins for several days.

More than one session is recommended, and a full series of sessions is optimal, depending on your needs.

Benefits of PHP sessions:

- Dissolution of lifelong reactive patterns.
- Release of physical and emotional tensions.
- Presence and grounding.

- A greater sense of intimacy with self and others.
- The discovery of new and powerful life strategies.
- Inner sense of clarity, purpose and destiny.
- Spontaneous return to joy, peace and freedom of choice.
- Profound insight into the human condition.
- Stronger connection with the Divine.
- Return to the here and now, being present in the body, in the present moment.

Joy facilitates transformation.

For a traumatized person, the journey towards successful transformation leads to full life and a change in spirit and mind. Through transformation the nervous system learns to constantly regulate itself and releases immobilization.

You are always defining your reality. The reality you experience is as you have defined it. As a man thinks in his heart, so is he. It is relevant to notice that the presence and role of crystals in the body represent memories of positive and negative patterns that resonate with morphogenetic fields and energy systems. There is a need to learn to avoid resistance; by resisting, the negative pattern persists and situations are attracted that reinforce what is not accepted. PHP works on reinforcing Biological Transmutation and potentiating DNA level changes. It works on avoiding cell degeneration, toxic processes, physical and psycho-emotional exhaustion.

Once we understand how disease is cured, we can regain our health. True permanent healing of the physical body cannot occur without addressing the underlying causes in the emotional and mental aspects.

CRYSTALS AND BELIEF SYSTEM

Those who have undergone a PHP session, or reflexology treatments, know that sore spots on the hands and feet often feel like crystals under the skin. They may even feel like they break or melt during treatment. These crystals are like tiny computer memory chips, encoded with thought patterns, words and emotions, containing all the parts of our past that we have suppressed.

These crystals impede the flow of electricity and energy through the nervous system. By applying pressure to certain points on the body and holding them until the crystal dissolves, the memory that is the source of the pain is released and provides another opportunity for resolution. This allows us a new freedom and openness in our bodies, our actions and our understanding.

Each pattern is connected to an emotion and to a crystal. A crystal is a receiving antenna that works on several levels. Electromagnetically speaking, it emits frequencies that affect the body's relationship with the environment and, in turn, attracts the person to situations that resonate with that frequency that the crystal emits. If we are resonating with a negative belief, we will attract the same situations in different areas of life. So, the experiences that lead to failure or success are also associated with these frequencies.

When you manage to find a crystallization in the body, consider it a gift. This gift allows us to recognize that we have a limiting belief, which all our life has kept us under its spell. The crystal is linked to thought / word patterns, such as the following:

- I never have money

- Life is too difficult

- I've got a bad leg

- Nobody loves me

- Nobody believes me

- I'm not happy

- I'm not enough

- I'm bored with everything

- I don't have time

- I don't believe anyone

- I am afraid of everything

What is your Belief System? Which phrase do you always use?
Does it come from you or from your parents or ancestors?

The Inner Dynamic of Holding Points

In infancy, the child uses unconscious and primary defenses such
as tensing muscles or presenting restlessness, as well as sleep
disorders which, depending on age, could become the only
available defense against the terror of overwhelming pain and
helplessness. Such contracted muscles block the flow of energy
in the body, hinder the awareness of pain and produce the feeling
of not having enough capacity to keep in balance the energetic-
physiological system of your body.

In a PHP session with the aim of recognizing the sensations and
images that emerge from the past in the mind of the client, the
therapist pays attention to different signals, such as breathing
patterns, the response of the viscera and diaphragm, and the skin

tone. Emotions emerge from deep within and reconnect with the body. The therapist uses techniques that allow the client not to overflow emotionally, retraumatize, or generate catharsis. Through this approach, the client learns to sustain their process and feel their emotions in the body in a sustained, committed way. It is under these conditions that the renegotiation of the trauma occurs and, in turn, the reconstruction of the fragmented psychic processes. Expressions such as pain, fear, sorrow, rage, are a retained, disconnected, repressed whole, which the body and the nervous system naturally know how to reorganize. However, in trauma state, this natural process is interrupted, and what is done in session is precisely to awaken the innate genetic processes, in order to redirect and release what is not integrated. When the body relives the moment of impact and the client has the appropriate therapeutic support, it can integrate and reconnect the dissociated. The physical and visual contact, the facilitator's voice allows phrases, words, and above all beliefs associated with the trauma's moment, the impact, to appear. All this constitutes the necessary context to deepen the work in the session, to delve into the depths of the psyche and the memory of the body, and to understand how all this resembles a virus that consumes us and makes us sick.

The crystals, or calcifications, produced by the nervous system are like little computer chips, like a data bank, which store and activate the programming of memories and experiences. They act as subliminal transmitters that affect the person and their relationships, emitting restrictive beliefs that are translated into thoughts and behaviors. They also subliminally activate patterns that resonate in others. Likes attract likes, for example, anger crystals attract anger experiences. Whatever the crystal emits in a subliminal message will be attracted like a mirror. This creates a kind of recurring pattern that reinforces limiting beliefs about your experience of life. When we can understand this mechanism and recognize what is in ourselves, we will be able to break the reactive pattern.

PATTERNS OF RESISTANCE

The base thought patterns we emit resonate in others. We need to break these patterns before they crystallize, to avoid playing the role that programming imposed on us. When we are not aligned with the universe and go against the flow of situations, we generate resistance and create pain in our body.

Resistance creates pain. Resistance reveals a struggle between the conscious desire to change and the unconscious forces that stand in the way of that purpose. These unconscious forces are also at the root of suffering.

However, sometimes pain is the only way to realize that we need to pay attention to what is happening to us and resolve it. Resistance to change is picked up by the PHP facilitator through body language and eye contact.

When having points held, one can feel connected to an extra battery of energy. Breathing feels clearer and the process is easier. Muscles feel strong and you feel alive emotionally and mentally. The energy moves at a cellular level, and you feel connected to the whole body. This is when the memories of unresolved trauma are released.

The body is like a musical instrument that always plays a concert on the energetic scale. If this scale is fluid and resilient, this instrument will play well throughout the concert. When the emotional scale is not flowing, we get stuck experiencing, for example: pathological disorders, a catatonic state, which are the expression of blocked energy in the body.

Over the years, this constrictive response pattern becomes a kind of addiction, a way of relating to life that devitalizes and consumes large amounts of energy.

As in therapy we learn to hold ourselves and feel more prepared, more competent to confront, process and release the hidden causes of constriction, an uplifting sense of personal power emerges. Healing this pattern, which is like armor in the body, the muscles begin to relax, expand and the person begins to use their personal power more freely.

Facilitation of a PHP Session

The first requirement of a PHP facilitator is a full sense of commitment to the work and trust in the body and its wisdom. The facilitator is one who seeks to heal oneself and others through a recognition of the creative power of the mind, the heart and body. A permanent willingness to live in coherence and respect for healthy boundaries is needed. The facilitator maintains a posture of neutrality and healthy empathy, which provides enthusiasm to sustain the session, while respecting the process that emerges.

The essential purpose and goal of the facilitator is to open awareness, recognize the value and spirit in all people, and acknowledge all events as life-shaping experiences that can contribute to the greater good.

Creating a Safe Environment

We know that a hostile environment can cause people to relate to each other in trauma-induced patterns.

When people feel safe, they can return to the source of the problems and their limited beliefs, to address the release of the frozen energy that has been transformed into belief patterns. People can change if they feel safe. When a person does not feel safe, they shift their nervous system into Sympathetic Activation and perceive the context as a threat and this triggers the nervous system to go on alert. When this happens, the body switches to an adaptive behavior pattern.

When training in PHP, special emphasis is placed on different skills of the therapist. These include:

Empathy:

This is the awareness and realization of what is happening to the client in the session.

Attention-alertness:

Also, being aware of changes in tone of voice. If the client speaks softly, match that intensity. This will help you resonate. If the client speaks loudly or is angry, match that intensity.

Regulation:

Among other abilities is the power to modulate the intensity of the energy that is released when holding the points in the session, i.e., to avoid re-traumatization by emotional overflow.

It is also important maintain a proper attitude during a session:

- Keep a clear mind
- Keep an open heart
- Be present 100% of the time
- Empathy, not sympathy.

Things to observe during a session:

- Monitor breathing – abdominal, chest, restricted
- Monitor skin tone
- Track sensations
- Reflect and paraphrase, if necessary
- Forget absolutes or pre-conceived ideas
- Explore all options
- Go for the specific memory
- Find the exact thought / word pattern
- When in doubt, backtrack.
- Ask appropriate questions:

    - *What is happening?*
    - *What are you feeling?*
    - *Have you felt like this before?*
    - *Where are you?*
    - *What are the words?*
    - *What do you hear?*

- *What do you feel?*
- *What do you see?*
- *Can you describe it?*

Be alert to one's own sensations and intuitions:

- If a person has received anesthesia or has taken drugs, the therapist may feel a sensation associated with it; for example, the tongue goes numb and dry.
- Also, when holding points, the therapist can perceive changes in temperature, numbness in their hands, even pain, among others.
- Another skill involves reading the non-verbal language, which is observed in the movements, position and behavior of the client.
- Do not be afraid of silence, allow silence to be present in the session, so that the person can process their experience.
- Do not force situations. Do not try to make something happen.
- Do not cause more pain through pressure on the points than the person can bear.
- Endure everything with love and willingness.

Cycle of the Points:

During points holding, a cycle develops on each point, which can be perceived by the therapist through his/her hands. Remember that this happens at each held point.

Signals during the cycle that can be perceived by both the client and the therapist:

- Strong pulsation on the point
- Electrical sensation on the skin
- Pain in the hands
- Goose bumps
- Numb arms
- Cold winds
- Dry mouth
- Burning

- Heat
- Equalized / equalized pulsation at the point
- Cold
- End point
- Vibration at point location

When the therapist's fingers start to burn, this indicates that the client blood circulation in the body has been restored in various parts of the body. By regulating the nervous system, life is restored to the body. Unlike the heart beating, this pulse in the points when they are regulated.

When the emotions are released and the pain disappears from the points, they stabilize in a heart rate state of equilibrium at 72 beats per minute.

Pain is the repressed memory. Allow yourself to enter into it. Intensify the pressure on the points to gain more memory.

PRESENTATION OF THE POINTS TO HOLD

POINT'S NAME	FUNCTION	LOCATION	PURPOSE
STO	Accusation to the autonomic nervous system Releases	Betweeen trapezius muscle, sternocleidomastoid ideus occiput	Access to the limbic system
Heart	Stress and shock	Thorax, midline sternum, between 4th an 5tf rib, at the level of the breasts	Spiritual connection and love
Armpit	Open consciousness and heart	Dorsal high, axillary midline 4 to 5 inches under the armpit	Harmonization of emotions
Chest	First aid	See drawing pg #233	Heal deep emotions reconnect materialy, return to the body
Thymus	Unblock emotions	3 cms under yogular notch, midline of the sternum	Reconnect emotional alterations and immune deficit
Thyroid	Regulates metabolism and mood disturbances	3 cms under the point of the thymus on the sternum	Controls vital emotions: temperature, heart rate
Adrenals	Reduces stress	Under the last ribs of the thorax	Sedative and helps to calm

Stress	Regulates emotions linked to visceral somatizations	3 cms under the stress point	Elevates the mood unlocks eruptions of the digestive system
Trauma	Emotions that block the digestive system and diaphragm	3 cms under the stress point	Releases vital energy trapped or blocked in the abdomen
Fear and social engagement	For situations of inhibition of the ventral vagus system	In the middle of the viscera, on the left side of the body, under the left breast	Heal transform and reconnect the digestive and nervous system
Spinal	Release patterns of childhood and inherited blockages	In relation to the nerves of the spine: Cervical: 8 pairs Dorsal: 12 pairs Lumbar: 5 pairs Sacrum: 5 pairs Coccyx: 1 pairs	Reorganizes transgerenational inheritance and trauma

Recommendations

It is relevant to hold points carefully and with awareness, consulting permanently about how the client is feeling in the process, which are the markers or somatic signs and how the experience is lived.

In the book, you will find applications of personal points (which we have called SELF-HELP) and others that are specific to the therapy, which are described according to each application need.

PHP IN PRACTICE: SELF-HELP

By strengthening and awakening in yourself the capacity to reset your own nervous system, you can begin to access that healing power. When you can relate your physical symptoms and pains to repressed sensations, suppressed emotions and thoughts, you can release the tension, release the pain and amplify the healing vortex of energy.

The pattern of trauma, with all its physical, mental, emotional and spiritual symptoms, will be transformed.

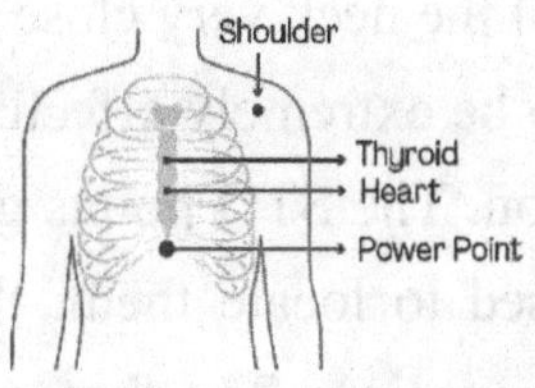

Choose one of these points (thyroid, heart or shoulder) and take it together with the power point that is one centimeter below the xiphoid cartilage).

Feel the energy of your feet and the rest of your body for 15 minutes breathing every time you hold the point sequences.

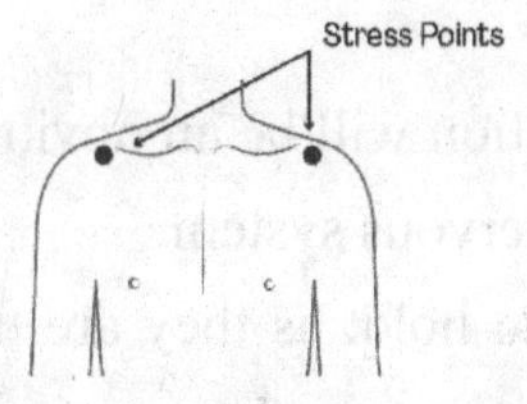

Stress point (under the insertion between the shoulder and collarbone) hold them together and breathe.

Exhale... Feel your stomach, solar plexus and navel.

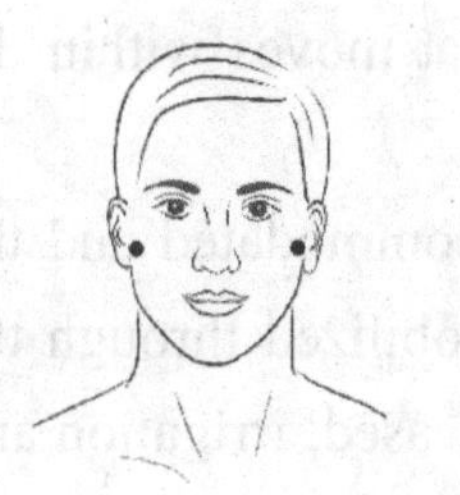

Press with your middle fingers both joints of the jaw (temporomandibular joint)

Connect with the back of your head in the brainstem.

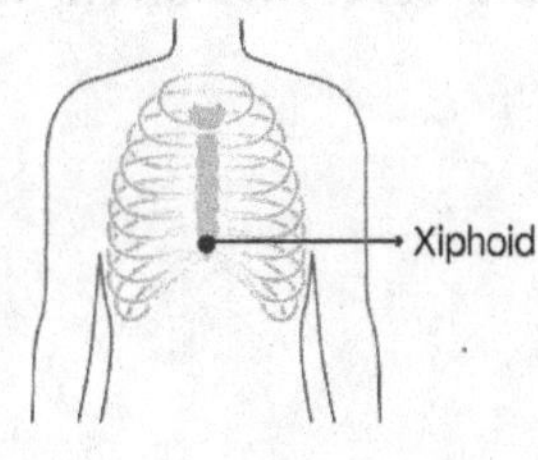

Place the 3 fingers of the hand together and press on the stomach area one centimeter below the xiphoid cartilage.

Hold the pressure of the points gently and breathe.

24

---

[24] Ref: Image, Catalina Ureta

The STO Points

The STO points are located on the back of the neck very close to the base of the skull, they have proven to be extremely effective in restoring the nervous system connection. The STO points get their name from the three landmarks used to locate them: the sternocleidomastoid, the trapezius and the occiput. The first two are muscles, while the third is a bone.

Having the STO points in the proper position will be an obvious improvement in restoring balance to the nervous system.

The STO's are the first points we need to hold, as they are the main access to the neurosomatic regulation system. They activate the rage, which is considered an energy that moves within the body.

By holding the STO points the head is accommodated and the scapulae open, the cerebrospinal fluid is mobilized through the spine, mobilizing the energy, the neck is released, irrigation and respiration are stimulated. It reconnects the cerebral cortex, the limbic system and the brainstem.

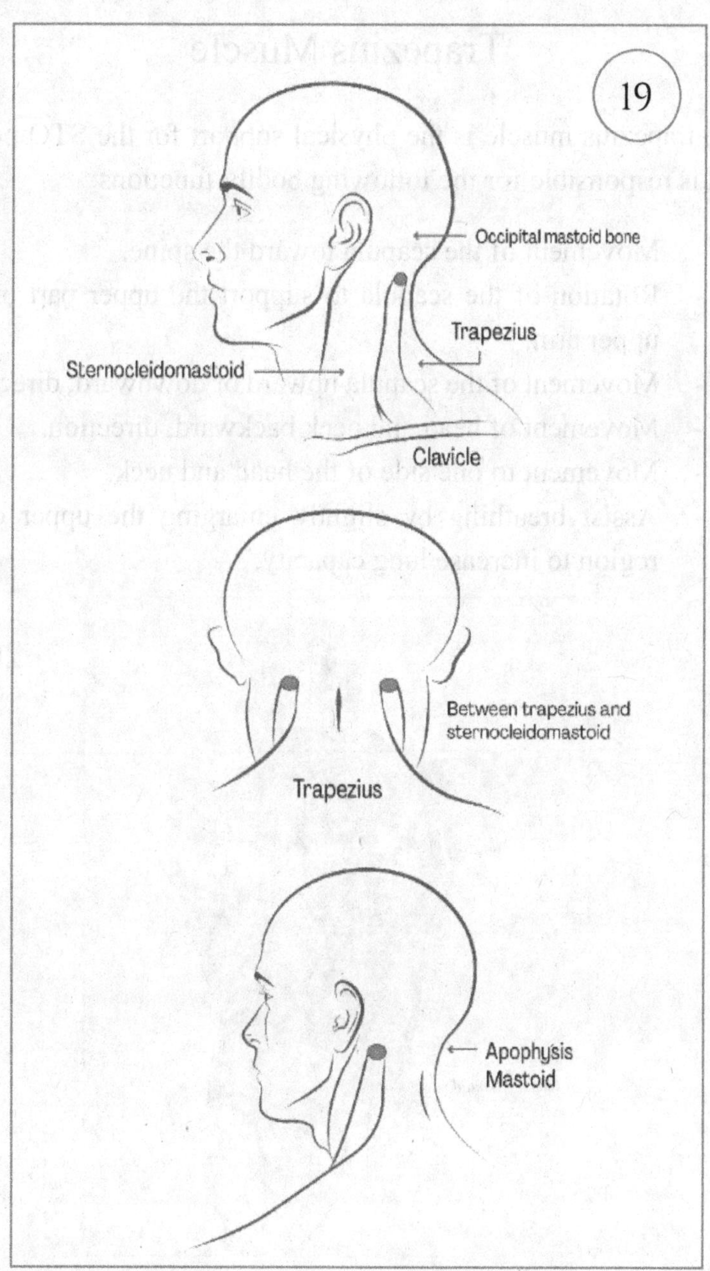

25

[25] Ref: Image, Catalina Ureta

Trapezius Muscle

The trapezius muscle is the physical support for the STO points and is responsible for the following bodily functions:

- Movement of the scapula toward the spine.
- Rotation of the scapula to support the upper part of the upper arm.
- Movement of the scapula upward or downward, direction.
- Movement of head and neck backward, direction.
- Movement to one side of the head and neck.
- Assist breathing by slightly enlarging the upper chest region to increase lung capacity.

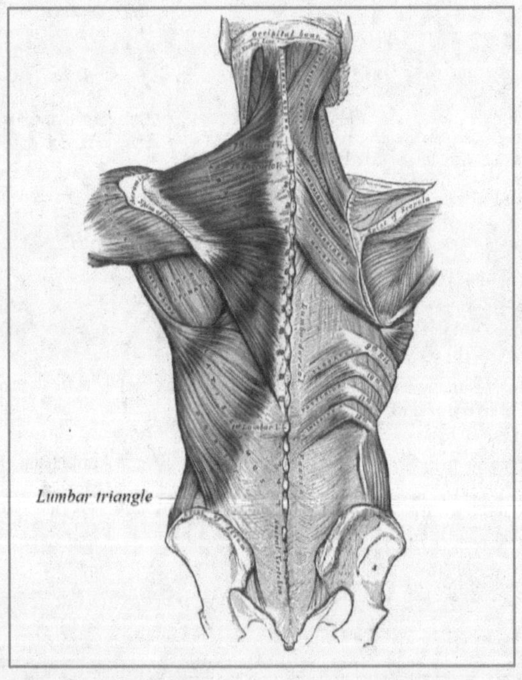

20

26

[26] By Mikael Häggström. When using this image in external works, it may be cited as: Häggström, Mikael (2014).
https://commons.wikimedia.org/w/index.php?curid=2892631

The Purpose of the STO Points

They are the main points for accessing the medulla of the brain.

- Activates and restores the vitality of the body, promoting the regeneration of optimal functioning in the nervous system.
- Assists in restoring nerve supply and blood circulation to the outer extremities.
- It provokes a deep integrative movement involving all aspects of the being.
- The limbic system circuitry is accessed. They give access to unprocessed information and inner knowledge.
- In Traditional Chinese Medicine, these points (Gallbladder 20) are known as "The Window in the Sky" and have been observed to bring information from the subconscious mind to a fuller level of consciousness.

The Heart Points

The heart is like our "spiritual brain". It gives us a connection to who we really are and connects us to our inner peace and love. That is what we all really seek in life, the connection and reconnection with the truth that resides deep within our spiritual heart.

Any stress or conflict has the potential to pull us away from all of that, because shock and trauma cause the body to contract and constrict, it leaves our consciousness separated from the energy of the heart. We lose strength, courage, root, and feel that we are not connected to life. Our connection to the heart, to Love, is broken. War, oppression, abuse, and all the pain, disease and misery that result are both causes and effects of patterns of separation between our being and the heart energy, and also of the toxic effect of living in a state of permanent survival.

For example, heart disease often originates when a person decides to close their heart, to close it is to stop the flow of love. Usually when working with the points around the heart we connect the chest, the sternum and the points in conjunction with the nervous system. We sensitively and intuitively get to the physical place where that memory, thought and decision that makes us close our heart is held. When the Love connection is lost, spiritual, emotional, mental and physical illnesses occur.

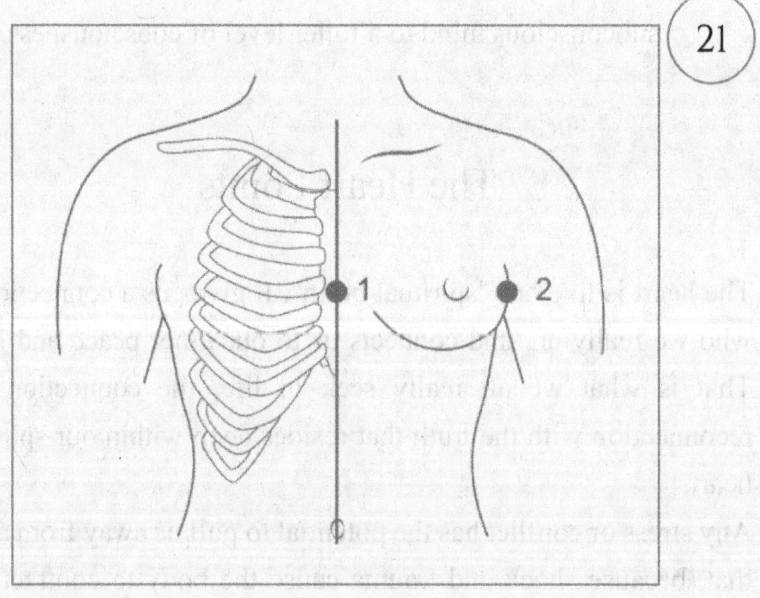

Location: In the midline, one inch above the rib in connection with the level of the sinuses and the center of the heart.

Technique: Apply firm pressure medially with index or middle finger.

Function and Purpose: Helps to access a higher connection to love, spiritual love, compassion and empathy.

It is important at the time of the session to make explicit the following questions, to know if the person is aware of the lack of these virtues:

- What problems prevent you from having compassion and empathy?
- What are the problems that prevent us from being in the heart?
- What thing or situation takes me out of my heart, out of my connection with myself?

The Armpit Point

The armpit point is taken in conjunction with the heart point.

Location: About 4 to 5 inches directly below the armpit; it is between ribs at chest level on the side of the body, approximately in line with the nipple. It can be accessed from the right or left side. The sensation of the client can be used as an aid in locating the point, as a person will usually have tenderness or pain when pressure is applied to that point.

Technique: Sitting facing the side of the client's body, the thumb or any other finger can be used to apply pressure to the point.

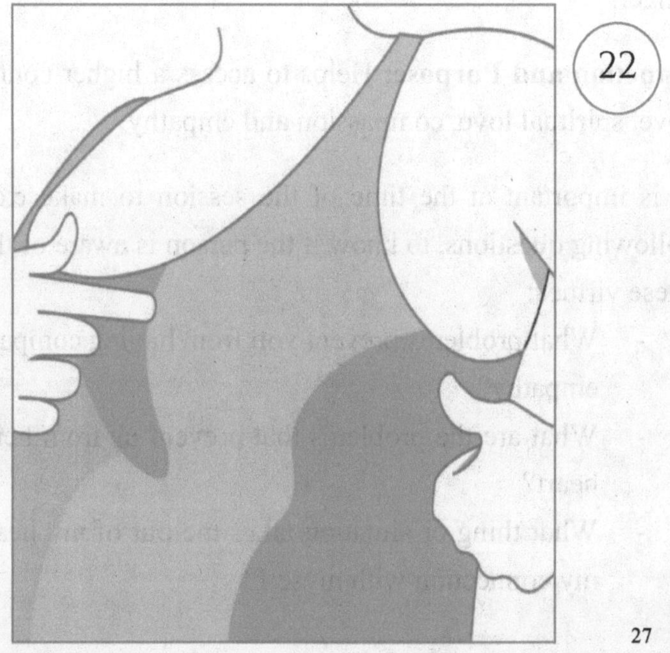

The Points of the Thorax

The points of the thorax are considered **First Aid points**.
One of the authors of this book, therapist Catalina Ureta, through her experience of more than 30 years, developed new sequences of specific points in the body to open the rib cage, work with the viscera and intestines, work with fear, mobilize respiratory

---

[27] Ref: Image Catalina Ureta and Judith Johnson

patterns in the diaphragm and connect with our heart and deep healing emotions.

When facing a first aid process, it is recommended to work with these points, especially to help the person to "return to the body", to recover one's connection with reality, to regulate the nervous system quickly, while reprocessing the overload produced by fear, stress or collapse.

Each point can be holding by itself. In children it is recommended to hold them very carefully and to be more aware of the degree of pressure on the body.

The points on the sternum are the door to openness, to reconnect with the heart, to be able to stimulate Thyroid, Thymus and heart.

Technique:

What we seek is to feel and find, with the fingertips, crystals or calcifications in the tissues. When they are detected, the client feels a stabbing pain.

We go from top to bottom holding the points: sternum, points under the diaphragm, stomach (trauma point) and viscera (fear point). In this last point, the point of fear, we can move the viscera carefully, accompanying the point with gentle massage of the intestines, releasing the tension.

We recommend, especially for these points, to be lying down when holding them.

First Aid Points

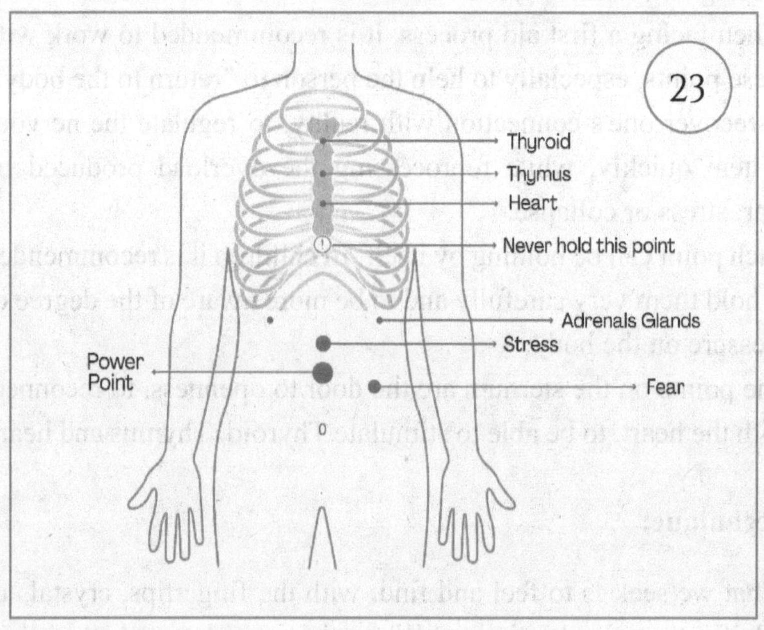

Points on the Sternum

Thyroid:

Point located three centimeters below the Thymus point on the sternum.

The thyroid gland produces the hormones triiodothyronine (T3) and thyroxine (T4), which affect all aspects of your metabolism. The pituitary gland and the hypothalamus, an area at the base of the brain, control the rate at which the thyroid produces and secretes these hormones.

---

[28] Ref: Image, Catalina Ureta

Part of the thyroid's function is related to the regulation of protein metabolism associated with mood disorders and is related to the non-adrenergic and serotonergic neurotransmitter systems. These hormones also influence the control of the vital functions of body temperature and heart rate. In diseases such as hypothyroidism and hyperthyroidism, cognitive problems, memory loss and mental confusion can result.

In PHP, the thyroid is related to the ability to express and communicate. It also works on emotional blocks about self-love.

Thymus:

It is located three centimeters below the jugular notch, in the sternum.

The thymus is anatomically located in the anterior superior mediastinum, in front of the heart and behind the sternum.

It is a specialized organ of the immune system. T cells mature within the thymus. T cells are essential for the adaptive immune system, which is where the body specifically adapts to foreign invaders.

The thymus is most active and largest in size during the neonatal and preadolescent periods. In early adolescence, the thymus begins to atrophy. However, residual T lymphopoiesis continues throughout adulthood.

In PHP, the immune system can be positively activated, connecting with emotional blockages that upset the chest, releasing tension in the rib cage. Retained grief that contracts, reduces the capacity of emotional expression, which crystallizes in the chest. [29]

Heart:

It is located in the midline of the chest, between the nipples. We can press it with the middle finger. It is the bridge that connects thoughts with emotions. This point allows access to issues of physical love.

Adrenals:

Points are located symmetrically in the middle of the number ten, bottommost rib, just below the rib. In PHP, holding these points reduces stress, calms, and regulates breathing, and relaxes the diaphragm. It allows the internal organs not to be affected by the internal tension caused by stress.

Stress point:

Located three centimeters below the nervous system point we find this point, which is over the stomach area, where it is common to feel discomfort and irritation. Digestion is affected; it increases the volume of hydrochloric acid affecting the gastric walls.

With PHP, being able to open this area also allows the body to reorganize itself, loosen abdominal muscles, synchronize the digestive organs, and distend the viscera.

---

[29] Ref: https://es.wikipedia.org/wiki/Timo

Power point:

Located three centimeters below the stress point, this point works to release the accumulation of vital energy trapped in the abdomen. It allows reconnecting, at the vagus nerve level, the instinctive responses of fear, anger and collapse.

In PHP, it is an essential point of connection of the upper and lower body and is located in the middle of both. Emotions that lodge between the diaphragm, stomach and colon cause gastrointestinal inflammation, constriction, and irritation.

Fear and Social Relationship Point:

Opening up to others is often difficult, as the vagus nerve may be inhibited, disconnecting us from others.

In PHP, we locate this point in the middle of the viscera, specifically on the left side of the body. By manipulating the viscera, we establish connection with the enteric brain and ventral vagal innervation, which relates to our ability to bond socially.

The enteric brain, also known as the enteric nervous system (ENS), is a complex and intricate network of neurons that exists within the gastrointestinal tract (GI tract). It is sometimes referred to as the "second brain" due to its extensive neural network and ability to function independently of the central nervous system (CNS) located in the brain and spinal cord.

The enteric nervous system plays a crucial role in regulating the digestive process, including peristalsis (muscle contractions that move food through the digestive tract), secretion of digestive enzymes, and absorption of nutrients. It is responsible for coordinating various functions within the GI tract to ensure proper digestion and absorption of food.

Furthermore, the enteric nervous system can communicate bidirectionally with the central nervous system, forming what is known as the gut-brain axis. This means that the brain can influence the functioning of the gut, and vice versa, leading to a strong connection between gastrointestinal health and mental well-being.

Research has also suggested that the enteric nervous system is involved in various aspects of emotional regulation and is linked to mood disorders and mental health conditions. This connection highlights the significance of a healthy gut in maintaining overall well-being.

Our interaction with the environment is often affected by the freezing of the enteric brain. The objective of sustaining this point is to be able to eliminate the fear of the viscera and thus reestablish our relationship with the environment.

Healing through this point allows transformation in people's lives, healing of risky diseases such as cancer, ulcerative colitis and irritable colon, among others.

Especially in children with Autism, it provides neurophysiological support to strengthen social interaction.

Breathing and Diaphragm
The essential
Principle of Regulation

The main muscle of respiration is the diaphragm, which maintains respiratory patterns that support the ability to breathe deeply or, sometimes, short and shallow; this affects the body due to its dysregulation, caused by trauma.

The diaphragm muscles arise from the lower part of the sternum (breastbone), the lower six ribs and the lumbar, vertebrae of the spine and attach to a membranous central tendon.

- It is domed, muscular and membranous. It is a structure that separates the thoracic (chest) and abdominal cavity in mammals.
- Contraction of the diaphragm increases the internal height of the thoracic cavity, thereby lowering its internal pressure and causing inspiration of air.
- The inspiratory diaphragmatic movement is spasmodic
- Relaxation of the diaphragm, the natural elasticity of the lung tissue and the rib cage produce expiration.
- The diaphragm is also important in expulsion actions, e.g., coughing, sneezing, vomiting, crying, expulsion of feces and urine; and, in labor, it assists in the delivery of the fetus.
- The diaphragm is innervated by the phrenic nerves, which arise from the ventral branches of the cervical roots C3, C4, C5. It also has vegetative fibers.

- The diaphragm is traversed by many structures, in particular the esophagus, aorta, and inferior vena cava.

In each session we work on reconnecting with the breath, to be present in the body and to be able to receive the points session.

Spinal Points

In PHP, we consider the spine as the realm of the unconscious: thoughts, beliefs and memories that are difficult to access. Its blockage or constriction by tension, inflammation or disease can affect the flow of the cerebrospinal fluid that runs through it, protecting it from impact. At night, the cerebrospinal fluid also assists in the release of toxic remnants from brain metabolism. Its blockage affects the spinal nerves, causes lymphatic congestion, low tissue nutrition and loss of electrical potential.

In the spine, according to PHP, there are inherited patterns of beliefs and emotions from childhood, which are reflected in crystallizations in the exits of the spinal nerves, from the vertebrae, this generates havoc in the spine. We say that unresolved problems are crystallized, and that the energy of the spine (called Kundalini) is blocked due to crystals.

When we perform sessions on the spine, the client must have a previous cycle of sessions, since previous work is required to be able to face the unconscious traumas that appear in the crystals that are located when reviewing the eighteen spinal pairs. The energy in the spine can be perceived as very strong when triggered by holding spinal points. This energy arises from the base of the spine and manifests as a deep sensation of heat.

When holding points in this area of the body, the therapist looks for the belief related to the spine and receives it from the information given by the client through words, images or sensations.

We work from the bottom up, holding points in the coccyx, which allows us to connect the whole spine, to root ourselves and feel connected to the earth.

In most cases, spinal deviation disorders can lead to calcification, which negatively affects the electrical supply to the nerves in various areas of the body. Working on the spine is important for healing. When we hold points on the spine one must check where the calcifications are located. The calcifications are located not on the spine, but on the edges of the spine, at the exits of the spinal nerves. When the calcification is located, both the right and left sides of the spine are worked on.

EMOTIONS AND THE ENDOCRINE SYSTEM

Emotional problems are regulated by the endocrine system. We have talked a lot about emotions and the relationship with the limbic system. Those problems that are unresolved will become much more evident as we begin the spinal work.

Those resistant to innovation or acceptance of all that is, was and ever will be, will create a crystalline structure in their body, thus creating an energetic misalignment.

The awakening of the energy or Kundalini:

- The first uprising of energies in the spine is intense.
- It can happen several times, according to the severity of the blockages.
- It can bring intense emotions and corresponding belief systems with currents of electrical sensations.
- It is different from the currents that correspond to the sensations.
- As we begin to access the energy flow in the spine, we access what is blocked, where the energy is interrupted and what needs to work, before we go to work with the cranial points, which are only worked on after taking certification as a PHP therapist.

Sensations in the Spine:

As we have discussed the energy, or Kundalini, will work its way up the spine until it encounters a significant blockage. This is usually common in one of the first three energy centers or chakras: the chakras of our own past, ancestry, deep emotions, and beliefs.

When the Kundalini is awoken, the energy rises up from the base of the spine, which in parable has been referred to as the base of the mountain. This huge amount of energy then erupts. The energy ascends to the peak, which correlates with the pineal gland. When the pineal gland is activated, a major change in consciousness is experienced.

As the body and energy are physical and energetic intelligence, cycles will be repeated until the pathway is cleared up the spine to the brain. Stored emotions and memories can be released. This process will end in a complete healing circuit.

The Foot Points

Every point on the feet represents a part of the body, as in reflexology therapy. Points related to organs can be stimulated, unblocked and activated for the purpose of healing.

This foot work promotes the movement of vital energy and revitalizes all the organs that are stimulated by each point.

Holding these points helps to balance blood pressure, stimulates kidney functions, memory, brain activity, relieves anxiety, pain, and trauma shock that is repressed in the body.

The importance of these points is that it allows the deeper parts of the brain and internal organs, hypothalamus, pituitary, pineal, sexual points and other structures that are not accessible with other points to be worked.

For each foot point, we need to locate the crystals that are detected by palpation in the soles, and then dissolve them with PHP work. It is also important to work the points on the feet when it is not possible to work other points on the body, either because they are contraindicated or because there are surgeries already performed or because of scars.

The Endocrine System and Reflex Points on the Feet

The points we hold reflect various organs, as well as the endocrine glands. Several points correlate with various emotions and repressed experiences. Cerebrospinal fluid flows through the connective tissue and the perineural and perivascular system. It is not limited to the area surrounding the brain or spinal column. Obstruction of the fluid causes a lack of electrolytes in the area, metabolically disrupting the area due to lack of nutritional factors. The crystal is usually at the end of a nerve fiber. Crystals dissolve with the help of nutrients, so mineral saturation is needed.

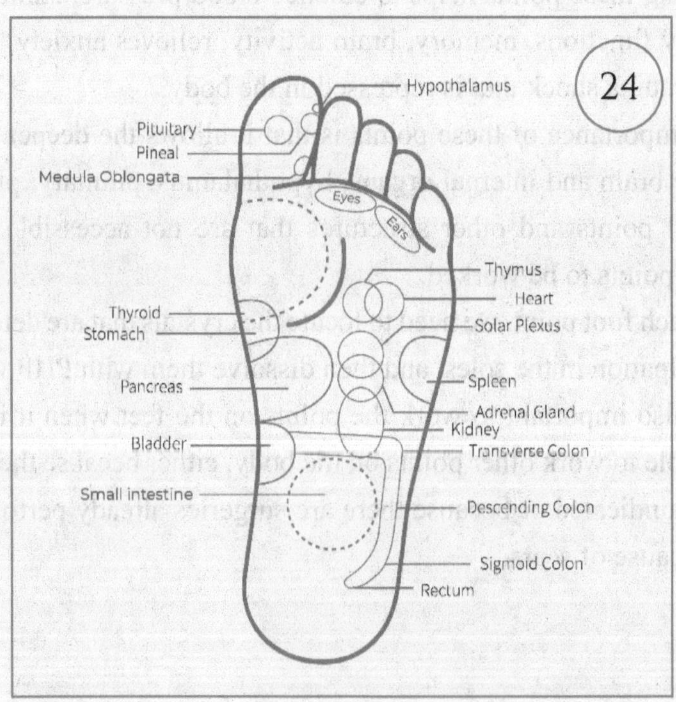

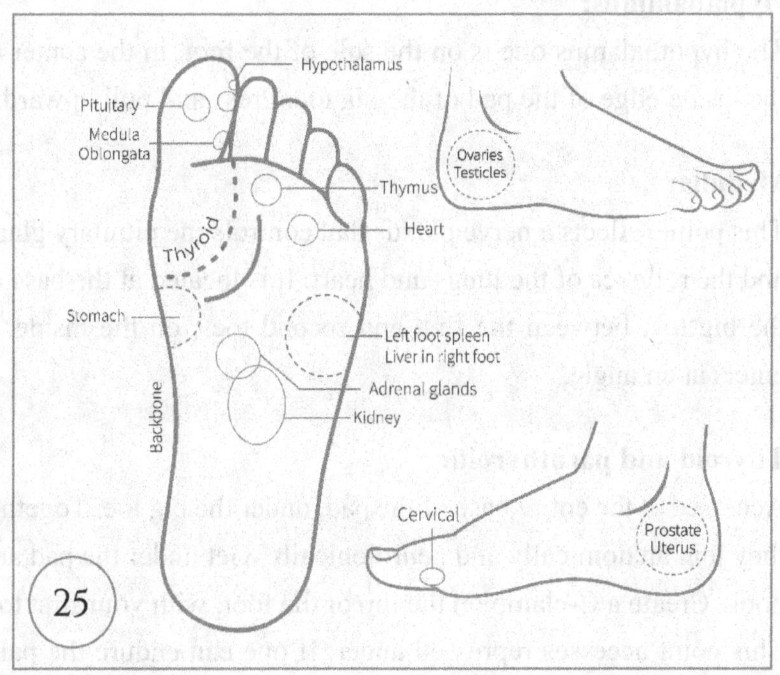

Pineal:

The point related to the pineal gland is located on the inside of the big toe. Press toward the nail. As the crystal dissolves on the right foot, the crystal on the left will dissolve, due to the bipolarity of the body.

Pituitary:

The pituitary point is located in the center of the pad of the big toe. Press and pull upward to dissolve the crystal properly.

---

[30] Image: Catalina Ureta and Judith Johnson

191

Hypothalamus:

The hypothalamus one is on the sole of the foot, in the center of the inside edge of the pad of the big toe. Press and pull upward.

Medulla:

This point reflects a nerve plexus that controls the pituitary gland and the reflexes of the lungs and heart. It is located at the base of the big toe, between the first and second toes, on the inside. It enters at an angle.

Thyroid and parathyroid:

Accessed at the entire base of the pad, under the big toe. Together they join anatomically and neurologically. Get under the pad and hook. Create a C-clamp on the top of the foot, with your first toe. This point accesses repressed anger. If one can endure the pain, all blockages will dissolve.

Thymus:

The thymus is reflected in two places. The first is between the second and third toes, up the canal to where the bones meet. Using a thumb and finger, make a C-clamp on the top and bottom of the foot. The upper part has to do with the outer part of the organ, and the lower part with the inner part.

The second place, thymus reflex, is located in the thorax, below the jugular notch in the sternum and manubrium. Put a finger on the point at a 45-degree angle and point downward. This is also a water retention point, as it deals with lymphatic congestion.

Heart:

This point is located between the third and fourth toes, both at the top and bottom, it represents the cardiopulmonary complex. The heart and thymus are attached to the cardiac plexus, which is located within the rib cage. Using a thumb and finger, make a C-clamp on the top and bottom of the foot.

Pancreas and adrenals:

Press above the navel toward the solar plexus, looking for a hard knot where repressed grief is stored. Also, that repressed grief can be stored in the bottom of the foot.

The entire inner middle space is the pancreas, which is an important organ of digestion and relates to the adrenals.

On the inside of the sole of the left foot, pull under the arch.

Spleen and liver:

On the left foot, on the outside of the sole, use a pinch for the spleen, and on the right foot, bottom outside, for the liver. Cirrhosis of the liver can be repaired.

Cranial Points:

At the end of the PHP training, activation of the cranial points is performed for the purpose of strengthening the therapist's skills. To reach this level, the therapist must be fully certified and have access to a specialized session in the Cranials.

EMOTIONAL SCALE AND SPECIFIC BLOCKS

The levels that emotions reach is called Emotional Scale.

The energy in our body is located in our organs and glands, in the endocrine system. When our energy is connected and open it will create a proper circulation of energy demand to all organs and nervous system circuits.

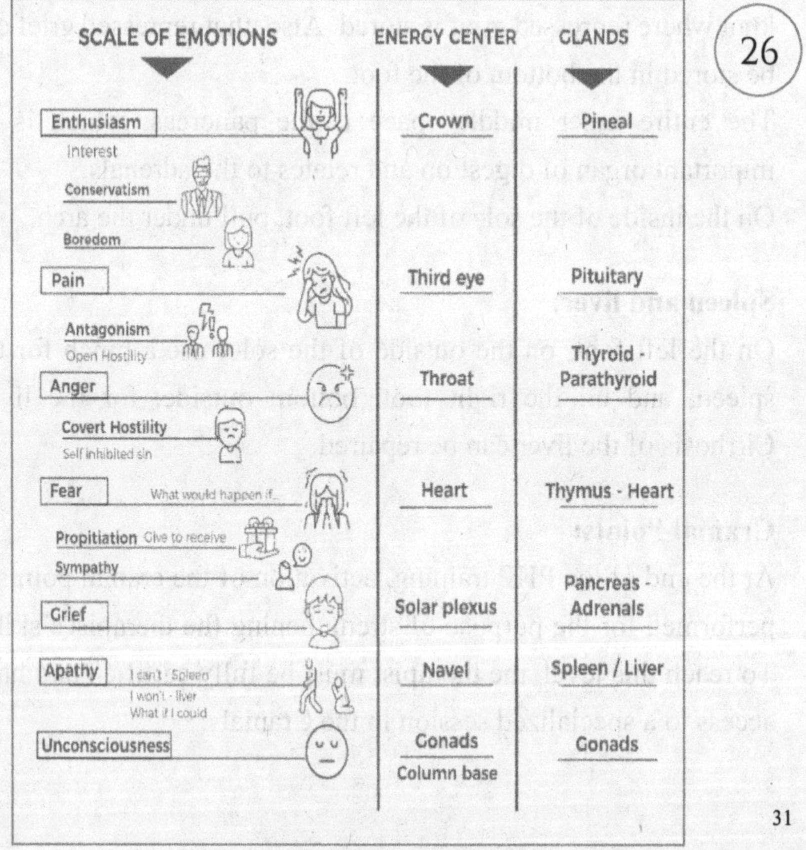

31

Level 1: Enthusiasm

Chakra: Crown
Gland: Pineal

Enthusiasm - Pineal Gland: *I can, I am, I want to love*.

This state of enthusiasm is like a small child, full of energy, happy, open and receptive to life, connected to God and his inner peace. Enthusiasm is associated with the feeling of joy, being centered and complete. Children see their parents as God in the physical form. If they are prevented from expressing enthusiasm and being who they are, through parental thought forms or actions, then the child begins to suppress their own energy. This is called "I" Containment.

Level 1.1 - Interest:

It hurts not to be in unity and with love. It hurts not to be connected to source. The child begins to question itself. The thought pattern becomes *"what is wrong?"* As the child tries to return to the state of connection. When they cannot reach that state of total love again, they doubt themselves, fear takes over and the thought becomes: *"something is wrong with me"* or *"something is wrong with the world."* For a young child, the world consists of themselves and their parents, so the thought can also be *"something is wrong with my parents"*.

195

Level 1.2 - Conservation:

The child, sensing that something is wrong and wanting to make a change, notices and is attentive to the parent's reaction. The child learns very quickly what actions and/or behaviors receive positive outcome responses, positive loving responses and what actions receive disconnected painful responses. Becoming reactive to what others think and feel about them creates a pattern in which we are called upon to please people.

Level 1.3 - Boredom:

The child no longer feels like things are working. Having to respond to the thought patterns of others, he becomes bored with life because there is no truth, and the life force cannot flow. Having to contain his true self causes boredom to become pain in the body.

Level 2 - Pain

Chakra: Third Eye
Gland: Pituitary
Pain - Pituitary Gland: *hurts a lot, very painful, very difficult.* When there is physical pain in the body, the natural response is, *"I don't want to feel the pain."*

When someone feels pain, they usually blame themselves. The thoughts are "I can't cope with this" and "it hurts too much". Because of the pain, they begin to suppress the energy causing it to move down the scale.

Level 2.1 - Antagonism:

When the pain becomes too uncomfortable to contain, it is projected outward by placing it on another person, creating blame. "You did this to me," then becomes the thought pattern.

Level 2.2 - Overt Hostility:

Once the pain moves to this level, it usually does not stay there for long, due to the reaction of the person toward whom the hostility is projected. Reaction to the hostility of another usually moves the energy downward.

Level 3 – Rage

Chakra: Throat
Gland: Thyroid / Parathyroid
Anger - Thyroid, Parathyroid - Throat: *"look what they did to me, they took from me."*

As energy moves downward, constriction is experienced within the physical body leaving less space for free flow of energy and breath. Anger has a strong effect on the physical body, especially the shoulders, neck and jaws. The thoughts are *"I hate you"* or *"I don't like what I'm doing to you."*
When the anger turns inward, it becomes guilt. The thoughts and beliefs then become *"I am not enough."*
Within the lower levels, there are fewer sub-levels.

Level 3.1 - Covert Hostility:

As the energy drops, it begins to feel less safe to express the anger that is felt. Anger is exhibited in a subtler way. This is experienced as passive-aggressive behavior or "teasing". This form of communication is where you get mixed messages.
They are saying one thing, but their tone and subtle body language says, *"I'm mad at you."*
Feeling unsafe to express anger creates a feeling of helplessness. The thought pattern is *"there is nothing I can do"*.

Level 4 - Fear

Chakra: Heart
Gland: Thymus / Heart:
Fear - Heart / Thymus: *it makes me nervous when you...what if it doesn't work...I have to leave...I'm worried.*

When anger is repressed, it becomes fear. The repression of fear is felt in the chest around the heart. Fear affects the immune system and causes a weakness in the body's natural defense system. The thoughts are *"what if..." or "I am afraid"*.

Level 4.1 - Enabling or Conciliatory:

This level of fear is manifested by not being able to ask for what is wanted. This person will give things or do things to get the same or similar in return. There is a belief or thought that *"you don't want to give me what I want"*. As a result, this leaves the person feeling empty. Many people use illness as a disguise to get what they want.

Level 4.2 - Sympathy:

This form of fear is the belief that the other person cannot do something for themselves. At this level, you will find the "caretakers." They are always doing everything for other people. Their belief or thought is *"they can't"* or *"they are not strong enough to do it for themselves."* This is a form of sabotage.

As they begin to rise to this level, they re-experience the fear they did not feel at the time, due to the shock. They may experience trembling, gasping, all the physical symptoms that accompany fear. They experience the fear of losing control, or that they lost control.

Keep the body and mind connected by moving between body sensations and thought. Resourcing is very important at this time. Organic resources arising from a person's natural words and experience are the best choice.

It is suggested to work with the client's inner resources, allowing and encouraging them to emerge spontaneously. By discovering his or her own resources, a person is regaining power and self-confidence.

Level 5 - Grief

Chakra: solar plexus
Gland: Pancreas / Adrenals

Grief - Pancreas / Adrenals – *"I have always felt this way. There is nothing I can do. I never…"*

There is an important dividing line between Level four (Fear) and Level five (Grief) in the tone of the scale at the energetic level. It is at this point that the energy becomes unconscious. There will be no awareness of the memory of the repressed fear. It is at this point that you may notice a drastic drop in energy, and not be able to explain why. Thoughts associated with this point are, *"Something is wrong, and I don't know what it is."* Tears are an important indicator for this level. Tears seem to easily flow from the eyes. As we move through the grief level, memories brought to the conscious mind can foretell a real breakthrough.

There is a major dividing line between level six and level five as you move up the level. It is at this point that unconscious repressed fear moves into conscious memory. As a person moves into grief, they begin to reconnect with the limbic area of the brain. As they connect with this part of the brain, they remember their connection to themselves, their inner resource, and in grief they can let go of the pain of not remembering. The activating event is usually remembered in the transition between apathy and grief. The facilitator will feel a "high" in energy - coolness, chills, warmth in the spots, alertness, goose bumps, an energetic awakening. This is the re-entry into the trauma vortex.

Tears are an important indicator for this level. These tears are not deep tears, but tears that simply flow from the eyes, tears of pain about losing the heart connection.

Then comes fear and the body may begin to tremble. It's usually the fear of losing control again and not having the resources, not knowledge. There is a tendency to go back to those old places of confusion. The purpose of the facilitator is to allow a person to feel the fear and go there anyway, and help them remember what their resources are, that in fear they also have resources and can make it safe for themselves.

Level 6 - Apathy

Chakra: Naval
Gland: Spleen / Liver / Kidney
Apathy - Spleen / Liver – *"I can't, it's too hard, I don't care."* The energy of this level is a mixed emotion. The thoughts and beliefs are *"I can't"* or *"I don't know how."*

When apathy is suppressed, it moves down the scale to a catatonic state. A person may notice a drastic drop in energy and not be able to explain why. Thoughts associated with this level are, *"Something is wrong, and I don't know what it is,"* *"It's too much,"* or *"I don't understand this"*. When the emotion affects the spleen, it produces a feeling of helplessness. The thought and belief is, *"I can't"* or *"I don't know how."*
When the emotion is affecting the liver it produces a feeling of stubbornness, sometimes accompanied by strong resentment.

Then the thought pattern and belief is, *"I won't do it"* or *"There is nothing I can do."*

The apathetic person has just given up; nothing matters to them anymore. They are in a state of hopelessness, helplessness and resignation, trapped in the belief that *"I can't make this happen."* At this level, the person begins to experience the mind/body split. The tendency is for the individual to simply let go of that which is resisted, which ultimately leads to the level of unconsciousness. In Apathy, a person has lost their connection to the inner source of power. They lack a sense of their value or an inner sense that they can have an impact on the world. While the words may be *"It doesn't matter,"* the deeper feeling is *"I don't care."* The purpose in life has been lost.

In this situation we can ask the querent, *"Do you remember a time when you did care?"*. This reflection invites the person to "pendulum swing" from *"I don't care"* to a time when it did matter.

The more significant the experience, the greater the impact of a negative response and the deeper the frustration. The reaction is to dissociate from the experience and downplay the event. At that moment the impact is so severe that the person feels that he/she has lost the power to act.

Level 7 - Unconsciousness

Chakra: Root

Gland: Reproductive organs, Spinal column

Catatonia - Gonads / Unconsciousness, *I don't know, I am not conscious.*

When this level is reached, it is as if the soul is not connected to the body. There is no connection to who you really are. These people have the appearance that the lights are on, but no one is home. There is no life force emanating from them. They are robotic. The pattern is *"nothing is happening."*

There are degrees of dissociation and unconsciousness depending on the severity of the trauma at any level. One face of dissociation is that of the talking head. This person is completely in his head, in his intellect, with no connection to his inner sensations. This lack of contact with the body is an indication of a mind/body split. Unconsciousness can also manifest as disconnection from life, from the soul, from the body. There may not be much sensation in the extremities. If you were to pinch the person, they would not feel it as much. The nervous system is deactivated. There is little connection to thought processes in this state. The word patterns are "nothing is wrong" or "I don't know." There is no problem because the person is in denial. An issue or resistance pattern is submerged to such a degree that there is a total lack of awareness. If the individual remains in unawareness, he or she will continue to react to the associated situations from a series of reactive patterns.

Level 7.1 – Catatonia:

This is a state of total and unconsciousness, helplessness. There is no movement unless someone stirs. Breathing cannot be detected. This is a severe state of contraction in which the life force is very weak, it is associated with altered consciousness.

In a PHP session, a person may believe that everything is fine and that they are simply relaxing, but the facilitator will sense that something is wrong, lacking light or presence. Energetically it is perceived as flat, static, without movement. The facilitator may also notice tastes in his or her mouth, perhaps a dry tongue, a feeling of being drugged, and drowsiness, a lot of drowsiness.

As you work with the points, the expectation is to move up the emotional scale, reconnect the energetic centers, and integrate the different emotional components with the organs and glands, forming a structured and organized harmonious whole.

CHAPTER III
CATEGORIES OF TRAUMA

"In the same way that Perseus used his shield to confront Medusa, many traumatized people may use their sense of 'perception' or an equivalent sensation's shield, to master the trauma. The sense of bodily perception contains the clarity, instinctual power and fluidity needed to transform trauma."

Dr. Peter Levine: Waking the Tiger

Highly Impactful Traumatic Experiences

A specific traumatic experience with certain symptoms and signs is classified as a category of trauma. Working with trauma, there are important differences in the characteristics of the traumatic experience. These situations require a specific therapeutic management in each person. In some cases, psychological alterations, dissociation and/or emotional blockages are observed that provoke obsessive or phobic behaviors. In each category, an evaluation of the type of trauma is required. Depending on its origin, we must consider whether the trauma also involves physical harm. For example, an emergency medical procedure or intervention, a tracheotomy, a car accident involving loss of limb, an exposed fracture or bite, a fall with head trauma, drowning, or beatings. In situations such as these, the intensity of the experience will lead the person to moments of high activation of their defense system and may disintegrate their sense of physical and psychological safety.

At the time of therapy, the following should be considered:

- Evaluate in each client the type of trauma category. If the trauma is of High Impact, a PHP facilitator should be used.
- The intervention should be accompanied by exercises and PHP points related to the specific category.

- Consider recommending and integrating supportive treatments to the PHP work: psychopharmacological, psychological or psychiatric, if necessary.

Traumatic Experiences and their Repercussions

In the process of nervous system dysregulation, internal patterns, systems, and mechanisms are activated at the cerebral level, which provoke multi-systemic responses. This affects the immune system and triggers high levels of stress and symptoms of anxiety to varying degrees. Recurrent post-traumatic stress symptoms become evident. What are the symptoms of post-traumatic stress disorder?

There are four types of PTSD symptoms, but they may not be the same for everyone. Each person experiences symptoms in his or her own way. The types are:

1. **Re-experiencing symptoms:** Certain triggers can evoke memories of the trauma, leading to the re-experiencing of sensations, emotions, or fear. Illustrative instances encompass flashbacks that immerse you in the event anew, unsettling nightmares, and distressing thoughts.

2. **Avoidance symptoms:** Trying to avoid situations or people that trigger memories of the traumatic event. This may cause you to: Avoid places, events, or objects that remind you of the traumatic experience. For example, if

you were in a car accident, you might stop driving. Avoid thoughts or feelings related to the traumatic event. For example, you might try to keep very busy to avoid thinking about what happened.

3. **Symptoms of hypervigilance, alertness, or reactivity:** These may cause nervousness or alertness to danger. They include: feeling easily startled, feeling tense or "on edge." Having sleeping difficulty. Having anger outbursts.

4. **Cognitive and mood symptoms:** Negative changes in beliefs and feelings are composed of various elements, including challenges in recalling important details about the traumatic event, harboring pessimistic thoughts about oneself or the world, experiencing feelings of guilt and remorse, a decline in interest for previously enjoyable activities, and difficulties concentrating.

Symptoms usually begin soon after the traumatic event. But they may take several months, even years to appear. They may also come and go cyclically for years. If your symptoms last longer than four weeks, cause great distress, or interfere with your work or personal life, you may have PTSD [32].

Mariann Dávila suggests that, before categorization, we consider a criterion to differentiate whether the trauma stems from internal or external conditions. This differentiation helps us ascertain the source of the trauma's impact and its corresponding physiological and/or environmental repercussions.

---

[32] Ref: https://medlineplus.gov/posttraumaticstressdisorder.html

Types of Trauma

Trauma types are defined according to the form and degree of impact of the traumatic event. A car accident is not the same as a fall from a bicycle, drowning or being the victim of a violent abduction. The approach to these categories is handled in a specific way and require specific exercises.

Some types are:

- Car crashes or accidents
- Falls
- Burns, fever, anesthesia and poisons
- Abductions, wars
- Fires, Earthquakes
- Fear of death
- Sexual harassment and violence
- Ancestral and collective cultural trauma

The work of elaboration and healing of trauma is a slow and complex process. It is like "peeling back the layers of an onion," one layer at a time. Through this method, the body slowly integrates the dissociated aspects and helps the nervous system to unload the tremendous overload of energy that deregulates it.

Today, it is evident that trauma refers to the response that the nervous system fails to discharge through its defense and survival mechanisms. This failure leads to a direct systemic dysregulation of organs and the neuroendocrine system. Simultaneously, it disrupts the autonomic nervous system and influences brain function by hyperactivating the limbic system. This hyperactivation results in thought disorganization, heightened vigilance, and tendencies towards aggression. This is reflected in the serious difficulties of not being able to release high stress loads, not being able to withstand a greater demand for tension, collapsing and generating an unconscious and autonomic defense of the Dorsal Vagus nerve, freezing the body's innate self-regulating capacity and disconnecting us from the social connection.

How do we recognize "Traumatic Imprints"?

- Chronic Stress
- Chronic pain
- Fear-based decisions
- Phobic behavior
- Uncontrolled aggression
- Lack of intimacy
- Socially unavailable
- Lack of joy
- Feeling disconnected from life
- Depression
- Overreacting to an ordinary situation
- Sympathetic nervous system reactions

Internal Aggression

Viewed through a physiological lens, the impact of trauma becomes apparent via the body's defensive responses, disruption of systemic equilibrium, and homeostatic imbalance. This can manifest as high fever, metabolic instability, electrolyte depletion, hypoglycemia, internal hemorrhaging, headaches, vomiting, acute dehydration, and in certain instances, life-threatening conditions. Such severe bodily reactions necessitate immediate emergency assistance as the initial course of action. A body in shock can lead us to experience internal chaos, delirium, space-time disorientation, muscle spasms, digestive problems, dehydration and even convulsions.

External Aggression

In external aggression, the body reacts with high activation response mechanisms on the immune system, the digestive system or at the nervous level through the blood-brain barrier.

- Vaccines, antibiotics and some drugs should receive medical supervision, as they can produce anaphylactic shock, fainting, respiratory arrest and may require emergency medical attention.
- It can also be highly risky and traumatic for the body and the person to accidentally consume toxic substances, poisons, or receive toxic inhalations.
- Many people have been bitten by a snake, for example, and their survival depends on whether they manage to receive an antidote for that specific venom.
- Another external scenario of aggression is when we are exposed to catastrophic news from the media and networks: deaths, violence, robberies, assaults. By witnessing these situations, we lose our sense of security, we permanently feel threatened.

- Also, in some cases we live in areas where we are at risk or threat of receiving an unpleasant surprise. We can be assaulted, kidnapped, stabbed, beaten, shot at the supermarket, at school or at work. Without leaving home, we see how street violence, drug trafficking and the lack of security make us feel defenseless and many times we become unconsciously aggressive, as an innate defensive mechanism. We avoid meeting others, we are afraid, distrustful and insecure.
- Trauma due to war-torn situations where torture and violence are part of everyday life.
- Situations of abuse and extreme psychological violence.
- Trauma stemming from catastrophes and natural disasters encompasses the profound loss of not only possessions but also cherished relationships, livelihoods, familial ties, and the very fabric of the life we once knew. We experience uprooting, loss and many times they lead us to experience vicarious trauma, where our suffering increases because we see others in the same conditions and are unable to give them help or defense, suffering the same or worse conditions. Our life feels permanently threatened.

CATEGORIES OF TRAUMA

For PHP it is essential to know which categories of trauma you are working with, to be able to control the behavior and behaviors that will occur in the session. Example: If you notice that the category of the trauma is phobia, you must be careful, because in their bewilderment when reliving the sensation of danger, the client will collect themselves and could react with anguish, crying or lack of control. As you work during the session, the energy that is trapped in the body is released and the therapist must reinforce the idea that there is no threat, delivering safety signals to the nervous system of the client.

It's crucial to highlight that certain severe cases may present intense symptoms, demanding meticulous and gradual care to aid in their recovery. This approach allows for the gradual restoration of energy and well-being.

Suggestions for working in somatic imprints:

1. Ask: What part of your body feels the least tired?
2. When an individual lacks sufficient energy, it's important to avoid hastening the process of corporatizing their experience. Instead, focus on gradually reintegrating dissociated aspects, enhancing the client's sense of security throughout the therapeutic journey within the body.
3. Work with her/his posture. It is very important to help integrate and achieve balance.

4. Through the pendulation of sensations. Teach the client to expand and contract the energy in the now, so the energy balances like the ocean. If you watch the waves, one after the other, you will understand that the ocean expands and contracts, and then again discharges outward. Waves of coherence move within our body like the ocean, organized, and connecting one wave after another.

As an illustration of the impact that traumatic experiences can wield over us, we propose an examination of the following films. These movies distinctly portray how trauma becomes interwoven into individuals' lives.

In the film "Hemingway & Gellhorn," the characters find themselves amidst the chaos of war, and amidst this turmoil, an intense passion emerges between them. This passion reaches its zenith during a bombing episode, occurring while they are in an intimate moment. Notably, their passion flourishes amid the traumatic backdrop of war, illustrating how trauma can serve as the very force that binds them together.

In the 1993 movie "Fearless," starring Jeff Bridges, the main character manages to survive a plane crash that claims the lives of most of the passengers. This harrowing survival ordeal propels him into a state of seeming invulnerability, bordering on euphoria. Consequently, he embarks on a path of radical behavior in his subsequent actions. Trauma strips away his fear and constraints, enabling him to transcend his previous limitations.

In the documentary "The Wisdom of Trauma,"33 trauma is presented as an imperceptible yet potent influence that molds the trajectory of our lives. Within the film, Dr. Gabor Maté emphasizes the pivotal significance of initially comprehending the origins of behaviors and ailments that take residence within the human psyche. This stands in contrast to the prevailing approach of solely issuing diagnoses, quelling symptoms, and passing judgment on behaviors.

1. Trauma from Medical Procedures and Surgeries

In the medicine field, medical procedures continue to represent, in some cases, trauma to the body, even though in many cases they can mean saving life or resolving illnesses. Anesthesia, drugs with radioactive isotopes, injections, incisions, cuts, loss of organs or changes in the physical or muscular structure will simply affect the structure of the body as a self-organizing system.

From PHP's point of view, we consider it relevant to prepare the body to be intervened by a medical procedure.

Although many times procedures have the purpose of saving life, healing specific ailments, or extending life, most of the time they confront a system that naturally maintains balance, homeostasis and is protected by the immune and nervous system that recognizes these stimuli as foreign and threatening. For example: it is known to all how organ transplants require immunotherapy support so that the body does not reject the new organ, since it recognizes it as an invasion, an intrusion that is not its own. With this example we would like to emphasize that the body is aware of itself in all its processes, through its physical intelligence, systemic body awareness, sustained by the integrated structure between the nervous, muscular, and circulatory systems, activation mechanisms as we have seen through the autonomic pathway, which leads it to constantly evaluate its interaction with the environment.

When we approach a medical procedure; surgeries, implants, examinations, lumbar puncture, basic check-ups, we are breaking a highly sensitive barrier, the skin, a tissue innervated and organized to perceive pain, heat, pressure. Fear, anguish, crying, dizziness, nausea and even loss of consciousness may appear. For these reasons, we can prepare the patient psychologically and psychosomatically to face these procedures. We work at the level of imagery and reprogramming of the brain amygdala responses. We prepare ourselves to visit the intervention site beforehand, touring the spaces, connecting with the staff and above all we recommend reinforcing the doctor-patient relationship in order to feel safe and in good hands.

PHP therapists address the body's ability to regulate itself. For example, through the application of specific exercises they can help the client, in case of surgery, to work on personal resources, to regulate stress, fear and uncertainty caused by experiencing the loss of consciousness due to anesthetics or sedatives. Also, to face the fear of dying in a state of unconsciousness during surgery or the worry of experiencing complications.

We make the following recommendations to prepare for invasive medical procedures with anesthesia and surgery:

- Get in touch with a doctor who allows you to feel safe and empathetic, who is a professional that gives you a sense of connection and trust. If you do not feel safe, change doctors.
- Seek to be accompanied by a person who can be attentive to your needs and who can provide support and emotional stability.
- Before the procedure, get to know the place.

We collaborate with the client to facilitate the acquisition of techniques aimed at cultivating tranquility. Our approach involves fostering the reestablishment of harmony between muscles and nerves through sensory engagement, controlled breathing, and the manipulation of the vagus nerve. This process aids in averting dissociation and fostering the gradual assimilation of consciousness, thereby preventing disorientation, particularly during the progressive emergence from anesthesia.

Our primary goal is to empower the individual to effectively manage a range of symptoms induced by anesthesia, including but not limited to nausea, dizziness, vomiting, headaches, and vertigo.

It is relevant to attend to the emotional aspects and behaviors before and after the surgeries. This will allow the limbic system to work with the regulation of emotions that are trapped in the body, the memories associated with fear, panic, terror and shame. We work on reorganizing the traumatic images by integrating images that represent safety. At the level of the amygdala, these memories can be reprocessed and allow the body to elaborate sensations and memories of flashbacks, of pains that have remained as tonic immobility in the muscles, provoked by fear or dissociation in defense of something lived as inescapable.

In the PHP sessions, we begin by visualizing what the surgery will be like, the route, the nurse, the stretcher, to connect it with images of safety. Recognizing and experiencing the sensation that everything is going to be fine increases the tolerance window of the Sympathetic and Parasympathetic nervous system. To regulate fear arousal responses, we can use breathing, neck movement, releasing and tensing muscles at times to release tension. We widen the margin of optimal activation, and the body responds with less difficulty to the procedure. Stress can be moderated as we learn practical exercises and use our own resources.

In children, the company of a loved one is essential. In more difficult cases, we suggest using a toy of the child's, which will provide security; for example, a doll or a teddy bear, a car, or a super-hero whom he/she admires, and who comes to save us. These images generated in a conscious way, show the amygdala what is going to happen, and reorganize the activations. Another recommended action with children is to simulate the procedure through a game that uses their dolls or objects as characters and context of what will happen. This helps the child to be clearly aware of the procedure and not be surprised.

In some cases, music or a friendly companion can make the difference at the moment of the intervention.

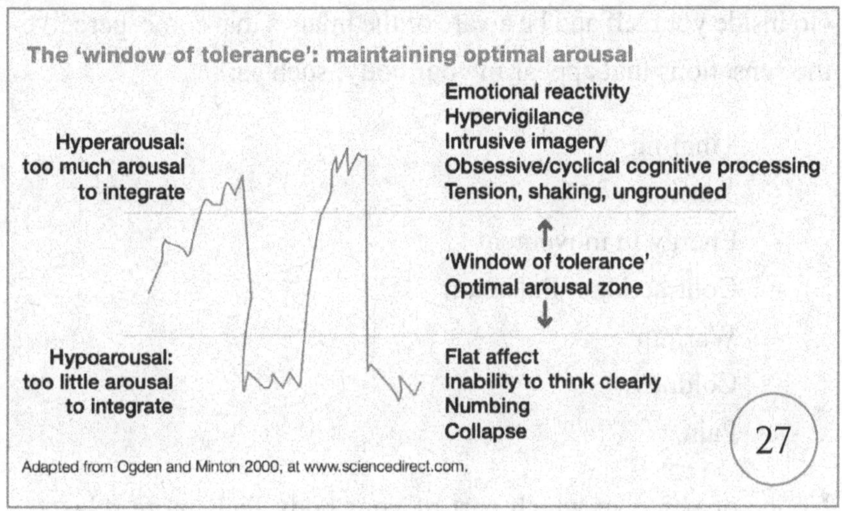

[33]

After surgery, it is important to mobilize, through the points, the energy frozen by the defense response that could not be completed. We can work on the regulation of the respiratory rhythm and heart rate, on the discharge of neurogenic tremors, on the fear of shock (especially if there is an emergency intervention), on the autonomic regulation, looking for a place in the body where we can feel safe, calm or at peace.

Exercise for anesthesia and surgery: Muscle Expansion

You can do this exercise lying down or sitting in a quiet environment. This exercise needs your full attention.

---

[33] Ref: https://www.hhri.org/gbv-training-manuals/women-manual/resources/window-of-tolerance/

Go inside yourself and be aware of the images that come, perceive the sensations that appear in your body, such as:

- Tingling
- Tension
- Energy in movement
- Contraction – Pulsation
- Warmth
- Coldness
- Pain

Notice or perceive which part of your body feels more relaxed. Accessing sensations helps to repair the connection with oneself. Just observe them and become aware of them through perception. What are you feeling? Thinking? Seeing images? Perceive and focus on how the energy changes in your body, and track it. Move your feet. How does it feel?

- If you feel stiffness take all the time you need for the stiffness to disperse, play with your feet, move them; remember when you were little.
- If you notice any pain in the body, you can put heat on it, with your hands (re-associate).
- Expand the sensations, just feel the edge of the pain (the border).
- If you feel any emotion, it is normal, after an operation the body feels anger and sorrow.
- It will relieve you not to judge yourself with this emotion.

Why is it important to do this exercise?

As the nervous system heightens arousal within the sympathetic division, intense stimulation or agitation can trigger prolonged headaches or stomach discomfort. Over time, these manifestations might escalate into conditions such as migraine syndrome or chronic gastric fatigue. Crucially, the key lies in discharging the agitated energy trapped within the body through the channel of sensations. By doing so, this restless energy can be guided back towards its innate equilibrium, restoring a natural balance.

2. Trauma from Dental Surgeries

The interventions of dental surgeries and molar extractions are in some cases overloaded with pain and inflammation. At the time of treatment, dental maneuvers may be recognized as a threat to the body, and a betrayal of its safety. Defense responses are disorganized, so that the body "does not understand" what is happening; without understanding or integrating it, it experiences it as an "impact wound", a damage, rather than a relief or help. This is the case of extractions or surgeries where there is loss of a tooth, with bleeding and inflammation, which provoke intense terror, accompanied by a hyper arousal or high impact activation response. You can feel your heart rate increase, your palms get sweaty and your chest may tighten.

At times, a visit to the dentist becomes an inevitable necessity. In our attempts to evade it, we might endure intense discomfort and even delay seeking treatment until symptoms escalate to the point of fever, inflammation, and infection, demanding immediate attention. It is in these moments of urgency that we are compelled to seek the relief we had initially resisted. In dental trauma, the importance of providing the client with environmental elements that reinforce safety is currently recognized. The relevance of the tone of voice, the dentist's contact with the client's gaze and the physician's ability to sustain the crisis will make a difference. When a dental trauma is experienced, confronting another dental session can elicit heightened stress-related behaviors. This might encompass fear, tears, gastrointestinal distress leading to diarrhea, migraines, and often, an altered heart rate with instances of tachycardia. Sedation may be required.

In certain instances, orthodontic treatment involves altering the alignment of teeth, which can lead to discomfort and neurological issues. Clients may exhibit nocturnal jaw adjustments and bruxism as their jaws, mouth, tongue, teeth attempt to reestablish harmony. Additionally, pressure on the palate, tension within the temporomandibular joints, and persistent pain can occur during sleep. This type of treatment often disrupts the harmony between the facial bone structure and the positioning of teeth and surrounding tissues. While it is true that this treatment is necessary in some cases, there is a physical cost behind it that must be considered.

In dental implants it is possible for the body to experience a foreign body, loss of sensation, disconnection with a part of itself, in addition to the loss of an original tooth.

The mouth is a sensitive area in which we often reflect nerves, tensions or worries. Any intervention within it will create some temporomandibular joint (TMJ) disorder. This not only involves the jaw or teeth, but also the muscles in the area, the head, even the neck. Often people affected by pain blame it on a cervical problem or a headache, without imagining that it is a consequence of the intervention.

Tip:
In the implant procedure, holes are drilled in the jawbone. We recommend that this type of implant, which is a type of surgery, be worked on therapeutically during the whole treatment, in order to prevent possible side effects in the long term, such as difficulties in the regulation of chewing, problems in the cardiopulmonary and digestive system, as well as in the system of social engagement.

Exercise for combating bruxism:
A problem that affects more than 20% of the population is clenching or grinding of the teeth, generally during sleep hours. The main factor is stress and will have the following consequences:

- Headaches
- Dental wear and tear
- Dental hypersensitivity
- Fractures and even dental mobility
- Inflammation and receding gums

- Temporomandibular joint problems (the joint that connects the jaw to the base of the skull).

Ask: Do you feel tension in your jaw when you wake up?

- Notice the temporomandibular joint on each side of your face.
- Notice if it is tight; notice if the right side is tighter than the left side and vice versa.
- With your index finger press for about fifteen seconds at the point where the jaw meets the side of the head, then open your mouth and yawn.
- Again, with your index finger lower your lower jaw for fifteen seconds and let your voice sound outward, saying ah, ah, ah. Put your hands gently on top of your jaw (temporomandibular joint), feel the warmth of your hands and relax.
- If an image or emotion comes up, observe the colors and shapes. Breathe three times.

Why is this exercise important?

The jaw is connected to the dorsal vagus nerve and this is stimulated when eating, starting the peristalsis (the movement of the intestine) that helps digest food. The jaw is where we usually store our frustration and anger. If you start paying attention to your body you will notice that when you clench your jaw, you clench all the muscles in your body. Many people clench it when they sleep and need to wear a dental plate.

Catalina case:

During the pandemic in 2020, I did several Zoom sessions on my computer.

John, a forty-year-old man, was working with me in therapy every week. One day he called me very early in the morning because he had to go to the dentist that day and he was very upset and in a state of panic. He told me that when he was a child, he was very afraid to go to the dentist, and, for the same reason, he was put under anesthesia with every visit. In our session, I used the Somatic Release Technique™ (STR) and several exercises with the vagus nerve and nervous system. I also used imagery; I proposed for him to change his mental scenario and mentally place himself in the consultation room. I guided him to imagine going into his dentist's office and to visualize creating a very comfortable chair, full of nice cushions, with his favorite color. I said, "feel in your body how your feet are your support; notice your sensations and do abdominal breathing".

That day, after the session with his dentist was over, he called me. He was happy and he laughed. He told me he had a wonderful experience, no anesthesia was necessary, and he did everything I told him to do. Even his dentist could not believe it and became interested in PHP to help his other clients be calmer and more cooperative with the treatment.

3. Trauma and Anesthesia

In cases of anesthesia trauma, the body is left feeling that it has not fully "returned" to a natural state of alertness. A discontinuity is provoked between the self-awareness and the body. This void of information causes a break in the continuity of consciousness that disorganizes the synchronization between the body and the traumatic event. It is important to recognize these symptoms: feelings of lethargy, a sensation of fear that runs through the body, and diffuse anxiety without a direct reason. These are all symptoms of being "taken by anesthesia".

Anesthesia can at times induce dissociation at a psychological level. Beyond merely suppressing consciousness through drug effects, it can create a void in awareness. This vacuum disrupts cerebral processes, occasionally on a temporary basis, while in other instances it can disturb the autonomic nervous system, triggering a state of "shutdown." Such a shutdown can manifest as feelings of profound fatigue, a lack of energy, and may even result in symptoms like vomiting and dizziness. In some cases, it might lead to a sensation of slow and challenging recovery of consciousness. During PHP sessions, it is not uncommon for individuals, upon being positioned on the massage table, to trigger a reawakening of memories related to their surgical experiences. Sensations, sounds, and intrusive images may appear that cause us to relive this experience. In the session we try to incorporate, through the stimulation of the points, the power to reconnect the body with the memory and the dissociated emotions or sensations.

In certain sessions, we have noticed variations in respiratory patterns, instances of persistent pain, and inflammation in areas that have undergone surgery. These manifestations are occasionally linked to the trauma associated with surgical procedures. Furthermore, as an aftermath of post-operative trauma, we have observed occurrences such as panic attacks, chronic and traumatic stress, post-traumatic stress disorder (PTSD), and reactive depression stemming from the surgical intervention. We pay attention to body language and posture. We seek to recognize body and emotional blocking, for example, getting stuck in unconscious patterns of fear, shame, or guilt and thoughts of helplessness and other unconscious behaviors.

Dissociative freezing is often seen as "collapsing posture," muscles that lose strength, an unsteady gait, and difficulty looking into another's eyes. These postures reflect debilitating belief patterns and thoughts associated with chronic depressive states, mood disorders, and social difficulties.

After undergoing surgery, there's a sense of the energetic body losing its vitality. This condition of energy depletion can result in a sensation of floating, disorientation, and a lack of grounding. A diminished awareness of bodily sensations can lead to feelings of frustration and helplessness, accentuated by the perception of being unwell and unable to control the situation. This internal turmoil can trigger hostile reactions, directed both inwardly and outwardly, manifesting as aggression, intolerance, irritability, impatience, conflict, and a lack of empathy. These behavioral disruptions have the potential to disrupt the individual's life, causing a state of chaos. Certain emotions can become entangled with traumatic symptoms, leading to confusion. Some individuals resort to using alcohol, sex, or drugs as a means of releasing tension, which can result in addiction. Conversely, others may experience emotional numbness, rendering them incapable of feeling anything, ultimately contributing to long-term anxiety. Dissociation is common among traumatized individuals, and this detachment can lead to a prolonged state of emotional anesthesia within the body.

Exercise for anesthesia:

Touching or tapping is very good for the skin.

1. Using one hand at a time, gently bent in a concave fashion, start tapping with your right hand, go up from the wrist, towards the left arm up towards the neck. Then, with your left hand, go up the wrist, the right arm and to the neck; do the same with the right foot, the leg, until you reach the right hip; then, with your right hand tap the left foot until you reach the left hip. Gentle touching or tapping helps the skin to wake up.

2. Identify the STO points. These points are instrumental in releasing stored tension and revitalizing depleted energy. They play a crucial role in the restoration, replenishment, and rejuvenation of both nerves and blood circulation. It's important to note that the effects of anesthesia can linger within the body for an extended duration.

3. Visualize yourself standing by a serene lake adorned with crystal-clear blue water. Adjacent to the shore, a sizable buoyant platform awaits you. As you step onto the float and recline, you discern a subtle undulation coursing

through your body, harmonizing with the float's gentle motion. Gazing upwards, the sky reveals a medley of clouds; gradually, your imagination propels you closer to these formations, like a drifting balloon, allowing the tranquil breeze to carry you. A sensation of contentment envelops you. Gazing downward, you observe your own form, serenely at rest. With a gradual descent, you shift your focus inward, descending into your physical being. Pay heed to the nuances of sensation. Observe the rhythm of your breath, a testament to your vitality - the essence of being alive. Slowly move down into your body and notice how it feels. Notice your breath, I am alive.

4. Trauma from High-risk Childbirth

Today, unlike in past decades, good treatment, gestational support, mental care of the mother, her physical health and the health of her pregnancy are promoted. Generating conditions for a gestation period is profoundly important. At the time of delivery, it is possible to have complications and vital risk for both the mother and her fetus.

Mariann:

"I remember my first normal delivery; I was very young. I had symptoms of preterm labor and was hospitalized for a month in order to sustain the pregnancy, which came to term at seven months. At that time, I was without emotional support of any kind. I remember that a nurse, when taking me to the delivery room, was aggressive to the point of intentionally bumping into the door of the delivery room, which caused me great physical pain. Then at the time of delivery, they had to do a maneuver to turn my baby over and make a tissue cut in order to have more room for delivery, since I was not dilated enough. At that point they realized that I was not reacting to the epidural anesthesia and was experiencing great pain. Finally, at the end of labor, I was in deep pain, with lots of anesthesia in my body and multiple pricks in my arms and hands. I spent several hours recovering in the postpartum room. At the time of the check-up, to return to the ward, the head doctor realized that a needle from my epidural anesthesia had been left in my back. I still remember how the head doctor called the medical team in front of me, and explained to the other doctors what was wrong, which led to a summary report due to the seriousness of the situation: "I could have been disabled. My son and I emerged without major after-effects from an experience that was terrifying."

In the case of deliveries and cesarean sections, the effect of anesthesia also reaches the fetus, inhibiting its survival mechanisms, weakening its immune system, and causing disorganization in the enteric or visceral system. The baby is born numb and intoxicated, so it is important to take these considerations into account when making the decision to have a cesarean section. However, it is expected to be performed in necessary and unavoidable cases.

It is very common for the mother to prefer a natural birth; however, difficulties arise, such as a coiled umbilical cord in the baby, problems in the birth canal, which lead to emergency maneuvers and cesarean sections. In these moments, both the mother and the baby experience intense fear and anguish, leading to heightened activation. These situations of elevated emotional intensity can have a profound impact on both individuals. Unable to mitigate the intensity independently, the mother undergoes a profoundly terrorizing ordeal. Offering the mother comprehensive containment and unwavering support during these critical moments is of paramount significance. This support extends beyond the immediate period of vital risk and encompasses the vital task of reestablishing the connection with her baby. Concurrently, addressing any traumatic aftermath that the mother might have encountered is a crucial facet of the holistic approach.

A relevant consideration is to be aware that, in a cesarean section, there is manipulation of the organs and the intestine. The viscera, highly innervated by the ventral vagus system, suffer physical trauma, and the internal organs are disorganized. It is recommended that this trauma and disorganization be worked on in session.

Caesarean section - Guilt:

Many women feel guilty after a cesarean section.

Guilt is a natural and paralyzing emotion for some people. Many feel guilty because of something they have done, or because they have failed at something. Some have excessive guilt, suffering and depressive thoughts, feeling that they failed because they could not have a normal delivery.

Exercise for childbirth or cesarean section:

1. Imagine three events. In each one you will perceive the sensations they provoke in your body. Take your time to feel them.
    - First event: think of a moment of pain and injury that you have not yet integrated.
    - Second event: think of an experience in which you had a lot of help and support. Evoke an image, thought and emotion.
    - Third event: think of a difficult situation that you have lived through, but that made you stronger and more powerful.

At the end, integrate the sensations that these three events produced in you, which can be associated with heat, cold, pressure, and/or pulsations.

2. Sitting on a chair, sofa or on the floor, feel your sit bones and breathe seven times, squeezing your vagina as you inhale and releasing your vagina as you exhale. Take your time; notice your feet on the floor and feel the articulation of your hips. Relax them and notice if any sensation goes up your legs.
3. As you lie on the floor, position your feet against the wall and gently exert pressure. Notice the sensations coursing through your body and acknowledge the occasional necessity for this liberating movement. Often, energy becomes confined within the hips and pelvis, precipitating

complications in the pelvic bone and hip joint, which interconnects with the spine, sit bones, sacrum, and coccyx. Engaging in this exercise facilitates the release of tension, offering relief.

Dissociation states in surgery:

During a PHP session, the client might revisit and reexperience events from the surgery that had been dissociated or suppressed in their memory. This process can evoke feelings of fear and a sensation of coldness. In instances of clinical death during surgery, after resuscitation, it's not uncommon for individuals to share accounts of experiencing vivid imagery. These testimonials often describe encountering scenes of light or tunnels, which serve as pathways guiding them back to their body and the realm of life.

In these cases, it is necessary to integrate the experience by "corporealizing" it, making the person feel that life is in the body, now, in the present. This allows the nervous system to reorganize itself, recovering security and stability in the body.

Reorganization of the contents that emerge when coming out of dissociation:

We can work on a complete cycle of reorganization in the following way:

- Consciously pendulate between the body's present state and the felt sensation; between what is dissociated and the felt sense. In Peter Levine's Somatic Experiencing®, pendulation is described as the natural pulsation between states of expansion and contraction in the nervous system.

- Gradually we invite the client to reconnect through sensations, from the periphery to the center, from a pleasant sensation to the disconnected, until they can come out of the dissociation.

- During the exercise, thoughts, images, emotions, feelings, memories, affections, and sensations that were buried in the unconscious will appear. This facilitates the "unfreezing" of the dissociation in a gradual way, so that the fear responses frozen in the body can be reorganized and discharged.

This completes a cycle that had been retained, deregulating the person's life, preventing them from understanding what we refer to in therapy as "the floating anguish," or the feeling of being isolated, without mobility.

It is also important in some cases:

- To make contact through the touch of the hands, gradually integrating the dissociated area. Connecting with the warmth of the hand on the affected area can be deeply healing.

Finally, through holding the points, the client on the worktable is given space to reorganize their experiences and integrate what emerges.

Recommended exercises after surgery:

1. Take a yoga ball (that fits your size) and sit on it. Notice how your body seeks the center of balance of the body and keep your feet connected to the ground, along with the feeling of stability. Notice how the body feels centered, stable and secure. Repeat the exercise as many times as necessary.

2. Walk on the grass and feel the sensations under your feet, feel your own inhale and exhale; make a sound "uuuwaaahhh" to reconnect your digestive system until you feel the stomach as it responds to this sound.

5. Trauma from Loss and Traumatic Grief

Losses are part of life. The human being experiences them many times, with a feeling of emptiness in the body. Something is gone, there is emotional pain, discouragement, despondency and, in some cases, depressive states. Grief is a process, where denial, anger, and feeling unable to accept the loss is what we all go through. Many people live for years with the symptoms of emotional and psychological trauma. Over time their world becomes smaller and smaller. The effect of untreated psychological trauma can be devastating and infiltrate almost every aspect of a person's life. Some of the most common effects of untreated trauma are uncontrollable reactive thoughts; unconscious patterns of ruminative, invasive and repetitive

235

thoughts that generate distress, stress and anxiety on many occasions. Many times, the person is left in a state of abyss or a state where nothing exists. Something dies within oneself. When the person is an adolescent, they remain in that adolescence.

We recognize that the trauma appears through the physiological symptomatology; the body experiences the loss, collapsing without being able to avoid it. At the behavioral level, the physical and emotional emptiness of the loss is experienced by retaining memories, routines, taking care of significant objects, which allow us to maintain contact with the loss.

The stages of grief are denial, anger, negotiation, depression and acceptance.

In the PHP sessions, we work on integrating grief, identifying the emptiness left in the body after the loss. We work on closing the cycle of grief, completing what the person feels is pending with the person who is no longer with us. What happened during the Pandemic is exemplary. Words full of emotion were not spoken and farewells were not possible. Not being able to accompany and say goodbye to loved ones left a deep impact on families and friends.

These traumatic experiences disorganize and cause deep systemic wounds, but we can integrate the different manifestations of grief.

Physiological:

- Emptiness in the stomach
- Tightness in the chest
- Hypersensitivity to noise
- Feeling of depersonalization

- Shortness of breath
- Palpitations
- Muscle weakness
- Lack of energy
- Headache and dry mouth

Behavioral:

- Sleep and eating disorders
- Distracted behavior
- Social withdrawal
- Dreaming of the deceased
- Crying and/or sighing
- Searching and calling out loud
- Carrying and hoarding objects
- Visiting places, the deceased frequented
- Hyper or hypo activity

Reconnection exercise:

Hold the heart point and remember all the good moments you had with the loved one. Perceive a place in your body that "feels good" and take a deep breath. As you hold the heart point you will feel a slight stinging pain, like a little pinch or small ache. Leave your index finger there for about five minutes doing abdominal breathing, and then release it. You will notice a new feeling of more fullness and connection.

6. Inescapable Attack Trauma

It is inevitable that those experiences where we cannot react in time often provoke a high psychic and somatic impact. All defenses are disorganized.

In animal attacks, fear, helplessness and often physical damage generate a response of dissociation and extreme freezing. After these events we do not want to go out in the street, we cannot have a pet near us because we feel distressed, in danger. It is important to be aware that many times we are socially inhibited to scream, cry, stay in a moment of weakness, instead of shivering and releasing fear and rage, which is the discharge of the nervous system and, therefore, indispensable to non-traumatization.

We also feel terror and high vulnerability in the moment of experiencing assaults with blows, robberies with weapons, kidnappings or abductions with isolation, without being able to respond to our instinct that drives us to escape or attack the enemy.

The high intensity must be worked in layers, backwards and forwards in time, in a line of situations of a lower emotional and psychosomatic charge until the moment of impact can be addressed, previously creating, as we have mentioned, resources and techniques that protect from dissociation and re-traumatization.

Reducing the load on the nervous system, modulating the memories that appear, observing in the body how the trauma appears through layers of sympathetic and parasympathetic activation, is the way to return to the body. We relive moments of guilt, fear, resentment, impotence, which must also be integrated into the process. Discharging hypersensitivity to these events is an important focus of work. If we don't do this, we stop feeling safe and, in some cases, paranoid thoughts may appear that flood our mind, change our routines and leave us once again contracted and trapped.

Exercises:

In this exercise we are going to use our imagination:

1. Our superheroes like Superman, Tarzan, Superwoman or some person that you felt safe can come to help you and save you.
2. You can become a huge giant that will grab your shoulders and throw the attacker or predator away, far away, to another planet, to the ocean, or inside a locked box, but far away from you.
3. Perceive the sensations of your hands, how energy emerges from them, push this energy; you can visualize it in colors or energy going outward.
4. Feel your feet and visualize that you are running, away from the attacker, running in a meadow or mountain, or across the sand watching the sea, until you are completely away.

7. Trauma Due to Catastrophes, Fires, Earthquakes and Disasters

Burns, falls, fractures, asphyxia, wounds, head injuries are some of the situations that we may experience during earthquakes, fires, tsunamis, hurricanes, volcanic explosions, floods or hazardous or toxic explosions. We may experience more than one trauma in these conditions.

In these cases, we always apply the criteria of medical and psychological first aid, which prioritizes saving the life of the person and being able to get out of the state of danger. After stabilization we can go step by step bringing the person back to reality. We can do this by establishing contact with their feet. If appropriate, place our feet gently on the client's feet, asking them to look us in the eyes, to breathe and, in some cases, we may ask permission to place our hand on their shoulder, holding and supporting it while we trace the body's sensations. At the level of breathing, we can ask client to take a deep breath, feeling the breath with his/her own hands on their abdomen. In this way, we seek to release the energy trapped in the head and regulate the heart rate. We then place the client on the table, holding the points that are required.

It is important to consider that this type of trauma category is intimately linked to post-traumatic stress disorder whose symptoms may appear long after the event occurred, even up to several years. With the passage of time, the person stops relating the symptoms to the event and they become more complex until they end up in syndromes of greater complexity that affect personality and health.

The National Institute of Mental Health USA classifies symptoms into [34]:

A. Intrusive memory symptoms:

- Experiencing flashbacks, or mentally reliving the traumatic event over and over again, even accompanied by physical symptoms such as palpitations or sweating.
- Having recurring memories or dreams related to the event.
- Having distressing thoughts.
- Showing physical signs of stress.
- Thoughts and feelings can trigger these symptoms, as can words, objects, or situations that bring back memories of the event.
- Avoidance symptoms
- Staying away from places, events, or objects that bring up memories of the experience.
- Avoiding thoughts or feelings related to the traumatic event.
- Avoidance symptoms may cause the person to change his or her routine. For example, after a serious car accident, you may avoid driving or riding in a car.

---

[34] Ref:
https://www.nimh.nih.gov/sites/default/files/documents/health/publications/post-traumatic-stress-disorder-ptsd/20-mh-8124-ptsd.pdf

B. Symptoms of hypervigilance and reactivity:

- Easily startled.
- Feeling tense, being on alert or being "hyper-alert".
- Having difficulty concentrating.
- Having trouble falling asleep or staying asleep.
- Feeling irritable and having outbursts of anger or aggression.
- Showing risky, reckless, or destructive behaviors.
- There are often symptoms of hypervigilance that can lead to feelings of stress and anger and interfere with daily living tasks, such as sleeping, eating, or concentrating.

C. Cognitive and mood symptoms:

- Experiencing problems remembering important details of the traumatic experience.
- Having negative thoughts about oneself or the world.
- Having distorted thoughts about the event that cause feelings of guilt.
- Experiencing ongoing negative emotions, such as fear, anger, guilt, or shame.
- Losing interest in activities in which you used to participate.
- Feeling socially isolated.
- Having difficulty feeling positive emotions, such as happiness or satisfaction.

Exercise:

In the face of an earthquake, for example, the flight reflex appears. To resolve this internal hyperactivation, we will perform the following exercise:

Sit on a chair or sofa, close your eyes and establish contact with your sit bones, hips and feet. Now open your eyes and keep them open for five seconds. Close them again for five seconds and simultaneously make a rocking motion on the sofa or chair from side to side. Repeat this exercise six times. Breathe deeply.

8. Trauma Due to Burns

In relation to the skin and burns there is a greater exposure to pain, to lose sensitivity later and to have to survive with scars, which also represents a psychological trauma. Avoidance behaviors, shame, apathy, and frustration appear. Many times, burn recovery procedures are accompanied by other surgeries and treatments can be long, slow and painful. It is advisable to seek in the body the sensations of calm, stability and to work on the emotions, images and sensations that feel trapped in the body.

We work on how to find a new emotional balance, reconnect to oneself, become aware of what caused the most suffering, stress and fear in the experience and how to deal with the aftermath. We bring to consciousness the unconscious patterns of negative thinking, fears of survival and difficulties in affection, so the exercises of self-containment, self-support help to create strength in oneself.

9. Trauma Due to Falls and Fractures

We have the habit of falling and getting up again quickly and abruptly; sometimes because we are in the middle of the street or among other people, or simply because it is a habit. However, falls require giving the body time to become aware of itself. After a fall, it needs to recover from the pain, the shock, the feeling of loss of stability and control. At the level of balance, the vestibular system perceives the change of position and seeks to recover it together with the spatial orientation and the center of gravity in the body.

We may feel disorganized, bodily unstable and insecure when walking. In addition, it is not the same for a child or young person to suffer a fall as it is for an adult or elderly person. Children are more flexible and may have a greater capacity to reorganize the impact of a fall than an older adult with less flexibility, less bone strength and a greater possibility of fractures (which take longer to heal).

The most advisable thing to do is to stay in the place of the fall and maintain the position while we check how the impact has been on the body; together with perceiving if we have any damage or injury, evaluate the degree of involvement and pain, see if we need to ask for help, or we can give the body time to recognize its state through its capacity of body awareness.

When there is trauma, the body normally repeats the fall and becomes more unstable, as if it lost a pattern of stability. We can work on the floor, on the top of the carpet or on pillows replicating the posture when we fell and reviewing what is remembered before, during and after the fall. We can also work with yoga balls, where we restore feeling balance in the body and recovering the sense of gravity. By working with somatic sensations, we can allow the body to regain a sense of orientation to offset the defense mechanism response.

In the specific case of fractures, through the points we help the body to recover the sense of integrity and connection between its parts. This integration reinforces the body's ability to heal. We work on the whole process, from before the fall, from the moment of awareness of the fracture, the procedures and interventions, the first aid received and what was most significant in the process of the fracture. Many times, in the sessions we experience pulsations in or around the fracture, we may feel warmth, a residual pain, numbness, or a void between one part of the body and another.

10. Trauma Due to Asphyxiation, Drowning and Immersion

These types of events are considered highly traumatic and dangerous. We cannot be without breathing for more than three or four minutes, without beginning to experience serious consequences at the level of brain oxygenation. After a while, the state of loss of neurons can lead to a deep coma, with total loss of consciousness in an irreversible way.

An accident where we are left underwater without being able to come to the surface can be terrifying. The drowning sensations are of deep impact and are accompanied by high intensity activation of the defense system, movements to try to overcome the difficulty. Intrusive images, sense of disorientation, swallowing water and feeling in this situation should also be worked on at the time of the sessions. It is of vital importance to recover normal respiratory patterns, to reprocess high intensity discharges, to unload extremities and to reorganize neck movements, to work on the dissociation that may have been provoked; it is also necessary to help the person to face fears and the fear of reliving these memories.

In some cases, it is advisable to have a therapist to sustain a field of stability and to attend to the activations that can be massive or of high intensity. It is very important to maintain eye contact, to maintain contact with the present moment and to reduce the activation, so as not to create conditions of re-traumatization.

11. Trauma Due to Blows to the Head, Closed and Open Cranial Traumatization

Traumatic Brain Injuries or ECTs are considered serious injuries, which can generate inflammation, hemorrhages due to the impact, increased intracranial pressure and in some cases loss of consciousness, which is why they are recognized as accidents of high severity and life-threatening. Emergency medical assistance should be sought.

In this type of accident, the effects of the concussion severely alter the processes of consciousness, balance and sense of reality. Losing consciousness causes a lapse of awareness that alters memory processes, causes dizziness, nausea, headaches due to swelling accompanied by vomiting and overall physical weakness.

In relation to the effects, these are classified according to the type of blow, if it is a closed ECT, when there is no rupture of the meninges and there is no damage to the skull; and in the open ECT there may be rupture of the meninges, damage to the skull, penetration of the object of impact if it is the case, so we are facing an eminent vital risk. In both cases we have the following symptoms identified by the ACHS (Chilean Safety Association).[35]

Mild symptoms:

- Altered level of consciousness (drowsiness, difficult to awaken or similar changes)
- Confusion, feeling absent or not thinking clearly
- Headache.
- Loss of consciousness
- Loss of memory or amnesia of events prior to the injury or immediately after the person regains consciousness
- Nausea and vomiting
- Seeing flashing lights
- Sensation of missing periods of time

---

[35] Ref : https://www.workerhospital.cl/detail-news/2019/everything-you-need-to-know-about-tec-or-encephalo-cranial-injury

Severe symptoms:

- Changes in alertness and consciousness
- Seizures or convulsions
- Muscle weakness on one or both sides of the body
- Persistent confusion
- Persistent unconsciousness or coma
- Repeated vomiting
- Uneven pupils
- Unusual eye movements
- Gait abnormalities.

In PHP sessions and before events such as those mentioned above, we work the musculature associated with the neck and scalp in order to reorganize the exploration response and the defense orientation. We need to connect the neck, spinal cord, sacrum, coccyx and feet. We renegotiate through sensation, working the symptoms we have described in the order they appear throughout the sessions, as it is likely that we need to work very deeply on all the elements of dissociation, loss of consciousness, loss of memories and balance, sexual problems, fear of heights, loss of balance and body center of gravity.

Catalina case:

Jules was 10 years old when he had an accident. He fell from a tree and his leg was broken in several parts. He had many surgeries and had to be in a cast for almost a year. Because he had so many surgeries, he lost the connection between his leg and his hip, which made it impossible for him to maintain relational stability.

We worked by proposing an imagery to his body, he would be a kite gliding through the sky very gently and falling on a mountain of cushions. In that session for the first time, he managed to connect again with his leg and then gradually resumed his soccer practices without problems.

Exercises:

1. What emotion do I feel when I have fallen?

   Remember, it can be anger, sorrow, fear or pain. Take into account the way in which you fell and remember the emotion of that moment. Move your diaphragm by placing the four fingers of your two hands in the center of your chest. Move them backwards, as if circling your ribs, towards your back, breathing deeply five times. This exercise will help you to reorient the defense response and reestablish a good connection with the body.

2. Use a yoga ball and five cushions. You will place the yoga ball in the center and the cushions around it. You will stand on the yoga ball and simulate the way you fell. Gradually, slowly and consciously, find the position you need to regain your balance again. Repeat these movements, sensing the sensations of the body, breathing consciously and observing how you stand upright.

12. Car Accident Trauma

This type of trauma is, unfortunately, more common than we think. It occurs daily and involves different degrees of physical and psychological damage. At the moment of the accident, the fact of being accompanied by other people or alone, has affective implications and puts us in a situation of intense vulnerability.

In certain instances, when confronted with accidents, the individual becomes conscious of the situation and realizes their inability to escape. In other scenarios, everything unfolds suddenly and swiftly. We might find ourselves forcibly ejected through the windshield, experiencing the impact of an airbag, or even losing touch with reality entirely. These impacts can result in various injuries, exposed fractures, and extensive physical damage. There's also the possibility of becoming trapped within the wreckage.

The collision occurs rapidly, often accompanied by violent jolts and a cacophonous noise. It can lead to rollovers, a loss of control over the vehicle, and even a loss of consciousness. The extent of the damage varies widely, ranging from mild fright to instantaneous fatality. Frequently, we're not in the driver's seat; we occupy the co-pilot position or the back seats, which exacerbates the sensation of helplessness and contributes to an experience where we feel adrift and devoid of control.

In massive accidents we may witness the death of one of those who accompany us or have to attend to other people who are also injured. In other words, surviving a car accident has many elements that activate the psychological defenses; the emotional dissociation of those who collaborate in the rescue appears.

We work on reorganizing the body movements of shoulders, elbows, neck, legs and hands. In addition, we separate the different moments that accompany the accident, we work on the discharge of activations, the movements that remained frozen in the body. Emotions are addressed, especially terror, fear, and the anguish of becoming aware of the accident.

At the moment of the accident, we may have had to attend to another person. This causes us to put aside for a moment our own experience of trauma to focus on the other person.

During the session, we once again deconstruct the event into its individual components, allowing us to regain a heightened awareness of the personal experience. We engage in targeted exercises aimed at regulating the autonomic nervous system. These exercises work to desensitize the body from the grip of emotions, sounds, pain, and the sensations of fear and anxiety that might have become lodged within it.

This therapeutic approach proves especially valuable in accidents where circumstances require us to await assistance. In these instances, individuals often navigate through moments of solitude, entrapment, and abandonment as they patiently anticipate help's arrival.

The consequences of the trauma could cause nightmares, sleep problems, restless sleep, pain, dizziness, feeling disconnected and disoriented. This can lead to sleep disorders, anxiety, fear of driving or other means of transportation.

Mariann's case:

"In a car accident, my head hit the base of my skull. I remember the exact moment when I started to turn left in my truck. The next moment I see myself lying in the passenger seat, and the car was moving in the middle of a ditch on the side of the road. I woke up with a huge headache, glass everywhere, a sharp pain on the side of my body and I didn't understand what had happened. A bus had hit my truck and I didn't feel any noise from the impact, nor did I know how I ended up without control of the vehicle. I could never understand how I was hit, what happened at that moment, who hit me or how long I was unconscious. When I got out of the vehicle, I felt dizzy, my vision was blurred, and I felt that all sounds affected me. I was disoriented and had a bad headache. At that moment the police arrested me and the bus driver for injuries. I was in the police station for more than two hours, until I was taken to the hospital and hospitalized for two weeks. I remember having yellow spots in my vision, persistent headaches and dizziness, as well as pain in my neck and bruises on the left side of my body. Within weeks of leaving the hospital I had to take a mechanic exam, and when I read, I immediately forgot what I read; "it was the hardest exam of my life." My inability to remember what I read lasted more than two months, and I was left with a calcification where I received the impact. When I was discharged, I had to go back to pick up my truck and take it with me from the police station, where it had been left.

At that time, I didn't know about trauma and I didn't have any therapy, so, shaking from head to toe, with my hands sweating and my mouth dry, I got into the vehicle until I calmed down.

Once I managed to get behind the wheel, "I gathered my courage and drove home feeling that I could overcome the terror of driving again."

Patterns of accidents have been observed to repeat themselves, like an unconscious traumatic pattern. Many times, people had more than one and do not remember it. Usually, the tension is frozen in the shoulders and they acquire a contracted position, shoulders up, and tightening the neck. This is the energy accumulated from the trauma and needs to be released, or else symptoms will appear in the body.

Catalina case:

A psychiatrist in California learned that I worked with Somatic Experiencing® and PHP. She came to see me as she had been suffering from back pain for many years. When I start my sessions, I usually ask about the issue to be worked on and begin the session with somatic work or exercises with the Vagus Nerve. "This time, because of her pain, I decided to do Somatic first. I read in her intake form, that she had been in a car accident in Europe. I asked her if she agreed to work with this accident event, and she said yes. I asked her if she remembered what the day was like and where she was going". She said, "My husband was driving, we were not doing well, we were thinking about divorce. It was a cloudy day and I was feeling disconnected". As she said this, she raised her right arm up above her head and I took the opportunity to ask her: "I want you to keep your arm up there and feel the sensation that is inside your arm". She tells me she feels cold and burning. I tell her: "keep feeling it" and she says "Oh, now I remember that with this arm I was passing some French Fries to my friend who was in the back seat, and when I passed them to him, we crashed. He died in that accident."

At that moment her whole body began to tremble. I told her that it was her nervous system regulating itself and not to be scared. She lay down on the table, hold the points of her heart and she lay down there until she finished regulating. She never came back after that session; her back pain was gone.

Exercise for car accident:

Let's start by recalling the incident in parts. Recall what you were doing before you got into the car. Notice your sensations in your head, limbs and the rest of your body. Remember whether it was day or night when you encountered the other car; remember the sound of the impact and imagine changing it to a soft one, like the sound of a bird chirping. Notice if there are currents of energy moving in your body and let them move, they are a sign that the muscles and joints are reconnecting and resetting. Lay down and rest.

13. Trauma from Sexual Violence

Sexual violence can intrude into our lives during childhood, and its grip might feel inescapable. Often, the memory of such traumatic experiences resurfaces gradually over time rather than immediately.

In certain cases, as parents or caregivers, we might remain oblivious to instances of sexual violation that a son or daughter endures, sometimes repeatedly or persistently. This silence may stem from their reluctance to disclose the ordeal or their inability to comprehend what has transpired. This constitutes a violation not only of their physical autonomy but also their psychological well-being. Predicting the extent of the psychological impact on the child and the enduring imprints of such sexual trauma on their life remains elusive.

There exist what we term as traumatogenic contexts, intricate family situations characterized by elements such as domestic violence, problematic drug use, poverty, and mental health challenges among caregivers or parents. Within these contexts, there's a heightened likelihood that a child will be left defenseless and neglected, potentially exposing them to severe physical transgressions including beatings, maltreatment, manipulation, and sexual assault.

Emphasizing the early detection of sexual trauma becomes paramount. Some symptoms that might manifest include heightened stress, anxiety, nocturnal terrors, engagement in play with traumatic themes, premature sexualization, and/or self-inflicted harm. Particularly when abuse occurs at a tender age and information is scarce, establishing a connection between these behaviors and sexual abuse or relational trauma proves challenging.

Frequently, instances of abuse inflicted by the very adults entrusted with responsibility are downplayed or even denied within the family dynamic. In such scenarios, the child experiences profound disorientation in response to the absence of protection and support.

Abusive situations may be carried out covertly during the child's care, at bedtime. These moments of unprotecting may occur in places that are not considered risky: in the nursery, at school or in family social activities.

The impact of sexual abuse on the child can be a "disorganizing" factor when changes in the child's body occur, especially in adolescence, when there is a greater possibility of problematizing the experience of abuse. Restlessness, maladjustment, low self-esteem, overweight, anxiety, fears, insecurity, are painful, non-integrated traces that

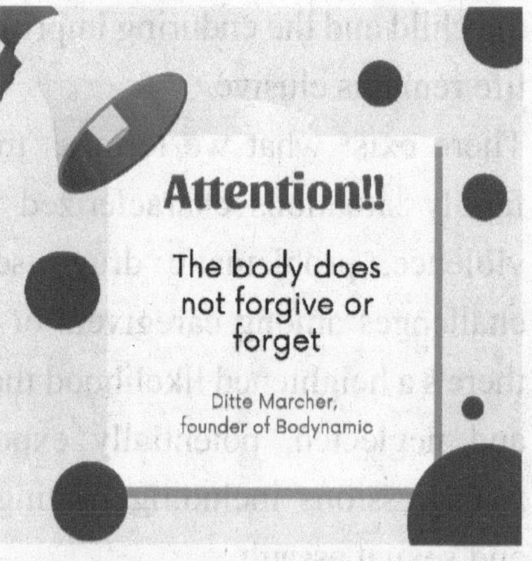

become trauma, post-traumatic stress disorder and are lived with much suffering that is only shared in contexts of "protection-repair".

It is very common that around the age of eighteen there is already an awareness of having experienced a type of sexual abuse or harassment. Usually, in therapy, the client must deal with self-rejection, with emotions of rage and helplessness, flashbacks and also with the first symptoms of PTSD. There is a persistent feeling of unprotectedness and unavoidable shame, which disorganizes unconscious internal aspects. It is even possible to observe an impact on the organization of the personality.

Through therapeutic intervention, the affected person can express the trauma and, with the accompaniment of the therapist, find the voice to recognize the pain, the impact and get rid of guilt.

In working with the body from the point of view of adaptive responses, the memories of sexual trauma are installed in different parts of the body. In certain instances, simultaneous with the occurrence of the traumatic experience, patterns of memories, somatic sensations, emotional responses, visual imagery, and sensory signals are formed. These leave imprints that necessitate identification in order to reorganize the body's defense mechanisms in response to danger.

We cannot separate the symptom from the environment and the affective conditions of the client. We cannot work the sexual trauma only through the psychopharmacological management of the sequelae of anxiety, terror or anguish, without looking at the history "written on the skin". We need to give the unheard voice a chance to begin the path of integration of the sexual trauma.

The therapist needs to understand the aspects of the Autonomic Nervous System overload responses; it requires observation of posture, gestures, looks, in order to open a therapeutic space.

Self-regulation, neuroception (+) and the ability to reorganize the defense response, are the context that accompanies the essential elements of the Polyvagal Theory and somatic work.

In sexual trauma intervention, somatic touch can be a working strategy that acts on the boundaries broken at the moment of sexual trauma; however, there must be work prior to the PHP session in order to stabilize the client.

In the therapeutic approach to sexual trauma, a considerable degree of specialization is essential. It entails addressing intricate aspects such as dissociation, emotional distress, the erosion of personal boundaries, restructuring defense mechanisms, and the pivotal task of reestablishing a connection between the body and a wholesome sense of pleasure. This connection often becomes disrupted, pushing the body into a state of immobilization.

Through a gradual process of reconnecting with the body, we facilitate the integration of intense emotions such as rage, pain, vulnerability, fear, and shame. These are intermingled with sexual sensations that contrast with the experience of sexual trauma. By articulating and narrating these sensations, we establish a bridge between different psychological processes.

Furthermore, by guiding the individual's attention toward recognizing their immediate surroundings and jointly assessing the absence of danger, we send reassuring signals to their neuroceptive system. This in turn widens the individual's window of tolerance, contributing to their stabilization. To manage and regulate arousal, it's imperative to mitigate stress and anxiety by employing techniques like controlled breathing and heart rate regulation.

Catalina case:

M is a woman in her forties. She came to see me more than a year ago because she had been suffering from migraines for almost ten years. She had consulted doctors, nutritionists, and psychotherapists, she was not getting relief. She spent a fortune trying to find a solution. She cried constantly and could not attend activities with her preteen daughter. Her migraines would disappear for a few days and then, without warning, return.

When we started working together, I noticed that not only did she have a headache, but she also experienced a lot of embarrassment. She shared that from the age of twelve she had been in a cult in India and was sexually abused by many men in the cult. She came every week and cried constantly. She had never had a social life, nor attended parties, and was in the habit of dressing very conservatively, covering herself with a head scarf since a young age.

We started the therapeutic work by doing Somatic Experiencing® sessions, vagus nerve exercises and holding the points associated with sexuality, shame, fear and the STO points. M began to learn to move the energy outward and not inward in her body. After a while she noticed that the migraines began to fade. Slowly her body began to open up and reconnect; the fear faded away and she became more open to social life. She left the cult and wrote a book exposing her traumatic experience. She also decided to make a documentary on the subject with HBO. Today she is a PHP practitioner and has a boyfriend for a year. Her daughter has also had productive sessions with me.

Exercise:

1. Sit in a chair or on the edge of a couch. While rocking forward, squeeze your anus. Then while rocking backward, release it. Repeat the exercise seven times. Use your breath and feel the connection with your sit bones, hip bones and buttocks. Rest and repeat two more times.
2. Using four fingers of each hand, from the center of the chin, gently and lightly stroke the skin upwards past the

cheeks until you reach the forehead. Rest. Repeat about five times. This exercise is for the vagus nerve to reconnect the system of social engagement and to remove the shame.

3. With the index finger and thumb make like a crab claw. We will hold behind each ankle one at a time, where the sex points are located. Squeeze the points for about five minutes breathing deeply. Perceive how the energy goes up the legs, and rest. You can do this exercise as many times as you need. This exercise is to unblock sexual traumas.

14. War Trauma and Collective Trauma

When we are confronted with war and collective trauma, there is a context of permanent risk, of extreme threat that leads us to feel threatened, terrified, disorganized, hyper activated in the survival mode and disconsolate before the suffering of loved ones and the community.

The need to behave aggressively, to attack in self-defense, to shoot another human being, is usually a break in the psychic life of a person. Whoever makes use of his/her instincts, without being able to avoid it, is subjected to destructive impulses. This state of struggle represents a vital limit. Being in a permanent state of flight, hypervigilance and terror affects the nervous system and disorganizes the psychic structure. Survival becomes a burden, guilt floods us and we feel that we do not deserve to be alive. The expression of the violence of war makes us lose our sense of reality and the meaning of life. These experiences are sometimes accompanied by torture, imprisonment, physical and psychological abuse, and extreme cases such as being present at attacks and the death of close significant others.

Over time, war trauma leads to loss of social contact, to avoid connecting with others as at all costs, with clear symptoms of PTSD. Specialists are required to address these highly complex processes. Renegotiating survival, reprogramming memories, returning to the body, repairing broken bonds and boundaries, will allow us to return from the internal hell in which this terror remains encapsulated.

Catalina case:

In 1998, I worked in session with a man who at the age of four had been in the holocaust in Germany. While holding the points, he remembered the moment when he was separated from his parents. They wrote his name on a piece of cloth pinned to his jacket and put him on a train. After that he remembered no more. I helped him reconnect with his body. I remember one day he commented to me: "For the first time at my age, sixty-five years old, I feel joy". As a teacher and practitioner, that special session will be etched in my memory because it made so clear to me the value of this work that allows me to help others reconnect and feel their heart again.

Trauma and Neurodevelopmental Disorders

The PHP approach in special situations

The disease is not the person. Personality disorders, psychological problems, or having grown up with a traumatic imprint or acquiring a genetic condition, leads us to face personal challenges. We need to address our conflicts, pains and emotions from a healing perspective, where we deserve to feel stable, secure and with psychological and social resources that allow us to be autonomous.

Many times, we need to understand that in childhood and adolescence there are different processes occurring simultaneously: the development of the nervous system, social learning, learning skills, personality structure; all this supported by biological cycles determined by DNA and hormones that make our brain increase its volume and develop its structures, stimulate the sexual organs, secondary sexual traits appear, and we have a harmonious growth of tissues, muscles and bones. However, there are genetic and environmental predisposing factors that can affect these cycles, which should be detected as soon as possible in order to address these conditions and provide the necessary support so that the child or adolescent can develop to his or her full biological, psychological and social potential.

Neurodevelopmental disorders are diverse; however, to some degree we can accompany these children and young people in the stimulation of the nervous system through the points.

Many times, children with neurodevelopmental disorders can experience episodes of trauma that originate from the vulnerability of their condition, they are more exposed to situations of traumatic risk. We know that so much can be done for them, so that they can face these situations, helping them to reduce their stress and significantly improve their quality of life. We want to emphasize the need to be alert to groups more vulnerable to traumatic situations and the application of therapies aimed at improving their quality of life.

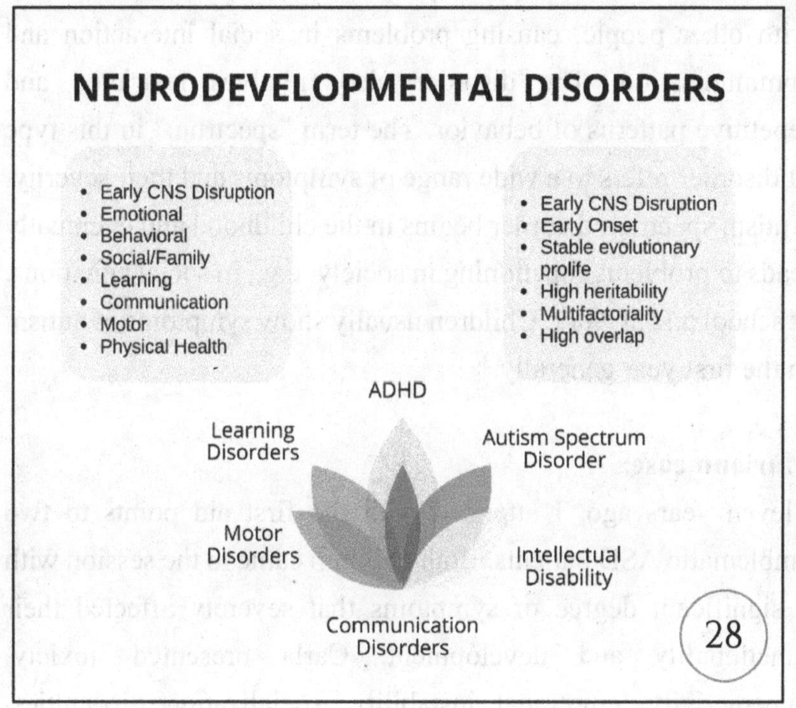

A. Autism Spectrum Disorder

Autism Spectrum Disorder (ASD) is incorporated within the neurodevelopmental disorders, included in the group of conditions with onset in the developmental period.

General description:

Autism spectrum disorder, is a developmentally related condition of the brain that affects the way a person perceives and socializes with other people, causing problems in social interaction and communication. The disorder also involves restricted and repetitive patterns of behavior. The term "spectrum" in this type of disorder refers to a wide range of symptoms and their severity. Autism spectrum disorder begins in the childhood and eventually leads to problems functioning in society, e.g., in social situations, at school and at work. Children usually show symptoms of autism in the first year generally.[36]

Mariann case:

Eleven years ago, I attended with the first aid points to two emblematic ASD patients. Both children came to the session with a significant degree of symptoms that severely affected their functionality and development. Carla presented anxiety, hyperactivity, emotional instability, socialization difficulties, symptoms that at six years of age seemed more like a hyperactivity problem.

---

[36] Ref: https://www.mayoclinic.org/es/diseases-conditions/autism-spectrum-disorder/symptoms-causes/syc-20352928

Camilo, ten years old, came to the session diagnosed with autism. He presented sensory difficulties, inability to pay attention to things other than what he was interested in and lack of social skills with his peers.

At that time, I was known as a therapist specializing in Neuroscience applied to trauma, Somatic Experiencing® and PHP and had only worked with adults. However, after five years of practice I began to work with children and young people because of an experience that I will now relate: I intuitively used the first aid points when a girl suffered an accident in the snow. I was there when she slipped in the snow. I went over and gave her first aid with PHP. She quickly came out of shock. By the time she received medical help, an hour after the accident, she was conscious and waiting calmly despite the pain of her injured knee. This experience made me feel that it was possible to approach working with children and youth and break ground for PHP therapy in age groups I had not worked with before.

Mariann case:

Carla came to the session wearing a ballet tutu and braids. Her mother was a schoolteacher and was looking for a way to help her daughter who was unable to sit in the classroom. As soon as I saw her, I was struck by how restless the girl was; however, her movements were not chaotic, but rather, exploratory, almost hypervigilant. When I lay down her on the table, the most important thing was to make contact with her through her eyes. While perceiving the sensations of her body, and to generate a dialogue, I asked her why she wore her braids, her ballet tutu and what it was like to go to school. Suddenly, she began to move her pupils gently back and forth, interhemispherically, regulating her brain. She took a deep breath, and her stomach began to pulse intensely. I asked her how she was feeling, and she replied that she felt that her teacher did not want her and that she was afraid to go to the classroom. I asked her to tell me what her room was like and how we could make her feel safer and calmer. She replied, "I would like to be able to go out when I need to, take a walk in the yard and come back to the room when I feel better." At the end of the first session, we coordinated with her mom to make a special request to Carla's school about her outings and we agreed to continue working weekly.

The following week Carla came into the session beaming. She threw herself on the table and as we began to work on the points, she told me that she had managed to sit in her seat at times. Weeks later she commented that she had also been able to engage in communication with a couple of girls and that her teacher did not seem so terrible and threatening to her. Thus, gradually, through working mainly with the viscera and fear, Carla was able to reorganize her stability and confidence. She learned to self-regulate by leaving the room, and the number of times she left the room became smaller and smaller. Eventually she was able to have a close relationship with her teacher.

Over the years, I always accompanied Carla during periods of stress. I came to understand her personality, her needs, and she went from being a hypervigilant child to an outstanding student. At the age of sixteen, she still felt she had significant difficulties in her social relationships. She was finally diagnosed with

Autism, a diagnosis that made a lot of sense to her and helped her to understand her processes and deal better with her anxiety and manias. Carla is currently studying law in college.

Mariann case:
Seeing Camilo was a treat. I could hear him from a far asking his mom to buy him cheese empanadas or ice cream after the session. Red-haired, green-eyed and ten years old, Camilo had been diagnosed with autism early on and his mother wanted him to be able to control his impulses better and socialize more.

Every time he came to my session, he would ask me to hold his points and gently caress the inside of his arms or wrists while I was holding them. These stimuli calmed him down and step by step he was surrendering to relaxation, to regulate his breathing, to better contain his anxiety and to make eye contact. For a year we worked on strengthening his socialization, improving his self-regulation and having more eye contact. He finally began to be calmer, more attentive to the outside world and less anxious. Within what could be improved, he was able to establish better bonds, reconnect parts of his body and feel more connected with others.

Many times, in the work with the points we see in people levels of changes and improvements that surprise us. The body is capable of strengthening and maturing processes that have been stopped, hindered, and, in a natural way, resolves through these stimuli processes of sensory integration, dissociation, trauma and stress.

Yes, in some cases, it is difficult to give a clinical explanation, since there are multiple factors that facilitate the change. However, at PHP we know that we are moving on the frontier of what we do not yet know about neurobiology, the body's capacity for adaptation and regeneration, and interdependent intra-psychic processes. Therefore, with each patient we open the way to new promises of improvement.

B. Attention Deficit / Hyperactivity Disorder (ADHD)

Attention Deficit / Hyperactivity Disorder is a neurodevelopmental disorder of neurobiological nature originating in childhood and affecting throughout life, characterized by the presence of three typical symptoms:

- Attention deficit.
- Impulsivity.
- Motor and/or vocal hyperactivity.

ADHD is a persistent pattern of hyperactivity and impulsivity and/or inattention that interferes with the child's functioning and is present in two or more settings, such as home, work, school, and social situations.

These behaviors are usually seen early. Difficulty in sitting still, sustaining constant attention and being able to concentrate.

Usually there is dispersion, restlessness, low ability to follow tasks and orders, executive functions may also be disorganized and in turn, these behaviors are considered disruptive at school level, so children often require pharmacological treatment to deal with these difficulties.

It must be considered that each child with this disorder manifests the same symptoms and with different intensity (being able to be mild, moderate or severe).

Mariann case:

When Nico came to the session, he was ten years old, he did not look directly at people into their eyes. His mother commented that he had no friends at school and that his self-esteem was very low due to his school difficulties. He had repeated a grade and was back in third grade, and they had asked him to leave school. He was unable to take notes on his homework in the classroom, nor was he able to complete the written exercises dictated by the teacher. He was considered disruptive, restless, talkative and distracted. He was frustrated because he fell behind in activities and was embarrassed to see that his classmates were making progress and he was not.

At the beginning of the sessions, we worked on the first aid points repeatedly for several sessions; in conjunction with coordinating with the school on how to do his homework and reinforcing support routines at home to study.

As we worked on the points, Nico began to loosen up and his mother said that after each session she noticed that he was in better spirits. As his nervous system became more regulated, he felt calmer. As he learned to feel his body, he felt more confident and relaxed. It was observed that he began to show more interest in collaborating with his activities, more willingness to reinforce his study habits, which gradually encouraged him to try not to repeat, since he had three months to make an effort to obtain better results.

When I worked the points, I noticed how his viscera was collapsed. There was a distension, a feeling of immobility, no vitality, little pulsation. His stomach was tight and closed, leaving the emotional tension inside the child. Children and young people experience life in early stages up to adolescence from emotion, these are like an active volcano that lives inside, added to the hyperactivity and stress he experienced at the time of being evaluated or having to perform. Deep feelings of anger, fear of not being capable and insecurity made him sad and unmotivated. Beliefs that crystallized in his handicapped mind only further reinforced the difficulties.

In this sense PHP really helps to discharge these emotions and feelings. It allows stress to be reduced and the child or young person can have a space for self-regulation and his or her nervous system to receive the necessary stimulation to enhance improvements.

Sometimes it is of great support for the child, however, it is necessary to complement with multidisciplinary treatments of an occupational therapist, psychologist, support teacher, neurologist, psychiatrist and/or doctors, if the conditions require it. Emphasizing that mobilizing the emotional contents of frustration, fear, anger, shame, are a tremendous burden and a barrier that separates the child from positive relationships, from a healthy self-image despite having this difficulty, which can be worked on.

C. Bipolar Disorder

It is characterized by changes in mood, as well as changes in activity and energy levels. The disorder often involves experiencing shifts between elevated moods and periods of depression. The elevated moods can be pronounced and are called mania or hypomania.

In the manic episode the individual feels extremely happy, euphoric, energetic or even irritable. On the other hand, in the depressive episode you may feel sad, hopeless, indifferent, depressed, or have very low energy levels. Also, you may have both manic and depressive symptoms simultaneously, also known as a mixed episode. In addition, it causes changes in thinking, sleep, behavior, energy, and ability to perform activities of daily living.

Types of bipolar disorder [37]:

- **Bipolar I disorder**: Defined by manic episodes lasting at least seven days or symptomatology so severe that it requires inpatient care. It also frequently includes

---

[37] Ref: https://blog.neuronup.com/bipolar-disorder-what-is-types-cause-symptomsdiagnosis-and-treatment/

depressive episodes lasting no less than two weeks. This typology may involve mixed episodes.

- **Bipolar II disorder:** Includes depressive episodes and hypomanic episodes, less severe than manic episodes. Psychotic symptoms may appear during depressive episodes.

- **Cyclothymic disorder:** Also known as cyclothymic, it is characterized, as in bipolar II disorder, by depressive and hypomanic symptoms, but with the exception that they have a lower intensity or duration than the aforementioned episodes. There are differences in the duration of the episodes (crises) according to age, being at least two years in adults and one year in adolescents and children.

- **Unspecified bipolar disorder:** This refers to those bipolar conditions that do not coincide with any of the diagnosed categories.

Catalina Case:

The importance of a specific memory in 2009. Tiff, a 42-year-old woman diagnosed with Bipolar Depression, came to see me for treatment. She called me on the phone to have an interview and tell me about her case personally. I spoke with her for 30 minutes and she asked me a lot of questions, checking up on me. She had been to different types of therapies and treatments and was very afraid to take on a new one. She had a fear of losing control of her life. She told me that when she was a little girl, at the age of five, she was diagnosed with Bipolar Depression and they started her on antidepressant medication. They progressively increased the medication, and she felt worse and worse. She became very upset that they were constantly changing her medication to stabilize her. As a child, she was very afraid to go to school; she was also afraid of teachers. Her parents had separated. Medical treatment gradually allowed her to connect with more people. She even had a complex marriage, with abuse, fights and manipulation.

I explained to her that trauma work is done by regulating the nervous system and the Vagus Nerve. Certain exercises are done with Somatic Experiencing® and PHP, which work with different organs and glands that connect with the three parts of the brain: reptilian, mammalian, and the neocortex. Through this process it is possible to achieve internal stability. At the time of the session, she had symptoms of immobility (activation of the dorsal pathway). I explained to her that we would work on regulating the system and mobilizing the fight and flight responses. She left that day and called me after three months to begin working with me regularly. We first explored her feelings and started doing grounding work, which means coming back into the body. In her case, there was dissociation from the body, because of medications and fears. With Tiff, I did basic exercises, using simple techniques to bring the nervous system to relaxation, and release the viscera. I usually teach my clients to perform an exercise protocol themselves. The goal is to have a connection with the person.

During her divorce mediation stage, I did a supportive intervention between her and the husband to reach agreements. I told her that we could work for only two hours on this process. She did not listen and in an act of uncontrolled behavior, she assaulted her husband by throwing a plastic bottle at his head. Firemen were called. I asked them to let me work with her. I put my hands on her feet and looked her straight in the eyes until she regained her emotional stability. The firemen who were already at the scene were surprised to see the sudden change, and as a result, they asked me to instruct them on this work methodology. It is necessary to establish an atmosphere of safety, refuge, hope and the possibility of healing so that people with trauma can open up to connect with their bodies. The story comes from their heads, from their thoughts and memories, creating dissociation and re-traumatization.

D. Anxiety Disorders

The anxiety disorder is a psychological disorder that implies the anticipation on the part of the subject to a sensation of a future threat.
It is characterized by fear, worry and anxiety. It is a persistent disorder that alters behavior. Fear involves an emotional response to a threat, whether real or imagined.

Types of anxiety disorders:

- **Generalized anxiety disorder (GAD):** This disorder is characterized by excessive worry about everyday events. While some stress and worry are a common part of life, GAD involves such excessive worry that it interferes with a person's well-being and functioning.

- **Social anxiety disorder:** Social anxiety disorder is a fairly common psychological disorder that involves an irrational fear of being watched, judged, humiliated and/or embarrassed. The anxiety caused by this disorder can have a major impact on an individual's life and make it difficult to function in school, work and other social settings.

- **Specific phobias:** These phobias involve an extreme fear of a specific object or situation in the environment. Some examples of common specific phobias include fear of spiders, fear of heights or fear of snakes. The four main types of specific phobias involve natural (thunder, lightning, tornadoes), medical (medical procedures, dental procedures, medical equipment), animal (dogs, snakes, insects) and situational (small spaces, leaving the house, driving) events. When confronted with the feared object or situation, people with phobias may experience nausea, tremors, rapid heartbeat and even fear of dying.

- **Panic disorder:** This psychiatric disorder is characterized by panic attacks that may seem unexpected and for no reason. Because of this, people with panic disorder often experience anxiety and worry about the possibility of having another panic attack. People may begin to avoid situations and environments where attacks have occurred in the past or where they may occur in the future. This can create significant impairments in many areas of daily life and make it difficult to carry out daily routines.

- **Separation anxiety disorder:** This condition is a type of anxiety disorder that involves an excessive amount of fear or anxiety related to being separated from attachment figures. People are often familiar with the idea of separation. In these cases, the very idea of moving away from the attachment subject produces an irrational fear. For example, the fear of young children of being separated from their parents. However, older children and adults can also experience it. The person experiencing these symptoms may avoid moving away from home, going to school or getting married in order to stay close to the attachment figure.

In Points Holding Process (PHP), the techniques assist in regulating anxiety, addressing ruminative thoughts, excessive control beliefs, and inflexibility when confronted with experiences that necessitate adaptability rather than resistance. Being able to dissolve these patterns paves the way for the emergence of fresh patterns and novel ways to progress in life. This process aids in restoring a sense of security and vitality. Anxiety exacts a physical toll on our bodies; it exhausts us, overwhelms us, and restrains us more profoundly than we often recognize.

CHAPTER IV
POLYVAGAL THEORY AND NEURO-FLEXIBILITY.

"Every thought is a nerve impulse"

In the research conducted by Dr. Stephen Porges and his Polyvagal Theory, which we have presented throughout this book, he highlights that the distinction between emotional and social aspects stems from the evolutionary adaptations of the nervous system. The reptilian brain and the mammalian brain function differently, in relation to the autonomic nervous system. Human beings have developed the biological capacity to engage in social interactions with their peers. We can sometimes self-soothe and regulate instinctive impulses through social cues.

From the moment of birth, infants rely on care and co-regulation with their caregivers for survival. This evolutionary shift in the nervous system, from reptilian to mammalian, has led humans to cooperate, collaborate, and depend on trust in others. Intelligence alone is insufficient; we necessitate a positive neuroception. This state involves being attuned to active listening and meaningful interaction.

Our great difference with animals is to mitigate the defense reactions that one has when feeling threatened, a situation that animals do not inhibit because they are under a biological imperative system of instinctive defense.

Our relationship between the nervous system, the brain and the innervation of the cranial nerves allow the system of social commitment. This is manifested through facial expressions, eye contact, the musculature surrounding the eyes, the ability to express gestures, the smile, the tone of voice we emit, the rhythm of the voice or prosody. Everything that is expressed in the face, together with the movements of the neck, is connected vaguely to our viscera and to the regulation of the vagal brake of the heart.

As we come to understand how the brain, nervous system, glands, organs, endocrine and immune systems are organized, we come to understand the importance of the underlying dynamics of the "state" of the nervous system, and how this state affects the rest of the homeostatic processes, mood, social functions, psychological and physical health.

The Neuroscience of Security

The ability to be connected is an imperative biological need. This connectivity elevates social behavior and acts as a neuromodulator. Porges points out in his course "Polyvagal Theory: Neuro-exercises for Safety and Connection" [38]: *"Safety signals have to mutually and synchronously regulate and reduce*

---

[38] Polyvagal Theory: Neuro Exercises for Safety and Connection, Professor: Dr. Stephen Porges. 2021.

reactions to threats, to promote (psychological) accessibility and (physical) proximity."

In this process of evolution, the vagus nerve, will have two basic functions:

1. Protect in extreme cases, as a survival resource through its dorsal vagus pathway, unmyelinated, from freezing or bringing us to a state of dissolution or traumatic, where we are trapped in a state of immobility with fear. When a threat occurs, metabolic activity decreases. Often a "freeze response" occurs, as in death and disengagement behaviors, involving the unmyelinated visceral vagal unmyelinated vagal response system, via the dorsal motor neuron of the medulla root. This is the earliest autonomic nervous system (ANS) response to threat.

2. Via vagus ventral pathway, where we can find a vagal state of reciprocal interaction, and co-regulation appears, face-to-face contact, social skills connected from the viscera towards the face, cranial pairs V, VII, IX, X, XI, together with the brainstem, cortex, and neck. These are the components of the social engagement system: chewing muscles, middle ear muscles, facial muscle, larynx, pharynx, heart, bronchi and head movements. This system works if through the body we experience safety, which will allow us fearless immobility, proximity, contact and bonding.

Nervous System

The nervous system is involved with any problem related to sensation, perception, emotion, thoughts, actions or internal regulation.

Through the entire nervous system, we become aware of:

- Everything we feel
- Everything we process
- Everything we do

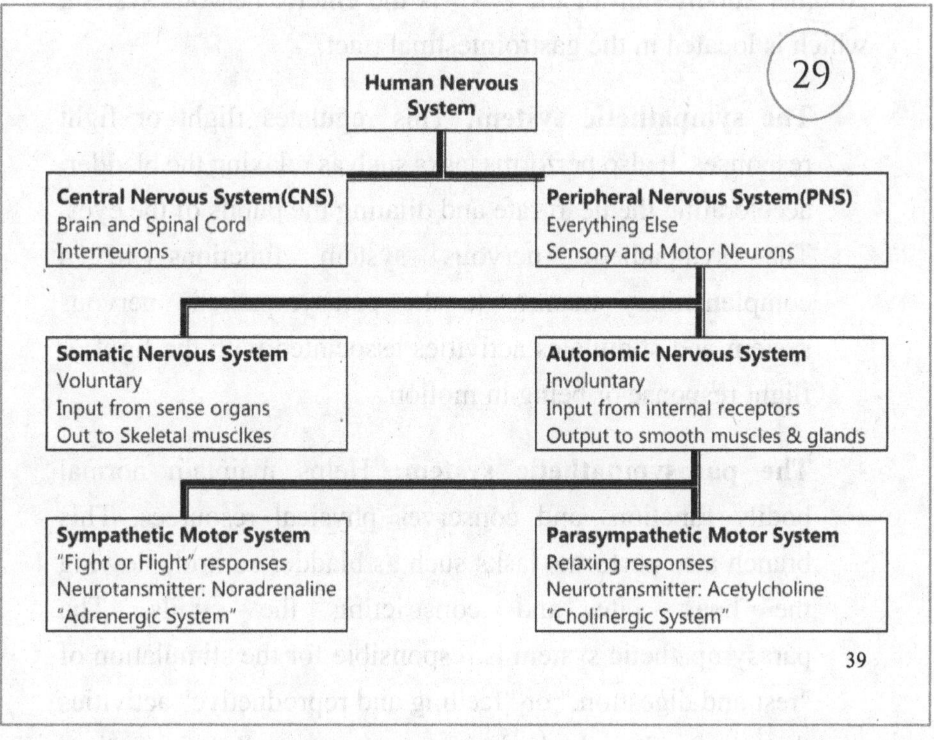

---

[39] Ref: https://solutionpharmacy.in/nervous-system/

Autonomic Nervous System

It regulates a variety of bodily processes that take place without conscious effort. The autonomic nervous system is the part of the peripheral nervous system and the central nervous system that is responsible for regulating involuntary bodily functions, such as heartbeat, blood flow, breathing and digestion. The Autonomic Nervous System (ANS) is responsible for regulating the body's unconscious actions and is divided into two subsystems: Sympathetic and Parasympathetic.

Another subdivision of the ANS is the enteric nervous system, which is located in the gastrointestinal tract.

- **The sympathetic system**: This regulates flight or fight responses. It also performs tasks such as relaxing the bladder, accelerating the heart rate and dilating the pupils of the eyes. The sympathetic nervous system functions in a complementary manner to the parasympathetic nervous system and stimulates activities associated with the fight or flight response or being in motion.

- **The parasympathetic system:** Helps maintain normal bodily functions and conserves physical resources. This branch also performs tasks such as bladder control, slowing the heart rate and constricting the pupils. The parasympathetic system is responsible for the stimulation of "rest and digestion," or "feeding and reproductive" activities that occur when the body is at rest, especially after eating, including sexual arousal, salivation, lacrimation (tears), urination, digestion and defecation.

The Vagus Nerve

It is the most complex of the cranial nerves. It is a mixed nerve. It is the main parasympathetic nerve of the body, originating in the brainstem and extending down through the face, neck, chest and abdomen, reaching the colon. It is the longest nerve in the body, originating in the brain, travels down from the neck and then passes around the digestive system, liver, spleen, pancreas, heart and lungs.

The vagus nerve provides the nucleus of communication between the PNS (Peripheral Nervous System) and the CNS (Central Nervous System). It is the core of the autonomic nervous system, connecting, monitoring and regulating the functions of organs and glands in communication with the CNS. It regulates the opposite nature of the sympathetic and parasympathetic through amyelinic and myelinic fibers; myelinic fibers conduct the neuron's electricity faster, and amyelinic fibers are slower, causing the electrical impulse to travel at a slower speed and the neuron's response to be slower.

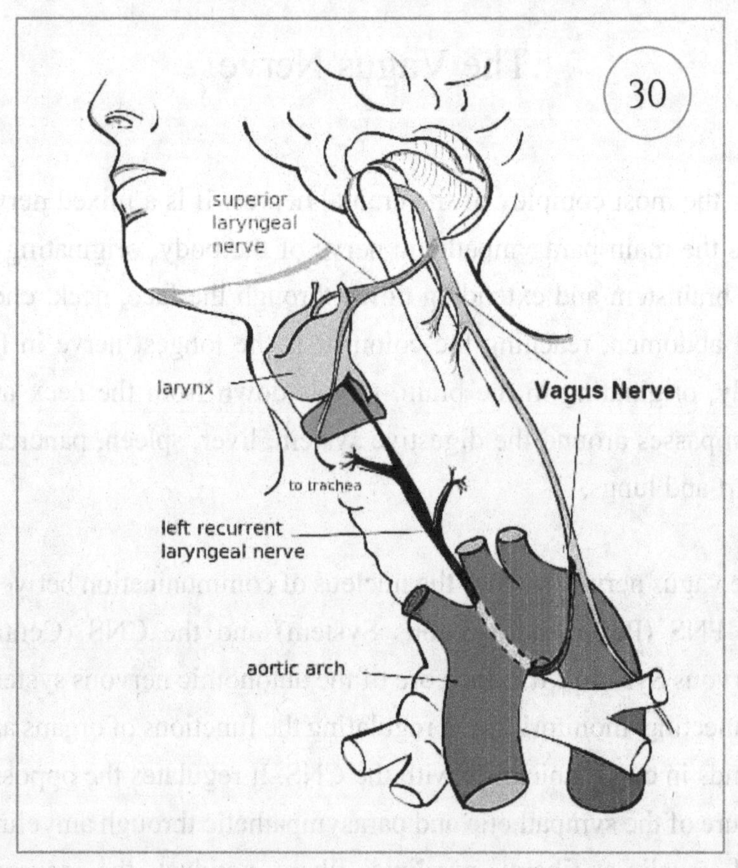

[40]

The vagus nerve carries communication from the enteric nervous system (the "second brain" in the gut) to the primary brain, the brain in the head. The autonomic nervous system plays a regulatory role in the expression of emotions and in the Social Engagement system, as described by Porges. It provides communication pathways between the medulla, amygdala and

---

[40] **Ref:** https://teachmeanatomy.info/wp-content/uploads/Overview-of-the-Major-Branches-and-Anatomical-Course-of-the-Vagus-Nerve.jpg.webp

hippocampus to access frozen energies and the source of memories.

This nerve is a major player in the parasympathetic nervous system, which serves the function of "rest and digest", the opposite of the sympathetic nervous system that is responsible for fight or flight.

The vagus nerve has two nerve branches that elicit different reactions when faced with danger.

1. **Dorsal vagus Branch (vd):** In evolutionary terms a much older part of the nervous system (vertebrates) that is activated under potential dangers, life threatening, shock, toxins, intrusions, overwhelm, neglect or other painful experiences. The nerve fibers are mostly amyelinic which produces a slow nerve response to the electrical impulse.

    - It originates in the dorsal motor nucleus in the brainstem and descends down the spinal column.
    - It mainly regulates the visceral organs below the diaphragm, such as the bladder, stomach and intestines, but also connects to the heart and lungs.

With activation of the Dorsal Vagus Branch, the freeze response is initiated and the "shut down" of metabolism and blood supply; this is a protection against hyper arousal (heartbeat, pain) and conserves metabolic resources, as it can cause a total collapse or partial freeze, such as the inability to think clearly or access words or emotions, or to move parts of the body.

The dorsal brake or dorsal vagal shift:

"If I cannot make my body safe, or if it is not safe to be me, then I will leave my body." This is a clear expression of the dorsal brake response when extreme danger appears. When this happens the ventral vagus system is inhibited, and the dorsal braking system is turned on. This allows energy to be conserved, tonic immobility due to fear to appear, allowing life to be preserved.

The parasympathetic nervous system is involved in relaxation or settling; this happens when the dorsal vagal switch is turned off; this process is also known as "rest and digest", which are states of fearless immobility, where the vagal brake is activated much more gently, allowing meditation or sleep.

Signs of dorsal displacement: Manifestation and mechanism of freezing.

This term is used when someone does not move. The term also implies a drop in body temperature. This is probably more than peripheral vasoconstriction from sympathetic shift, possibly representing a decrease in body heat production.
It occurs in the following signs of freezing:

- **Silence:** the speech organs, directed by the ventral vagal system, seem unable to coordinate when the dorsal vagal system is strongly dominant.
- **Dissociation:** this is possibly just the psychological correlate of freezing. Without movement, thought and

perception, the person loses his anchor in the body and in the here and now. He does not feel the body as his container. Involuntary defecation and urination: occur under extreme distress.

- **Fainting**: simple fainting is also known as vasovagal syndrome. While there is a great danger of injury from an unprotected fall, people who faint often feel fine afterwards. Fainting can function as an autonomic reset.
- **Shock:** Shock is a circulatory collapse. It is life threatening. We also speak of emotional shock upon hearing or witnessing something; it can be similar to fainting. Shock is manifested by speechlessness.
- **Sensation of strain**: muscles and limbs feel heavy.

2. Ventral Vagus Branch:

It is relatively new in mammalian evolution and is myelinated, i.e., the electrical impulse goes faster. It originates in the nucleus ambiguous in the brainstem.

- It is activated when it feels safe.
- It is the main actor within the Social Engagement System.

Social Engagement System or Ventral Vagal System

It consists of five cranial nerves, including the vagus nerve. It participates in most of the processes of social contact and pleasure. It is activated when we feel safe. We can control the regulation of the ventral vagus tone through our heart rate, manipulation of the heart rate through specific exercises that we will discuss later.

It guides eye contact, hearing, eating, speech (tone of voice), singing, breastfeeding, kissing, smiling, but also breathing and heart rate.

It is a bidirectional interaction system: receptive and expressive (sensory and motor nerves).

Prolonged stress or danger, or stress/danger early in life, tends to atrophy or impair the development of the ventral vagal system.

Vagal Tone

Vagus Nerve tone, or Vagal Tone, is key in the physiology of the Parasympathetic Nervous System. It is measured by tracking heart rate along with the rhythm of inhalation and exhalation. Your heart rate speeds up a little when you inhale and slows down when you exhale. The greater the difference between your heart rate when you breathe in and your heart rate when you exhale, the higher your vagal tone. A higher vagal tone means that the body can relax faster after stress.

What is a high vagal tone associated with?

High vagal tone improves the function of many body systems:

- Improved blood sugar regulation.
- There is less risk of stroke and cardiovascular disease.
- Lowers blood pressure
- Improves digestion through increased production of basic stomach and digestive enzymes
- Reduces migraine headaches
- Is associated with improved mood
- Helps reduce anxiety and increases resilience to stress.

What is low vagal tone associated with?

- Low vagal tone is associated with:
- Cardiovascular conditions and strokes.
- Depression
- Diabetes
- Chronic Fatigue Syndrome
- Cognitive impairment
- Much higher rates of inflammatory conditions.
- All autoimmune diseases (rheumatoid arthritis, inflammatory bowel disease, endometriosis, autoimmune thyroid, lupus and more).

How do we increase Vagal Tone?

The good news is that you have access to this on your own, but it requires regular practice. Here are some ways to tone the vagus nerve:

- Slow, rhythmic, diaphragmatic breathing.
- Humming. Since the vagus nerve is connected to the vocal cords, humming stimulates it mechanically. You can hum a song or repeat the 'OM' sound.
- Talking: useful because of the connection to the vocal cords.
- Washing your face with cold water.
- Meditation. Loving-kindness meditation promotes feelings of goodwill towards yourself and others.
- Balancing the gut micro biome through probiotics.
- The presence of healthy bacteria in the gut creates a positive feedback loop through the vagus nerve.

1.   Traumatic Coupling:

When arousal leads to a traumatic response of the nervous system, dysregulating it, what is called a coupling occurs. This involves a general stress response, which overcomes the level of response of the parasympathetic system, over the sympathetic or vice versa. This will depend on the intensity of the stimulus.

Acute Stress Reaction

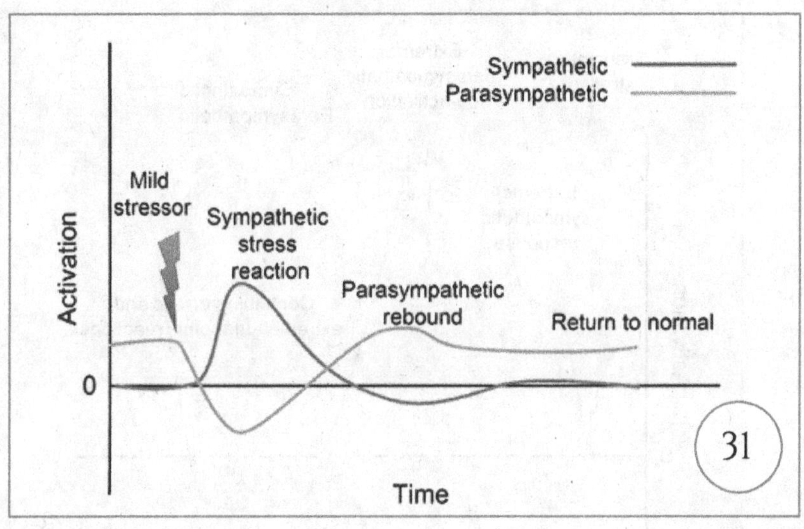

Chronic Stress Response

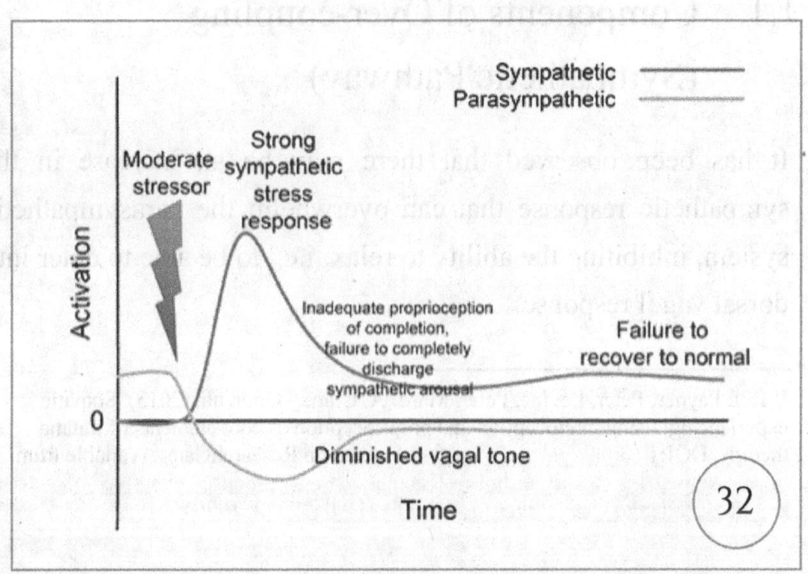

Traumatic Stress Response

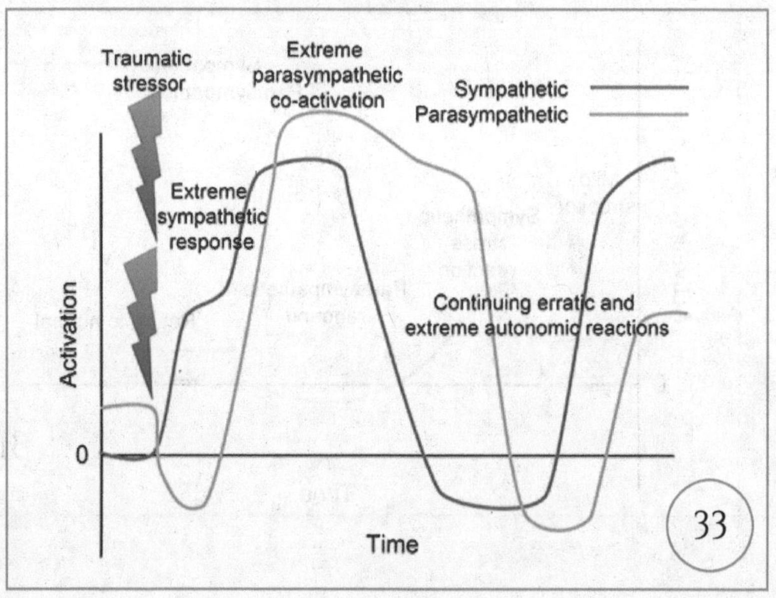

41

1.1 Components of Over-coupling (Sympathetic Pathway)

It has been observed that there may be an increase in the sympathetic response that can overwhelm the parasympathetic system, inhibiting the ability to relax, i.e., to be able to enter into dorsal vagal response.

---

[41] Ref: Payner, Peter, Levine, Peter, Mardi A, Crane - Godreau. (2015). Somatic experiencing: using interoception and proprioception as core elements of trauma therapy. DOI:10.3389/fpsyg.2015.00093 Figures on ResearchGate. Available from: https://www.researchgate.net/figure/Traumatic-stress-response-In-the-face-of-extreme-challenge-when-either-the-situation-is_fig3_272519064

The components of this sympathetic activation response are physical: Constriction and tension.

- The images are too fast for our brain and the nervous system is altered in response to them.
- There is a feeling of not being able to escape
- The fear of not flowing, of being stuck, of feeling that there is no way out appears.

1.2 Components of the Under-coupling (Parasympathetic Pathway)

At the moment of being able to stop a sympathetic hyper reactivity, the dorsal Vagus parasympathetic system, responds by rising above the sympathetic activation, generating a vagal brake; this represents the opposite of over coupling, as a form of maximal resistance to sympathetic activation.

The components of this under-coupling response are:

- Sensation of space, I feel empty, feeling of inertia.
- Haziness, confusion, apathy, darkness.
- No sense of orientation
- Disconnection, fainting, loss of consciousness.
- Dizziness

When releasing the blockages and allowing the energy to unblock, significant changes appear in patterns of compulsive and destructive behaviors, which made us unconsciously repeat negative situations in life. With PHP, new behavioral patterns appear, survival defenses, fear and emotions of sadness and emptiness are reorganized, and positive patterns are empowered, allowing us to make vital changes and create new life options.

PHP AND POLYVAGAL THEORY

In recent years, neuroanatomical discoveries have given us a basis for understanding how PHP work can induce dynamic, global, lasting, life-changing healing that results in less reactive responses and a greater loving sense of contentment, regardless of life circumstances.

We have examined how the brain functions as a high-speed processor capable of activating what Porges refers to as "Emergent Potentials." These potentials, like Neuro-flexibility, can be brought forth, triggered, and expressed through exercises that engage the vagal brake, regulate the vagus nerve, and modulate somatic indicators. We recommend evaluating these concepts using the Body Perception Questionnaire (BPQ, 2015), which Dr. Porges offers for free access on his website. This questionnaire can serve as a valuable tool for both you and your client in understanding the vagal state, acquiring somatic language skills, and gradually integrating the comprehension of the interconnectedness of the body, mind, and emotions.

Neuroception

Mammals have what Dr. Stephen Porges in his book "Polyvagal Theory" calls Neuroception: the ability to detect signals of safety, danger or threat to life.

Adaptations (or responses) are activated at the nervous system level, depending on internal (interoception) and external (exteroception) signals that an organism picks up, thereby eliciting corresponding adaptive neural responses. Generally, we will respond to danger or threat to life using the most recently developed system: the mammalian myelinated autonomic nervous system.

We have encoded into our behavioral patterns of coping with danger, at the brain level, certain strategies: first, social engagement, and, gradually, if we are unsuccessful, we will be forced to go into defense mode by activating the use of evolutionarily older and more primitive responses (sympathetic activation and minimal dorsal vagal braking).

In the PHP sessions, what is observed is a perception of the world as a place of danger, which leads to a nervous system in a potential state of unconscious defense. We observe the bodily triggers, the activation signals. We seek to modulate these defense signals to promote psychological and physical accessibility with the client. We seek to restore symmetrical relationships, to resolve difficulties in feeling safe with others. We also create a context of stillness and loving accessibility, of immobility without fear, which allows us to sustain vulnerability and work on the traumatic. In the treatment we are releasing the freezing response, which often releases a large amount of energy held in the system. Activated fear, in fight/flight mode, is transformed through interaction, support, point stimuli, co-regulation dynamics, tone of voice, eye contact, and, in children, sometimes through play or movements that clear immobilized parts. Singing, dancing or rocking can be very helpful exercises, which can also be reinforced at home.

By untangling this form of unresolved traumatic response from the nervous system, the person will begin to tremble from deep within. Sometimes the shaking is global and sometimes it is in a local area, such as a finger or arm. These tremors present themselves as a gratifying feeling of liberation and freedom. At the same time the primitive and limiting, associated, unconscious, traumatic beliefs that were assumed at the time of the event, are reevaluated from a new and broader perspective within a perception of safety, which allows re-signifying them, reorganizing the defense pattern, and activating neuro-flexibility so that the body, mind and emotions find a new way of experiencing reality.

The Polyvagal Theory shows the different neurocircuits we use to react to external or internal stimuli. It also shows how the brain and body are connected through the autonomic nervous system. It explains the freeze response at the neural level (heart rate drop). It shows what we need to feel safe, safety is predictable. And it shows the transition from the reptilian nervous system to the mammalian nervous system.

An illustrative instance of addressing a traumatic event and its impact on an individual's life involves the somatized freeze response. This response keeps the body trapped in a state of paralysis, and remarkably, it can persist even many years after the initial experience. However, through appropriate therapeutic approaches, this freeze response can be gradually released, allowing the individual to regain a sense of mobility and freedom from its lingering effects.

Dr. Peter Levine in his book, Waking the Tiger, points out that, unlike us, animals routinely shake off the terror of a threat or attack; it is an immediate and healthy response that makes them virtually immune to the symptomatology of somatized trauma.

CHAPTER V

SELF-HELP EXERCISES OF THE NERVOUS SYSTEM AND THE VAGUS NERVE

"If we believe we are going to be cured, we will be cured."
Catalina Ureta

Thirty Exercises to Reset the Nervous System to Help with Stress and Anxiety

1. **Exercise to relax the sympathetic system through the eyes**

The eyes are the root of the nervous system. The optic nerve NC XI, when relaxed, helps us to have better vision.

Sit in a chair or armchair, where you are more comfortable, you can breathe deeply, in a place without noise.

Take three deep breaths. As you inhale, you will close and squeeze your eyes a little. Keep them closed and, as you exhale, release them and open them. Notice if your face feels relaxed. Do this exercise six times.

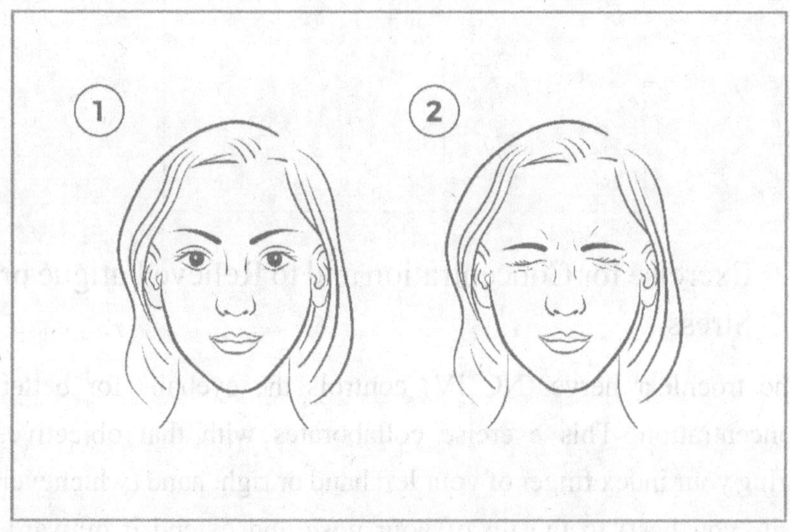

2. Exercise to Connect the Oculomotor Nerve

Helps your eyeballs to have clearer vision and connected with the breath. It also helps to relax the skin.

Put your hands over your eyes and all over your face, without moving them. Notice the connection between your hands (their softness and your sensations) and your face. Notice if your jaw begins to relax and if your breathing becomes lighter. Count six deep breaths. Hands on your eyes, fingers on the edges under your eyebrows.

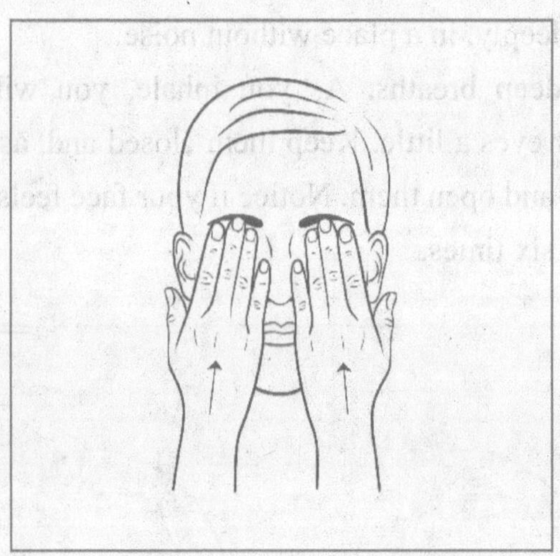

3. Exercise for Concentration and to Relieve Fatigue or Stress

The trochlear nerve (NC IV) controls the eyeballs for better concentration. This exercise collaborates with that objective. Bring your index finger of your left hand or right hand (whichever suits you best) to the tip of your nose and extend it outward.

Follow its movement with your eyes. Bring it back to your nose. Now bring it to your right side and, focusing on it, bring it back to your nose without moving your head. Bring it to your left side and bring it back to your nose. Rest and do this exercise three times. At each movement, rest and perceive your breath.

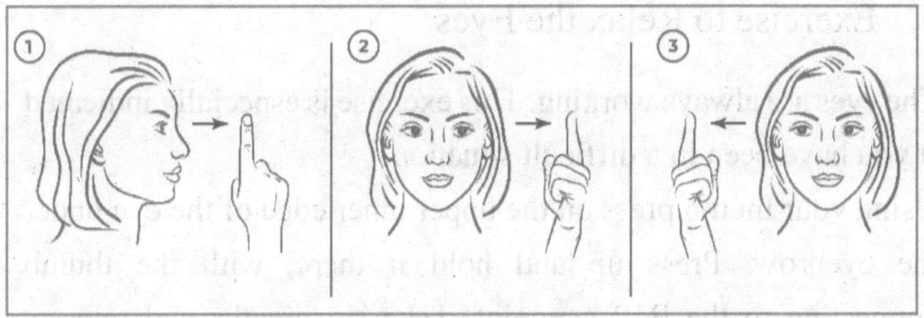

4. Exercise to Relax your fascial Muscles

Place the index finger of your left hand under your left eye and press gently looking for resistance (where you feel there is tension). Squeeze the trigeminal nerve (NC V) upwards, taking five breaths and then do the same with the index finger of your right hand pressing gently and again taking five breaths.

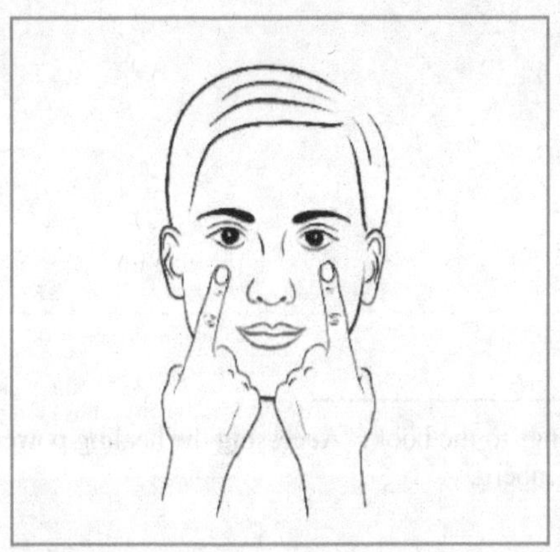

Another way to do this is to rest your elbow on your hand. With the other hand that is free, touch the point on the face that is on the cheekbone. Then move the point upward, just below the eye. Then repeat the exercise with the other hand. Breathe five times per side.

5.   Exercise to Relax the Eyes

The eyes are always working. This exercise is especially indicated if you have been in a difficult situation.

Using your thumb press on the upper inner edge of the eye under the eyebrow. Press up and hold it there, with the thumb connecting to the B12 acupoint. Take six breaths and release. Repeat the exercise with the right eye, always remembering to take six breaths at the end. Release and keep your eyes closed for a few minutes. Let your mind rest and, little by little, open your eyes and feel your body and its sense of relaxation.

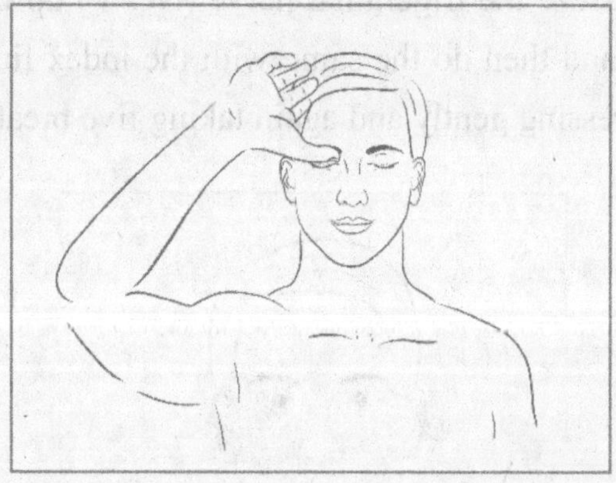

42

---

[42] This exercise belongs to the book: "Accessing the healing power of The Vagus Nerve". Stanley Rosenberg.

6. Exercise to Release tension, pain and frustration from the jaw

These emotions are what lead us to chew poorly and not relax the jaw during the night. We are going to hold the points of the jaw, press firmly, where the jaw meet. We will press each side of the face with the index finger, the right and left side of the temporomandibular joint (over the cheekbone). We hold the points by taking four breaths.

7. Exercise to Relax the jaw

We are going to place the index finger, or the one you prefer, on the lower jaw (mentalis muscle), squeezing and lowering it. Under the lips, in the center of the chin, place the index finger and press gently, opening the mouth and lowering the jaw. We are going to relax it as we breathe gently. This exercise is very good to do before sleeping to avoid bruxism or jaw pain.

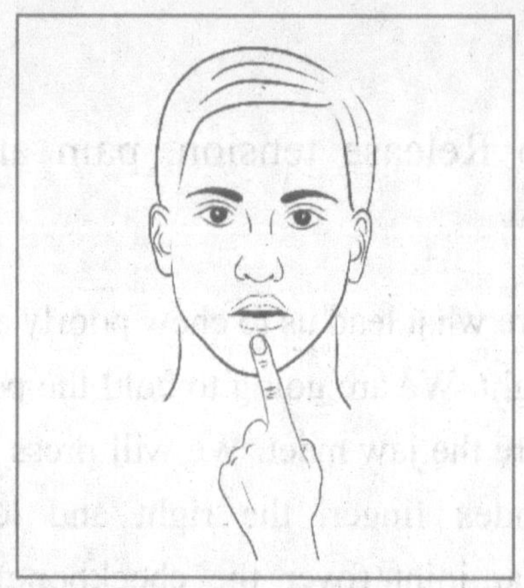

8. Facial Relaxation Exercise

Will positively stimulate the nerves that are part of the face and the system of social engagement. It helps to relax the face, the expression, and to have more facial movements.

We are going to use three fingers, and gently stretch the facial musculature towards the ear. From the edges of the nose, we stretch the skin bringing the fingertips towards the ear (acupuncture point both anterior and posterior). You will do this exercise five times.

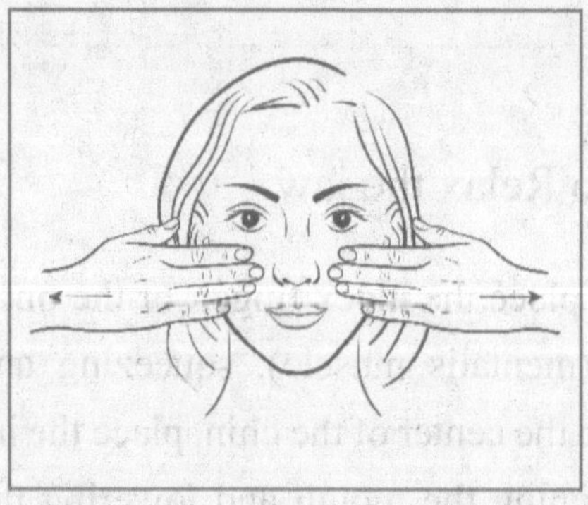

9. Exercise of Expansion of the Thoracic Cage

The vagus nerve is the X cranial nerve and it´s composed of sensory and motor fibers; it is the longest nerve in the body. This allows it to innervate organs of the thorax, abdomen, head and neck. This exercise will help digestion.

With the mouth open, bring the lower jaw forward (or outward). While leaving it forward stretch the shoulders backwards, then rotate shoulders and arms forward. At the same time, inhale and then blow hard through the mouth from the abdomen as you bring the shoulders and arms forward. Do this five times.

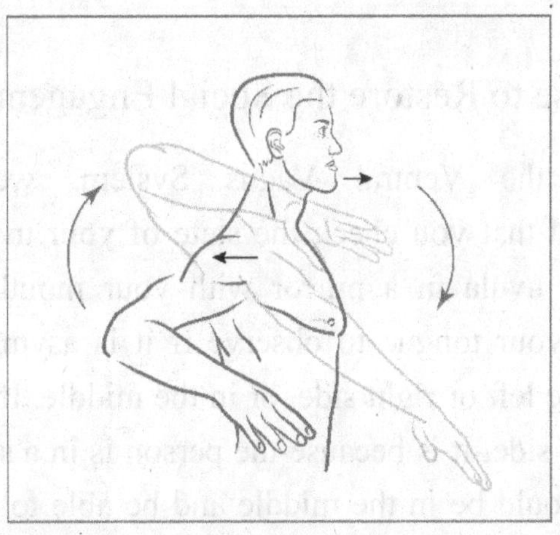

10. Exercise for the Tongue:

This helps us to improve health, it intervenes in taste, chewing and swallowing and improves the sounds of the voice; it helps us to communicate better, to establish links with others, to request, to thank, to persuade, to express.

We are going to stretch the tongue outwards as much as possible. When we are stretched out, we are going to breathe four times.

We bring it inward and breathe once; then we bring it to the left side and breathe four times. Then we bring it inward and take one more breath. Now to the right side and again take four breaths, come back to the center, take one breath and relax.

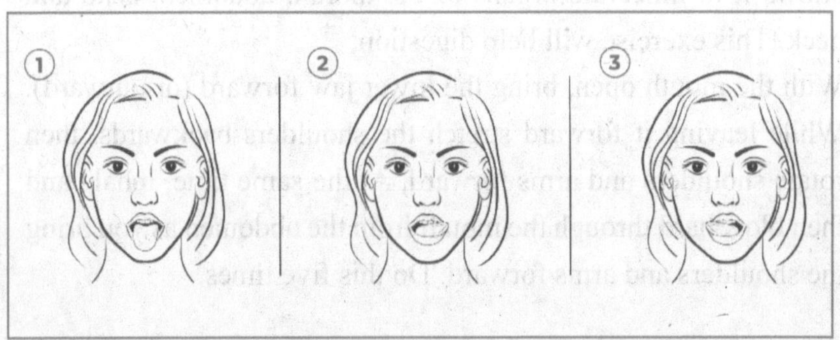

11. Exercise to Restore the Social Engagement System

To restore the Ventral Vagus System, we previously recommended that you check the state of your uvula. You can look at your uvula in a mirror with your mouth open while sticking out your tongue to observe if it is asymmetrical, i.e., hanging to the left or right side, or in the middle. If it is oriented toward either side, it is because the person is in a state of stress. The uvula should be in the middle and be able to move up and down.

With the mouth wide open, repeat three times the sound "ah, ah, ah", so that the soft palate (where the uvula is attached) can be lifted to allow it to return to its original central position. Observe if the uvula returns to the center. If it does not, repeat the exercise until the objective is achieved. Once the uvula is in its place, we can move on to the exercise of restoring the social engagement system.

In performing this exercise, we are going to work the sub occipital muscles which are related to the jaw muscles, the oculomotor muscles responsible for mobilizing the eye, and the per orbicular muscles that maintain the angle of vision as well as the balance, stability and rotation of the head. All this can be altered by stress and bad posture, especially with the overuse of cell phones and computer screens. With this exercise we will return relaxation to the system, recovering body balance and discharging stress.

This exercise can be done standing, sitting, or lying down.

With the mouth closed and hands clasped together behind the head, we first look to the left side towards the tip of the elbow keeping the head still and centered, turning only the eyes. We will make a yawn or a big sigh. Then we move our eyes back to the center and breathe once. We do the same procedure with the right side. We return the eyes to the center and rest.

This sequence is repeated three times. You might keep yawning or swallowing saliva afterwards, which is normal.

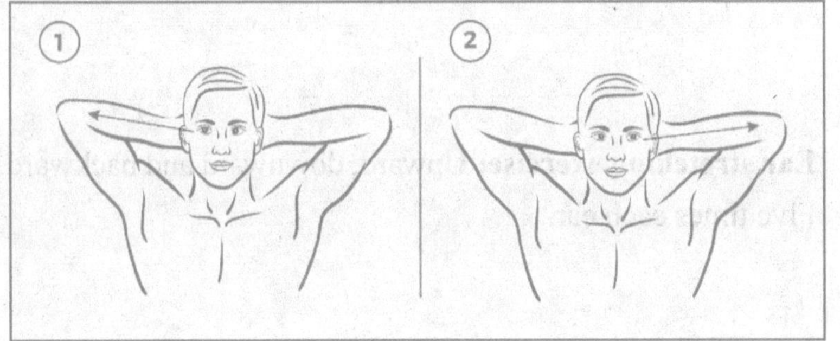

44

---

⁴⁴ This exercise belongs to the book: "Accessing the healing power of The Vagus Nerve". Stanley Rosenberg.

12. Exercise to Regulate the Vagal Tone

Sequence of three steps: Through the stimulation of these points (neck and ear) a regulation of the Vagal tone is generated.

- **Neck exercise:** From behind the ear, gently slide your index finger down the Trigeminal Nerve in the neck towards the collarbone. Press gently the point located on the collarbone, stopping there and breathe three times. Then, slide the finger back up to the point behind the ear and breathe three times.

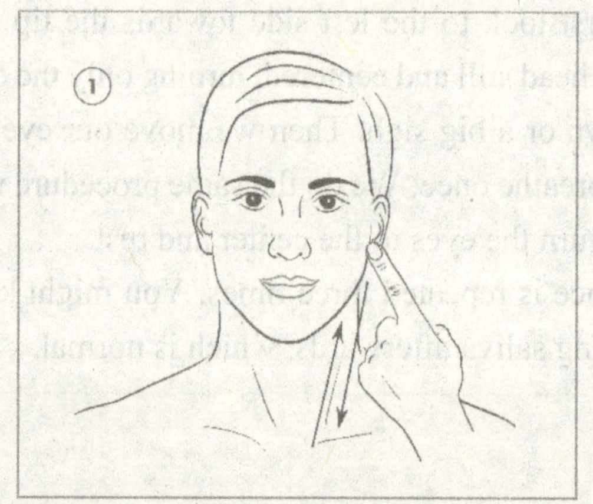

- **Ear stretching exercise:** Upward, downward and backward. Five times each ear.

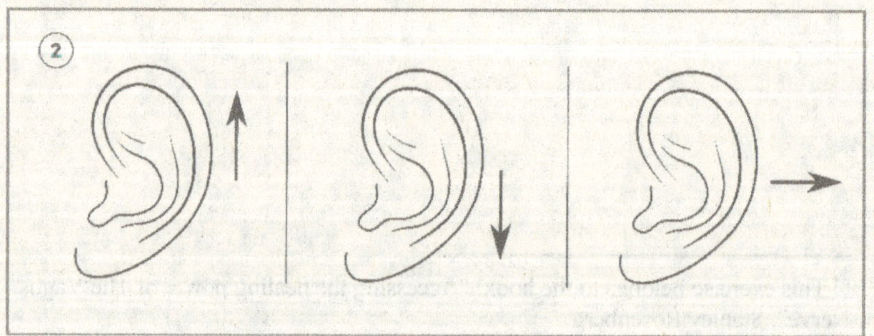

- **Ear exercise:** Circular movement within the ear, in the form of a rotary massage, generates a stimulation of the auditory ossicles (bones of the middle ear) [45] which improves hearing and, therefore, active listening. With one finger inside the ear, we move five times clockwise, and then immediately five times counterclockwise.

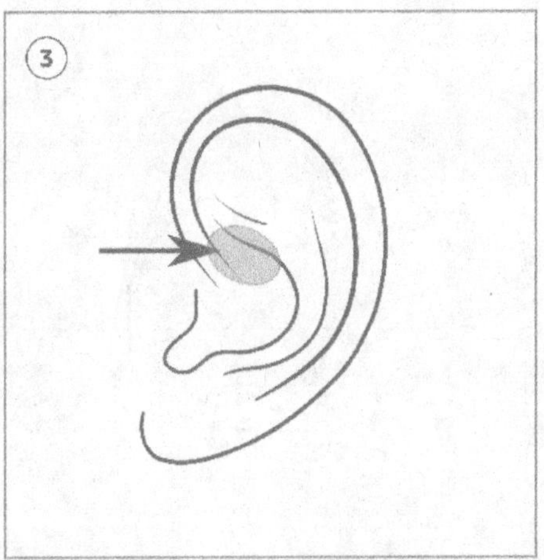

13. Yogi Exercise

Lack of oxygen is known as hypoxia and affects the cerebral hemispheres. The brain cells are extremely sensitive to the lack of oxygen due to tiredness and exhaustion, and many times also due to not drinking water.

With this exercise you will breathe better and send more oxygen to the brain. This will allow you to think more clearly and feel more expansion in your mind.

---

[45] The bones of the middle ear, hammer, anvil and stapes, form a chain located in the tympanic cavity of the middle ear.

We take the right flap of the nose and lift it outwards covering the left nostril with a finger on the other hand. Breathe in and out of the right nostril five times. Then, we let go and breathe normally. Then, we take the left nostril and stretch it outward plugging the right nostril taking five breaths. Release, breathe normally and relax.

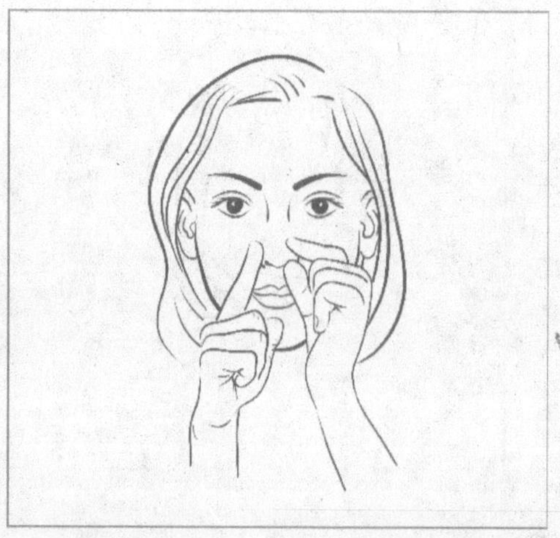

14. Exercise Vagus Nerve and Reset

The eyes are what connects the Vagus Nerve with the nervous system. Through this exercise the Vagus Nerve is stimulated and with it the exploratory orientation system is regulated. You can be more alert and perceive your surroundings more clearly.

We sit on a chair or sofa with a straight back and perform two sequences.

- We move our head as much as possible to the left side keeping our shoulders relaxed, and we look down to the left side as well; in that position we take five breaths. Then we bring our head to the center and breathe once. We move our head again, this time to the right side keeping our shoulders relaxed and look down; again in that position we take five breaths. We return to the center and breathe once.

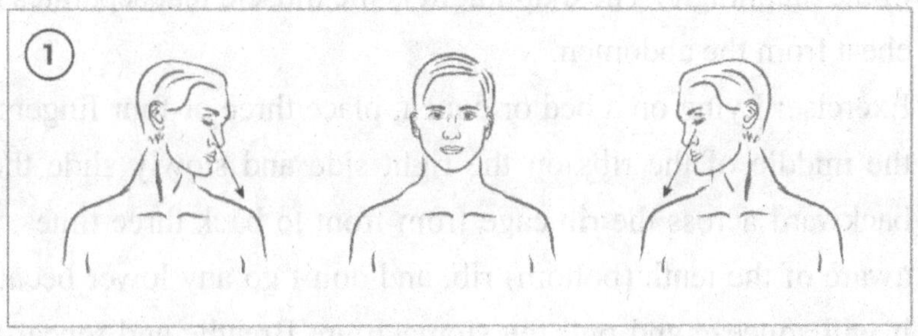

- Reset. Secondly, we are going to move our head as much as possible to the left side keeping our shoulders relaxed, but this time we are going to look at the opposite shoulder without moving our head; in that position we take five breaths. Then we move our head to the right side keeping our shoulders relaxed and we look at the opposite shoulder taking five breaths. We come back to the center and breathe once. We rest.

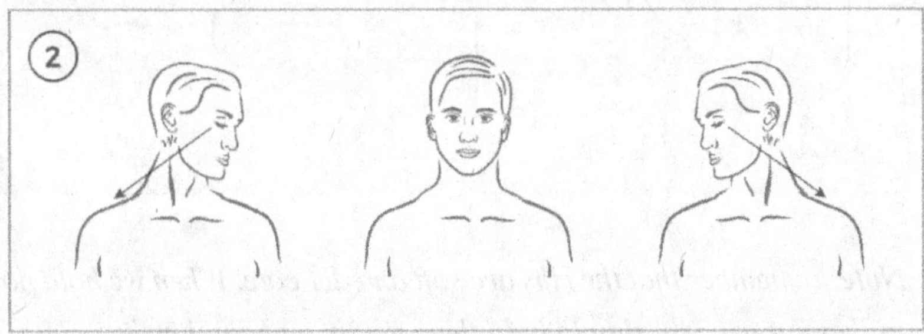

15. Exercise to Improve Digestion

Stanley Rosenberg says "the ribs squeeze the stomach under stress and create a hiatal hernia". This occurs when the upper portion of the stomach rises into the chest through a small opening in the diaphragm. The diaphragm is the muscle that separates the chest from the abdomen.

Exercise: Lying on a bed or couch, place three or four fingers in the middle of the ribs on the right side and slowly slide them backward across the rib cage from front to back three times. Be aware of the tenth (bottom) rib, and don't go any lower because it will squeeze and pull the stomach up. Breathe and repeat the exercise four times. Now do the same exercise on the left side. After this sequence, repeat the exercise with both hands, from front to back, along the sides of the rib cage. Breathe in. Repeat four times.

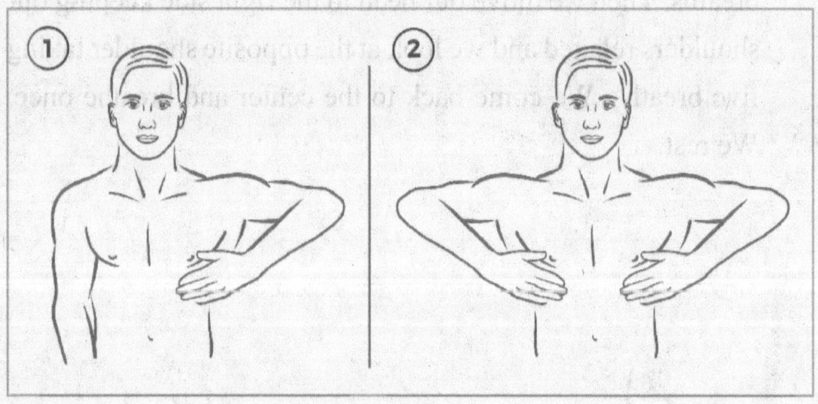

***Note**: remember that the ribs are soft and delicate. When we hold points in these areas, you should hold them gently and cautiously.*

16. Exercise to Release the Vagus Nerve

This exercise is to eliminate the stiffness of the neck and shoulders and to prevent the shoulders from crouching forward. In a crouched position, stiffness and constriction of the chest appears, reducing the space for the heart. This massage also manages to activate part of the trigeminal nerve that innervates the part of the neck related to the social engagement system.

1. Gently stretch the skin under the ear, on the outer edge of the face, over the neck. By doing this movement we separate the skin from the neck muscle and work the Vagus Nerve that is between the two. With your left hand you are going to gently pinch your skin from the top of the neck on your right side pinching your way down to the skin above the collarbone. Do this five times. Then, with your right hand, you do the same on the left side. Do this five times and rest.

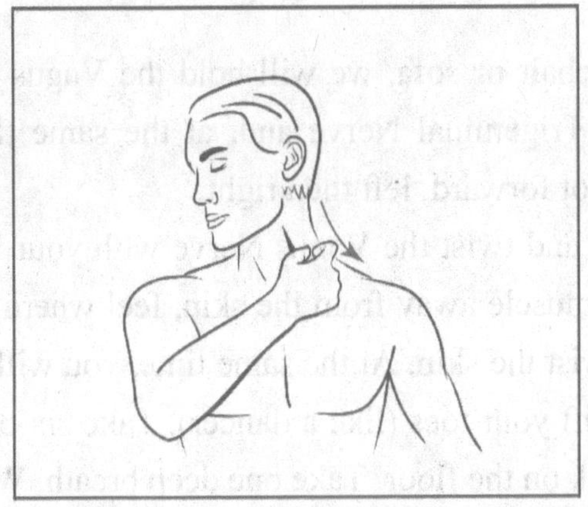

2. You will gently separate the muscle from the skin covering the neck, pinching from the bottom to the top. With the fingers of your left hand, you are going to gently pinch and release the skin of the cranial nerve IX glossopharyngeal shown below; do this five times. Repeat the exercise on the other side.

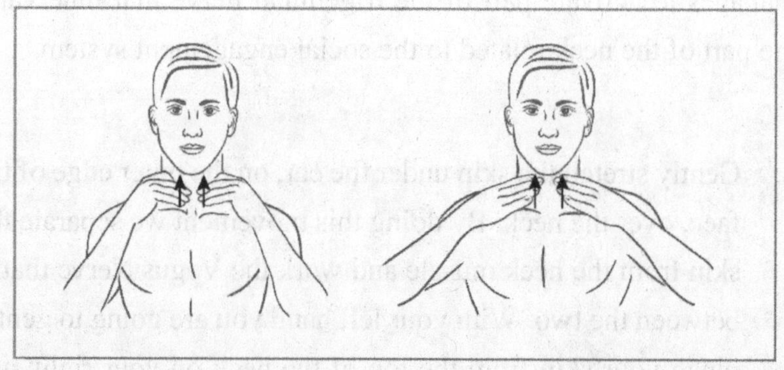

17. Exercise to Release and Hold the Vagus Nerve to the Foot. "Trigeminal Nerve"

Sitting on a chair or sofa, we will hold the Vagus Nerve in the neck, at the Trigeminal Nerve and, at the same time, we will stretch the foot forward, left then right.

Gently grasp and twist the Vagus Nerve with your left hand. As you pull the muscle away from the skin, feel where it is tightest, and gently twist the skin. At the same time, you will stretch your left leg and lift your toes (like a dancer). Take six breaths. Place your foot back on the floor. Take one deep breath. We will repeat the exercise with the other foot. You can repeat this exercise three times. Remember to do the six breaths each time.

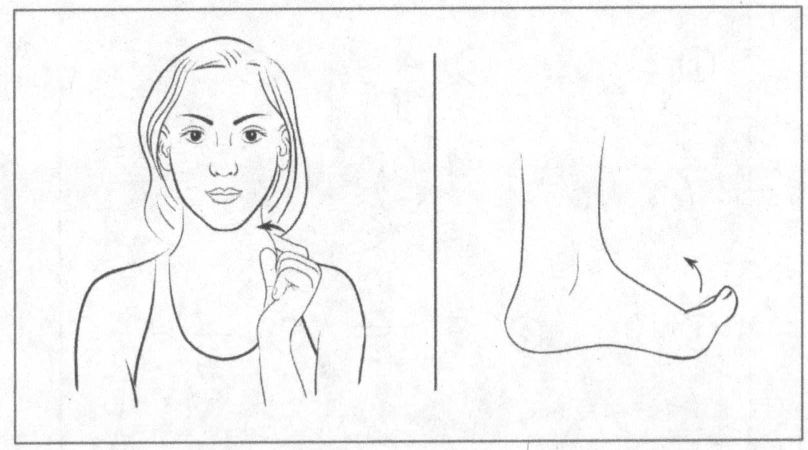

18. Arm Exercises to Release the Vagus Nerve and Nervous System

Raise your arms and put them one nested above the other at chest level. Move the arms, rotating to the right side without moving the neck, looking forward; breathe three times. Return with arms together to the middle of the body and take a deep breath keeping arms at chest level. Then, rotating arms to the left side without moving the neck, look forward; breathe three times. Come back with your arms together in the middle, take another deep breath and now bring your arms back up together above your head. This time you will rotate your arms to the right side along with your torso, without moving your neck. Breathe three times. Return to the center, take a deep breath keeping your arms above your head and rotate your arms together with your torso to the left, without moving your neck. Breathe three times. Return to center, take a deep breath and rest. This exercise is for neck pain and to keep the shoulders in good posture.

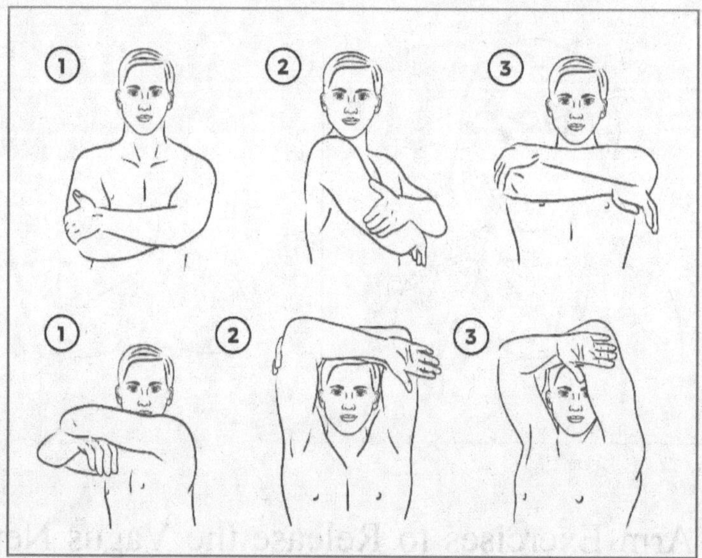

46

19. Exercise for Digestion and to Open and Expand the Ribs

Many times, the ribs trap the breath and contract if there is stress. In a standing position, put your right hand on the wall and raise it as high as possible, holding on to it, breathe five times; then lower it to the center and breathe five times; then lower it as low as possible and breathe five times. Change position and repeat the exercise with the other arm.

---

46 This exercise belongs to the book: "Accessing the healing power of The Vagus Nerve". Stanley Rosenberg.

47

20. Tapping Exercise for Emergencies

With your two fingers of the right hand tap gently on the edge of the bone, three-quarters of an inch below the right eye, at the level of the pupil. Repeat this twelve times, breathe normally; then switch eyes and repeat the exercise.

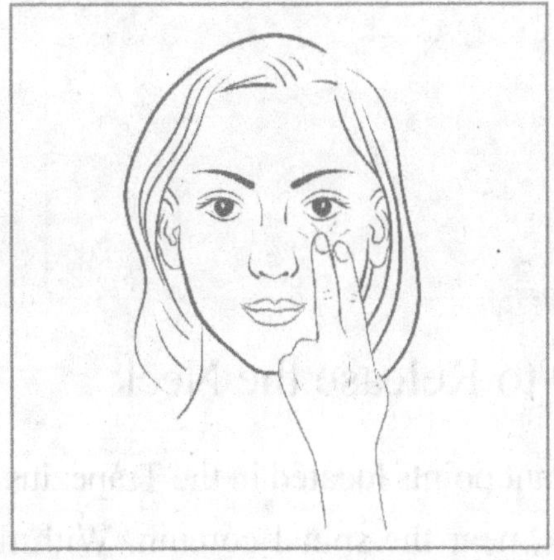

---

[47] This exercise belongs to the book: "Accessing the healing power of The Vagus Nerve". Stanley Rosenberg.

21. Tapping Exercise to Help the Lymphatic System

The lymphatic system consists of tissues and organs that produce, store and transport white blood cells to fight infection and other diseases.

This system includes the bone marrow, spleen, thymus, and lymph nodes. With the two fingers of your right hand, you will tap gently under your left armpit twelve times and, again, with your left two fingers you will tap gently on your right armpit twelve times. Lie down and rest for about five minutes.

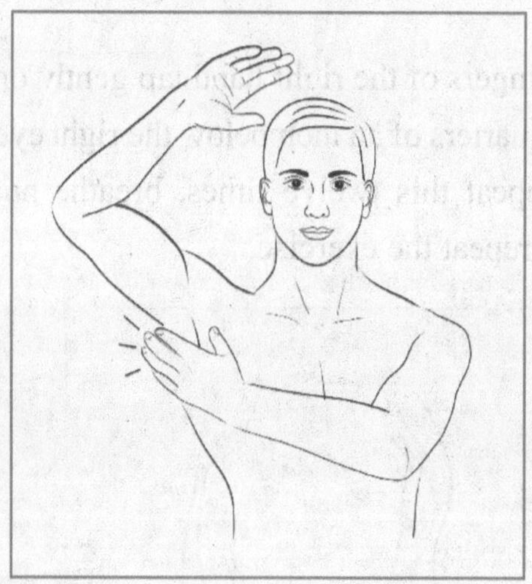

22. Exercise to Release the Neck

There are important points located in the Trapezius muscle, at the back of the neck, near the spinal column. With the right hand, pinch and release six times the left side of the neck going straight down along these points in the Trapezius muscle; then repeat the exercise with the right side. It helps the movement of the neck.

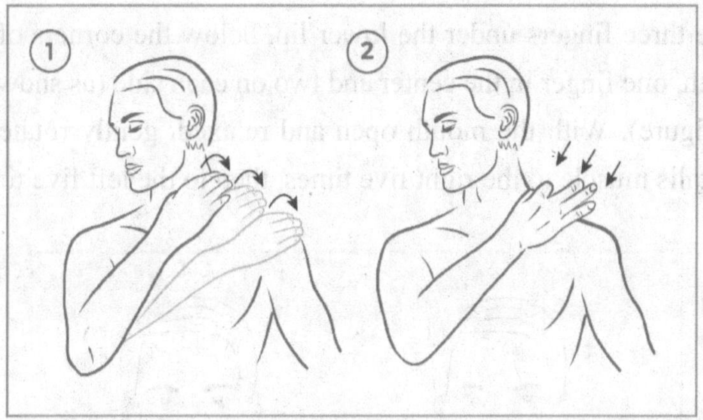

23. Exercise to Release Negative Emotions

The karate point (called Gama Point) is located in the center of the fleshy part of the canthus of the hand, between the top of the wrist and the base of the little finger. Tap the edge ten times with the opposite hand. Repeat the exercise with the other hand.

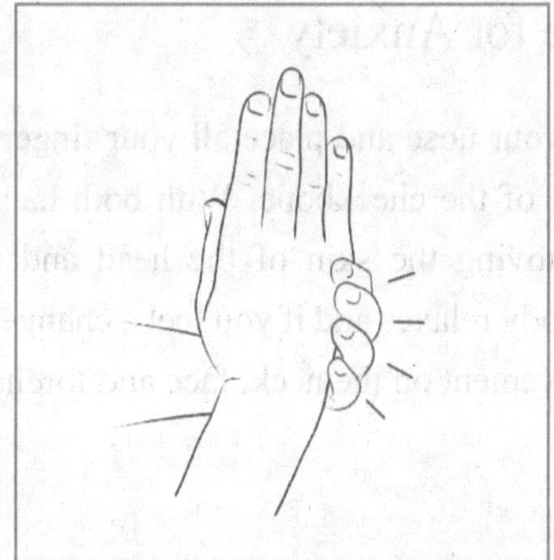

24. Exercise to Relax the Mentalis Muscle and Relieve Bruxism

Place three fingers under the lower lip, below the corners of the mouth, one finger in the center and two on each side (as shown in the figure). With the mouth open and relaxed, gently rotate the mentalis muscle to the right five times, then to the left five times.

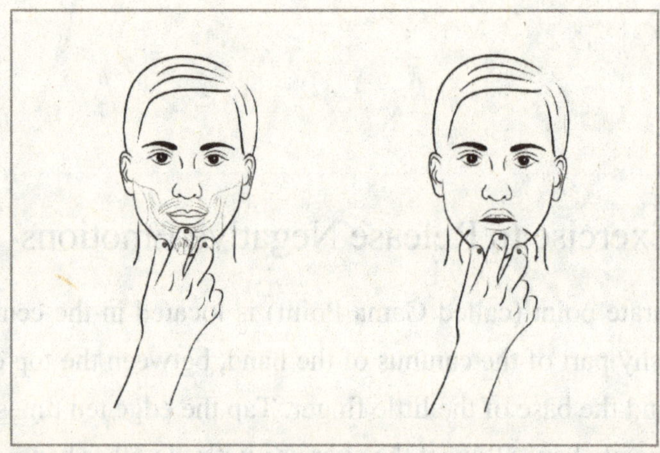

25. Exercise for Anxiety

Inhale through your nose and place all your fingers behind your ears at the level of the cheekbone. With both hands, slide your fingers back, moving the skin of the head and neck upward. Notice if your body relaxes and if you feel a change. Then we can do the same movement on the neck, face and forehead as shown.

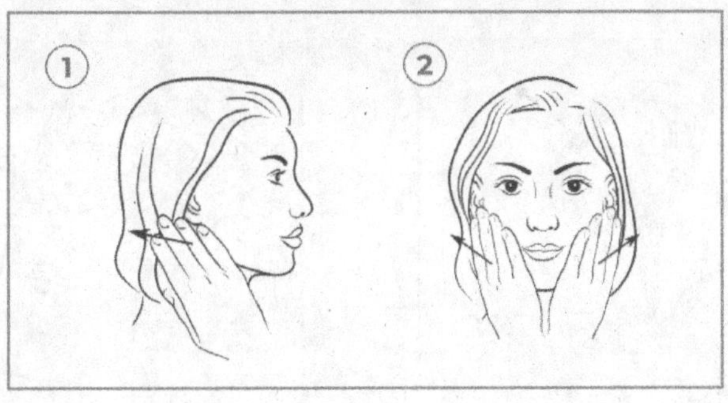

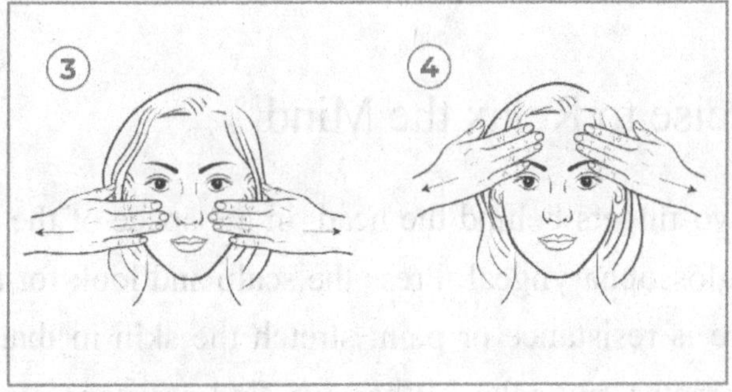

Note: *This exercise can be applied in newborns and children to stimulate social skills.*

26. Exercise to Relax the Rib Cage, and Loosen the Neck, and Shoulders

With the left arm, place two or three fingers on the head and tilt it gently to the left as far as possible; look up to the right side. At the same time, with the opposite arm, place three fingers on the ribs on the right side. Gently pull the ribs inward toward the right side of the body and count six breaths. Return the head to the center, take a deep breath and repeat the exercise with a change of sides.

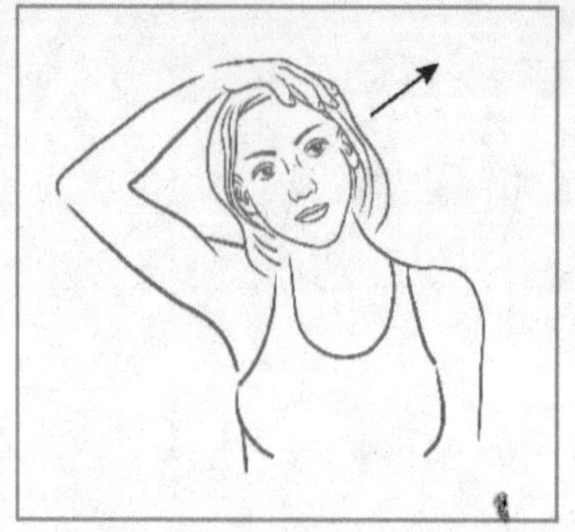 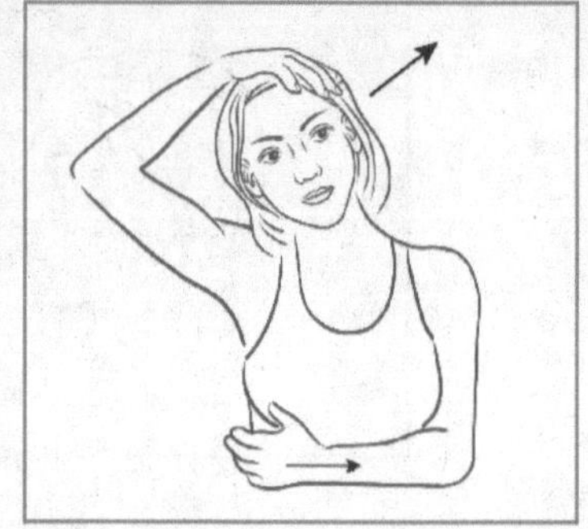

27. Exercise to Relax the Mind

Put your two fingers behind the head, in the space of the cranial nerve IX, glossopharyngeal. Press the scalp and look for a place where there is resistance or pain; stretch the skin in that place, take five breaths and relax. When we find resistance, pain, or tension in the body, you can help by putting a little pressure and then releasing. Repeat with the opposite hand.

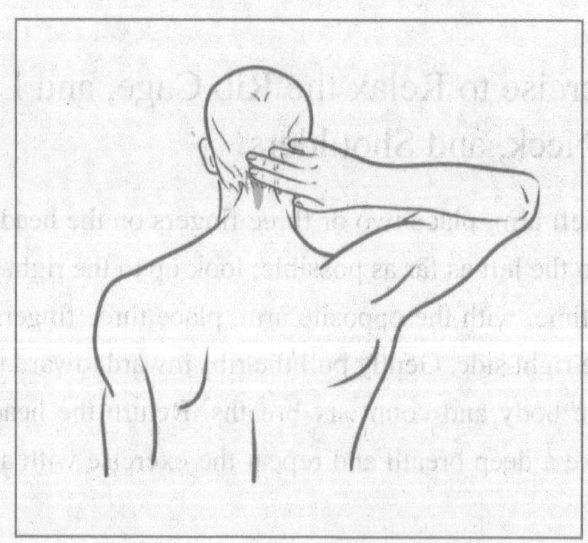

28. Exercise to Improve the Functioning of the Heart

Sitting on a chair, inhale stretching your arms and fisted hands forward, then exhale bringing your arms back in. Now reach your arms upward, inhaling, and exhale as you bring them back down. Stand up from the chair and inhale reaching your arms upward. Then sit down, exhaling and lowering your arms. Repeat each exercise three times, resting each time.

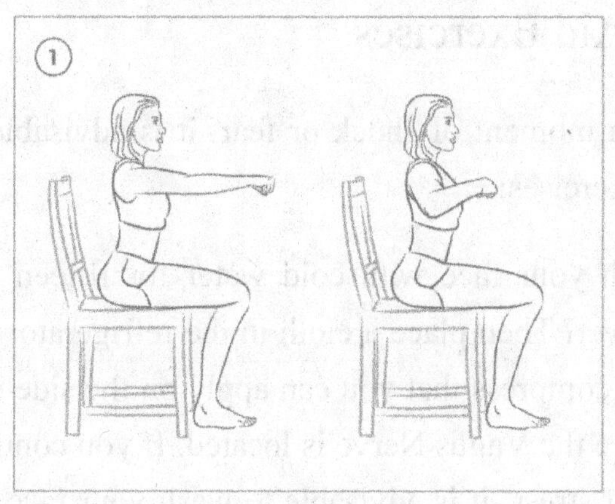

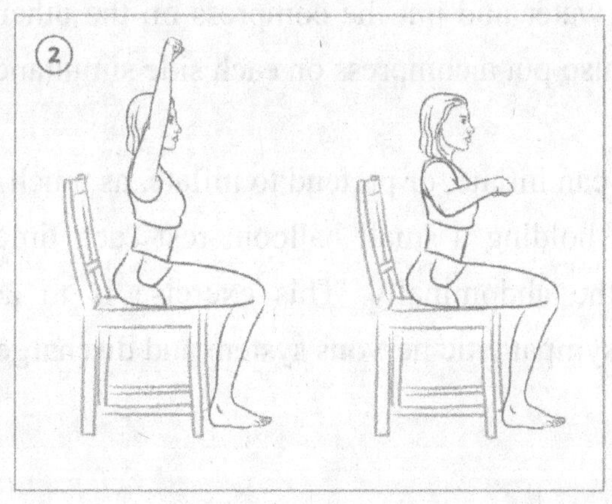

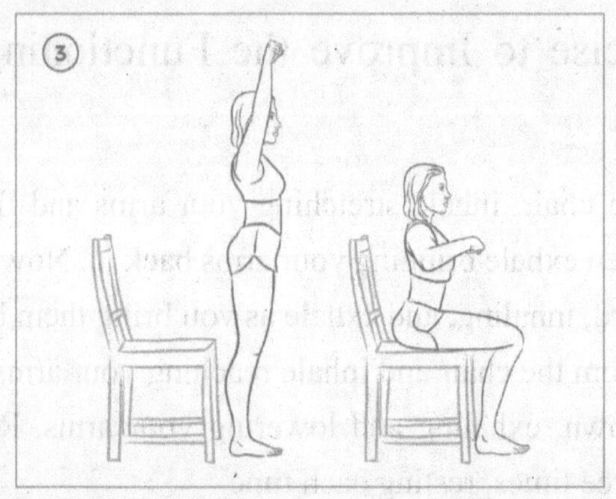

29. First Aid Exercises

If you had a moment of shock or fear, it is advisable to do the following exercises:

- Wash your face with cold water for fifteen seconds to recover. Then place a cloth in the refrigerator to use as a cold compress that you can apply on the side of the neck where the Vagus Nerve is located. If you continue with a lot of stress, it is advisable to wash your face again with cold water and put the compress on the other side. You can also put a compress on each side simultaneously.

- You can inflate, or pretend to inflate, as much as possible as if holding a small balloon; rest each time until you breathe abdominally. This exercise is to activate the parasympathetic nervous system and discharge.

- Lie down on the floor on a yoga mat, place a chair near your feet. When you are completely lying down, inhale, and when you exhale, put your feet up on the chair, then put them down and repeat the exercise four times. Rest.

- Take a deep breath and hold your nose closed with your hand. Lower your head down for a count of four. Then bring your head back up, release your nose, and exhale through your mouth slowly for four counts.

30. Exercise to Stimulate Digestion

Place the left hand above and the right hand below the navel. Gently tap above the navel six times with one of the fingers on your left hand. Then, gently tap six times again above the navel with the right hand. Finally, with one finger of the right hand gently tap six times inside the navel. Repeat inside with the left hand.

Author's Biographies

Catalina Ureta

I was born in Santiago, Chile under the shadow of the magical Andes Mountains. My father had married my mother at a young age, which was normal for those times. He had lost his father at the age of eighteen. My other grandfather had a large farm outside the city. My father had four sisters and two brothers and when he married my mother, he brought his mother to live with us. My grandmother's name was Cristina, and she made me very happy. She was a beautiful woman, very kind, loving, and she took good care of me along with the caretaker. When I was five years old, we moved from the apartment to a bigger house, as my mother had more children. My mother was very well educated, spoke English and French very well, and also wrote a book later in life called "The Crushed Woman." My mother was writing another book when she became ill. I came back to Santiago, Chile to be with her for few months, and my mother became very interested in my work with the body / mind connection. She asked me for therapy sessions every day in the last months of her life. At her final stage of illness, my siblings and I were at her apartment every day. One day we were all in the living room and my mother was in her room with her nurses. One nurse called me in and said my mom was having a heart attack. I ran into her room and my intuition guided me to hold her heart point. Immediately, the heart regulated back to normal. My sister and brother also came in and both of them started to hold her points. As I was looking at my mother's blue eyes, I noticed that her eyes started to change color from blue to violet, and then she became very calm. The nurses became very quiet and a feeling of peace filled the air; a moment that I will never forget.

An Inner Quest:

One day, when I was twelve, I remember telling my mother that I didn't need a doctor anymore because I knew that if I ate certain things or did certain things to take care of myself, it would help my body feel better. It felt like a certainty that I could take care of myself, that my body could heal itself, and that I didn't need any medication. This was a very deep feeling inside me and from a very young age I began to learn and become fascinated with questions like: What did the body have to do to get rid of a headache or a stomachache? I would just sit there, feel the pain and not take anything; not resist, but hold the pain, and then the pain would disappear.

At the age of nineteen while we were driving with my father and grandmother on a trip to the beach, we had a serious accident. My father and grandmother had minor injuries, but I went through the windshield and hit my head, received eight stitches in my forehead and fractured my wrist, which was put in a cast. During that accident, I was unconscious, and I had the experience of perceiving a tunnel of light, which I went through. There was no pain, only happiness. It seems that I was not yet ready to leave this world, because I woke up in the hospital after they had already put my wrist in a cast and closed the wound on my forehead. At that time, I did not know about trauma. After this accident I went to rest in the countryside with my aunt and cousins. I rode a horse every day. I felt in a place of peace, of healing, which changed my way of perceiving reality, I became more spiritual, more connected with God.

When my mother returned to Chile from France in 1969, I asked her if I can to go to the United States; I was twenty years old when I went to San Francisco, California. There, I met people from the community of Stephen Gaskin who was a counterculture activist, a hippie icon, and a professor at the University of San Francisco. Gaskin created a community called "The Farm" in Tennessee. A friend and I went to live at The Farm for three months; it was an unforgettable experience. There I learned to live naturally with herbs, lots of fruits and vegetables. I stopped eating meat, fish, eggs, milk, and sugar; no animal product consumption at all.

Fresh bread was made every day and everything grew naturally in the vegetable gardens. In that community, I learned to embroider, sew and play music. After three months my mother sent for me and I returned to Santiago, Chile.

When I returned to the city, I lived with my family again, I met Juan, father of my daughter Sasha Tadalinka. We fell in love and got married; I was twenty-one years old and Juan was nineteen years old. It was a gift to have my daughter Sasha. We lived in the city of Santiago in an apartment near Pedro de Valdivia, and we had a cabin at Vichuquen Lake in the south of Chile, and went there often.

One day while walking along Vichuquen Lake, I had an experience with my thoughts. I realized that my mind did not stop thinking. I, who had everything I needed in life, for the first time asked myself: Who am I? What am I doing on this planet? That night I had a dream about a boy riding on an elephant in India. All the people were kneeling in his path. I woke up with a very deep feeling of love, of divinity. I felt my heart longing for that divinity that he was radiating. The answer came to me immediately. Within just a few days, some friends said they were going to Mendoza, Argentina to learn about a teacher of Inner Peace.

In 1974, Chile was very tumultuous, and the communists made it very difficult to hold meetings. My friends were going to Mendoza to receive something called "Self Knowledge" which was taught by a highly respected master known as Prem Rawat. I could not go with them, but I did not lose that longing to know myself. I wanted to know what I was doing in this world, to understand my life and my mission, to experience that longed-for magic that I felt earlier.

It was then that Juan and I decided to go to the U.S. to raise our daughter Sasha, who was already three and a half years old. It was in Miami, that I was fortunate to meet people who knew about Prem Rawat and there, with great humility, I received the gift of Self Knowledge, on July 17, 1975.

In 1976, I moved to Malibu, California. It wasn't until 1993 that I began to study the healing arts with Judith Johnson and Dr. Peter Levine. For many years, when I was not in my office, I was traveling the U.S. doing workshops and individual therapy sessions in Chicago, Miami, North Carolina, and New York. In Detroit, I had a TV program called, "Listen to Your Body."

A few years back, I participated in a seminar with Dr. Edd Tick, PhD, a psychiatrist specializing in working with war veterans. As part of his work, Dr. Tick takes U.S. war veterans to Korea, to revisit the place where they lost their beloved countrymen. There they perform a catharsis, cry, sing and say goodbye to the fallen soldiers. For me, it was a very meaningful experience and I felt that they had enormous courage.

I started to go to Chile more regularly in 2003 to see my family and to teach the Points Holding Process™ (PHP). In 2006, I met Mariann with whom I was very happy to teach and work. My sister Monica and brother Max also supported me a lot and ultimately became PHP Practitioners.

It is with love and affection that Mariann and I have put together this quintessential information for your benefit so that readers like you can heal your body, mind and soul and live a life full of peace and affection.

JUDITH JOHNSON'S TESTIMONY

Psychoneuroenergetics.com

Catalina has a strong healing dedication. She has great strength and true ability to help change a person and hold space for their journey of healing. She is a magician in a sense as she can assist in magical transformations. Her magic is based on deep intuition, deep body knowledge and varied, multiple experiences with many clients, over many years. While there is nothing she cannot do, Catalina is especially adept at working with healing physical body from traumatic experiences. She very beautifully allows the trauma to dissipate and allows a person to return to their natural way of being.

I met Catalina about Thirty years ago in Malibu, California. She was then a student of my work called Energetic Cleansing Process, which has since evolved to become Psychoneuroenergetics Process™. She quickly began teaching with me and then, Catalina, began teaching her own course called The Points Holding Process™ (PHP) at her Somatic Institute. Catalina is also a Senior Teacher, Supervisor and therapist for Dr. Peter Levine's Somatic Experiencing®. The synergy that evolved from our relationship led Catalina and I to develop training programs that combine Somatic work with Body Electronics, first initiated years ago by Dr. John Ray and further developed as the Energetic Cleansing Process™. The combination of these two bodies of knowledge provided a foundation for true healing at all levels: physical, mental/emotional and spiritual.

But Catalina did not stop learning. She has since studied with Stanley Rosenberg and Thor Phillipsen, adding powerful tools for regulating and balancing the vagus nerve system.

Catalina and I are still teaching today and have been for many years. As a therapist, Catalina has a large following in the Los Angeles area, among them psychologists and other therapists, as well as entertainment moguls, celebrities, and others who yearn for true healing.

Originally from Chile, she has returned to her home country to offer many trainings and workshops. I am happy that Catalina has finally put together this magnificent collection of work and experience into a manual in her native language. I look forward to reading the English version!

Judith Johnson
Psychoneuroenergetics.com

Mariann Dávila

I was born in Chile in 1965 and for family reasons we went to live in Costa Rica for my childhood, where a long personal journey began in order to understand the meaning of life experiences.

As a child, I remember restlessness as a relevant aspect of my way of being. Today, I would rather call it something linked to an anxious and hyperactive aspect of my personality that led me to be in permanent movement, not only physically, but also internally. I can't say that I liked to stay at home, I rather liked to go out to play with others, to go around places, to talk to people and to take care of animals. My siblings were sensitive, warm and adequate children; I was rebellious, disorderly and with a compassionate heart, which innately led me to be close to people who suffered, where there was conflict and pain, abandonment and loneliness.

In 1980, I returned to Chile and this caused major stress, which I believe was the same for all my siblings. A strange place, new ways of communicating, new school, new everything. Many conflict processes took place and at the age of eighteen, I had my first son Esteban. Maybe because we were always going back and forth, surviving many difficulties, we are very close to each other. During that time, I had to work and study, which I keep to this day as the best of habits, since it allowed me to start a path of discoveries and meanings, to meet creative human beings that motivated me to write this book today.

At the age of twenty-nine, I had my second daughter, Constanza, who was a gift to my heart, however, a year later I was experiencing the traumatic grief of separation from my partner. It had been very difficult for me to maintain a stable emotional life I had struggled to complete college as an engineer and had worked at everything that came my way. Always dealing with stabilizing my children, getting ahead and continuing to learn, my life clicked when I turned thirty-three. Thanks to my cousin, Patricia Coggiola, who was a great support, I connected with the world of metaphysics and transpersonal development. Little by little I was able to recognize life as a path that I could better understand. While receiving her support, I was able to begin to change inside, to recognize my own processes and to heal my wounds and traumas. By now there were many people who had helped me along the way. I could write a book about so many people who made it possible for me to move forward. As my daughter's grandmother, Victoria Castro Rojas, would say, "I always believed in you, that you were capable", which, in my opinion, were those magic words, that meaningful validation, which would give me a lot of inner strength to move forward, after living through many problems due to lack of emotional support and stability early in life.

In 2001, I learned "Self Knowledge" with Prem Rawat; I participated in the Peace Education Program, and twice I coordinated his visits to Chile. Those were essential moments to make changes that would make my life take an unexpected turn. I would learn Essential Shamanism at Michael Harner's Foundation for Shamanic Studies in the USA and I would travel for more than six years around the world with Siberian shamans, learning to heal people through different energetic techniques. Finally, I would write my first book: Shamanic Logbook, a journey of knowledge into the world of the naturalistic cosmovision of the ancestral world.

In 2006, again my life would change radically when I met Catalina Ureta, with whom today we share the creation of this book. She led me to recognize the body, to connect with it and to heal traumatic experiences, to release the past, to recognize the strength and love that sustains us. I was able to train with her in PHP and Somatic Experiencing®, which allowed me to move from the dissociated to the integrated, recovering in many aspects of my personal life.

From 2007 onwards, I dedicated myself for years to teaching trauma in hospitals, clinical care centers, children's homes, schools, social projects and, above all, I worked training multidisciplinary mental health teams in trauma recovery, self-regulation and crisis management.

From 2010 onwards I dedicated myself to training in Executive Coaching, Team Diagnostics to work with teams and I decided to study Psychology, specializing in Psychopharmacology, Child Psychiatry, Mental Health and psychological support in Risk Management in Emergency and Disaster situations, since in Chile there are many recurrent situations of violations of territories due to disasters, social conflicts and catastrophes.

In 2015, I returned to take the Somatic Experiencing® training through the Peter Levine Foundation, creator of this work and it was unified with my path of more than ten years of studies in Neurosciences applied to trauma.

Trained by Ale Duarte in the Tuning in with Children Program, certified in Developmental Trauma by Dr. Liana Netto, I continued incorporating the gender perspective to my work. Graduated in New Contributions to the Psychosomatic Clinic from a Psychoanalytic Approach in 2018 at Diego Portales University, I would continue my training in Systemic Child and Adolescent Trauma therapy with Dr. Barudy and his Apega Network. Graduated in Neurosciences at the University of Santiago, I specialized in Psychosis, attending classes with Psychiatrist Alison Yung, at the University of Chile and it was in 2020 that I completed my clinical postgraduate degree in Severe Personality Disorders, Department of Psychiatry, University of Valparaiso, along with the course of deepening in emotional first aid from the Polyvagal Theory at the University Alberto Hurtado.

Currently I teach Cognitive Neurosciences at Universidad Santo Tomás and I have a Diploma in Gender and Violence, by University of Chile and I am in permanent training for three years in a Advanced Course in Transference Focused Therapy, International Society TFP Chile - Uruguay - Murcia, Spain. I currently participate as a member of the Association of Biodynamic Psychology (ABP).

For me, to do a therapy process is essential, especially in cases of trauma, complex trauma and dissociation. To give voice to the unsaid, to express what has been fear, to recognize one's own resources and to feel listened to, is a gift to oneself. Telling my story gives me "relief", sharing what I have learned in the reflections of this book gives me "strength" and, above all, being active in the participation of support networks for children, generating actions in self-care training for teams that work with trafficking and commercial sexual exploitation; all this has allowed me to work in technical supervision of street children's networks.

I also feel that I have been able to unify the work of PHP to clinical practice. This therapy brings us a field of research and development that is just beginning, supported by the advances in Neuroscience. PHP can be incorporated as a specific tool within the process of accompanying the patient, in an integrative way, generating possibilities of deeper and more significant changes in some cases. We can also structure different layers of work that go from somatic responses, going through the body, the nervous system and analyzing, according to the specialty of each therapist, the physiological, cognitive, behavioral, psychological and emotional aspects. We can educate about self-regulation, developmental life cycle, aspects of personality organization, self-care, dissociation and reconnect with life, feel valuable, centered, rooted with life and recover joy and peace.

For me:

> *"Resolving trauma is a journey of the soul that is worth taking, to feel free again from pain, anguish and loneliness. Trauma is the Odyssey of the human being, the inevitable that breaks the fragile and awakens the inner strength of each one of us and leads us to discover how extraordinary we are."*

Testimony of Ps. Ana Maria Castañeda Chang, Dr. in Psychology at the National Institute of Child Health San Borja, Lima Peru:

> *"Mariann is a woman with incredible strength, her commitment to improve the living conditions of children and adolescents has led her to jump borders repeatedly, here in Peru we have had the joy of learning from her, not only of her theoretical technical capacity, but also, of her being as a person. In the Institute she has contributed to make us one of the first groups to understand the neurological functioning in trauma situations.*
>
> *Personally, my life has been impacted by the warmth and affection that Mariann gives; she is an example for me."*

Suggested readings

- Hear Yourself by Prem Rawat
- Splitting the Arrow by Prem Rawat
- Bitacora Chamánica by Mariann Dávila Coggiola
- The Shift Now Master Fast by Tony Toney
- The 15-minute Pause by Michell Burke, Lilami de Silva
- The Inner Game of Stress by Timothy Gallwey, Edd Hanzelik, John Horton M.D
- Waking The Tiger by Peter A. Levine, Ph.D.
- Schizophrenia by Kevin Volkan, Vamic Volkan
- Accessing The Healing Power of The Vagus Nerve by Stanley Rosenberg
- Fear is Not an Option by Monica Berg
- The Call from Home by Anthony Torres
- The Ten Things to Do When Your Life Falls Apart by Daphne Rose Kingma
- How We Heal by Douglas W. Morrison
- The Divided Mind by John E. Sarno
- Unbinding The Heart by Agapi Stassinopoulos
- Ice Veil Tales by Ora Munter

INDEX

Los Angeles, California, USA

2023